MW00617007

FENTANYL
NATION

ALSO BY RYAN HAMPTON

Unsettled

American Fix

F E N T A N Y L
NATION

Toxic Politics and America's Failed War on Drugs

RYAN HAMPTON

with **CLAIRE RUDY FOSTER** and **ZACHARY SIEGEL**

ST. MARTIN'S PRESS
NEW YORK

First published in the United States by St. Martin's Press,
an imprint of St. Martin's Publishing Group

www.stmartins.com

Designed by Omar Chapa

The Library of Congress Cataloging-in-Publication Data
is available upon request.

ISBN 978-1-250-28893-6 (hardcover)
ISBN 978-1-250-28894-3 (ebook)

Our books may be purchased in bulk for promotional, educational,
or business use. Please contact your local bookseller or the Macmillan Corporate
and Premium Sales Department at 1-800-221-7945, extension 5442, or by
email at MacmillanSpecialMarkets@macmillan.com.

First Edition: 2024

10 9 8 7 6 5 4 3 2 1

For Kade, Alexander, Allison, Kaisa, Justin, and David

Kellen, Kianna, and Lev

And my godson, Cameron

CONTENTS

INTRODUCTION

One Friday night in May 2017, Officer Chris Green was putting in a few reps at the gym. Green, who had an athletic build and boyish features, worked for the East Liverpool Police Department as a K-9 patrolman and frequently encountered drug use and addiction on the job. Outside, the balmy air of an Ohio spring was on the verge of bursting into summer. It was the type of after-payday night that tempted folks to stay late at the bar, dancing to the jukebox and sipping ill-advised road beers. Green's fellow officers were probably busy pulling over intoxicated drivers. What Green didn't suspect was that his own life was about to be bathed in flashing lights as well—and I don't mean red-and-blue *wow-wow* lights.

He was in the middle of his workout when his phone rang: his partner, Rob Smith. Smith said that he'd witnessed a "hand-to-hand," with the suspected drug dealer driving a dark blue Chevy Impala. In moments, Green was behind the wheel of his unmarked car and zipping through the ghost town of East Liverpool's industrial district.

Known as the "City of Hills and Kilns," East Liverpool was once home to over 200 potteries that employed thousands of blue-collar workers who made ceramics that were shipped all over the country. At one time, this bustling little city along the Ohio River produced 50 percent of America's dinnerware. By 2017, there was only one pottery manufacturer left, and East Liverpool had become a shrinking working-class town with few opportunities and not a lot of hope.

Decades ago, residents of East Liverpool woke up each morning to the earthy smell of baking clay and a distant orange glow emanating from hot kilns. Today, the sights and smells of a thriving industry are gone. Like so many other Rust Belt towns, East Liverpool's manufacturing economy has collapsed over the last several decades. The 10,000 residents left behind now wake up to the ruins of abandoned factories and boarded-up homes. Those good-paying jobs with benefits have been largely replaced by low-wage service work in health care and fast-food restaurants. A long economic depression bred despair and the bad decisions that go with it. Opioid addiction is common. When Officer Green flipped on his dashboard siren, he expected to uncover illicit substances in the Impala. This wasn't a basic traffic stop—it had the potential to be a whole lot more.

The Impala's driver seemed to know it too. At the sound of sirens and flashing lights behind him, 25-year-old Justin Buckel panicked. He decelerated, taking his hands off the wheel so that he could grab as many small bags of white powder as he could. He tried ditching them out the window, but instead, they spilled everywhere, caking his car's gray seats and carpet with what looked like powdered sugar.

"When I got to the scene, he was covered in it," Green told a reporter for *Morning Journal*, one of the only surviving newspapers covering the region. "I patted him down, and that was the only time I didn't wear gloves."

With Buckel pulled over, Green and his partner Smith started to search the front and back seats. The inside of the Impala was littered with empty cans of soda, bright yellow boxes of half-melted Butterfinger candies, and a hefty dusting of white powder. That powder, it turns out, contained fentanyl, an ultra-potent synthetic opioid that was quietly replacing heroin on the East Coast. Street fentanyl was a cheaper, even stronger, alternative to prescription pills and heroin. It had been making its way across Appalachia and the Midwest. Now it was in East Liverpool.

Green went over to Buckel, who was handcuffed and drenched in sweat, to ask him what the powder was. At first, Buckel said it was cocaine. A moment later, he told the truth: it was fentanyl.

Buckel was still coated in chalky white when the cops arrested him and took him into the station. Two hours later, he was booked for possession of a controlled substance with intent to distribute, and tampering with evidence. Green and his fellow officers were elated, high-fiving each other because their arrest took some fentanyl off the street. Buckel was still sweating, but it wasn't just stress about an impending drug conviction. He told the officers that he wasn't feeling well.

Unlike other opioids, such as OxyContin or heroin, fentanyl wears off much faster due to its short half-life. The withdrawal comes on quickly and more intensely. Just a couple of hours without dosing can send someone into the worst flu imaginable. Muscle cramps, sweats, nausea, and anxiety—it is absolute hell. If you've never been through it, imagine your body is sore and exhausted but your mind is wide awake and restless. They call withdrawal "kicking" because your legs feel like they've run a marathon. This is typically what happens to people who struggle with addiction when they are arrested or head to detox: they're plunged into a gruesome sickness that lasts until the opioids leave their system. Despite being a dangerous medical condition, jails rarely treat opioid withdrawal as a serious matter.

Seeing that Buckel was in bad shape, the officers at the station called for an ambulance.

That's when the captain pointed out a white smudge on Green's uniform. Green thought nothing of it and brushed the powder off with his thumb. Moments later, he started feeling a little strange. "I started talking weird. I slowly felt my body shutting down. I could hear them talking, but I couldn't respond. I was in total shock," he said.

Within minutes, the athletic, healthy officer was falling into the door. His partner, Smith, held on to him.

"No way. I'm overdosing," Green, in frequent accounts to news outlets, said that he thought at the time.

The EMTs tending to Buckel were suddenly called over to help Green, who was sprawled semi-conscious on the station's cold tile floor. Uncertain as to what was causing Green to "faint," the EMTs sprayed a dose of the opioid overdose antidote naloxone (known as Narcan) up his nose. Green was rushed to East Liverpool City Hospital, where he received three more doses of Narcan—four hits of naloxone—just for brushing a smudge of powder with his bare thumb.

Green remembers waking up in a hospital bed surrounded by his family and colleagues. Many of them were in tears.

He was released later that Friday night. The next day, Green told a reporter that he still felt like crap. He said it felt like his head was caught in a "vice grip," that his heart felt like it got "kicked in the chest," and that his stomach was still in knots, "like I have a case of the flu."

He said, "I can't wrap my head around why anyone would take the drugs."

In the following days, Green's account of accidentally overdosing went viral. What started as a local news story in the *Morning Journal* exploded into a national sensation. It was the leading story for CBS's *This Morning*, broadcast to over four million viewers.

"The opioid crisis is not only dangerous for those addicted to the drug but also for first responders," the CBS anchor said sternly, looking square at the camera.

During an interview on the *New York Times*'s podcast *The Daily*, an astonished reporter asked Green, "You overdosed just by touching the back of your shirt to see what was on it? That's all it took?"

"Yes," Green said. "That's all it took."

Another *New York Times* reporter chimed in, "You see a lot of people referring [to fentanyl] as a chemical weapon. And I don't think that's an unreasonable comparison."

"It sounds crazy," Green said. "But at what point is enough enough? We're going to have to answer calls and traffic stops in biohazard suits—or a lot of us are going to end up dead. This stuff is as dangerous as anthrax. If I mailed you this stuff, it's going to kill you quicker than anthrax."

It's easy to see how this terrifying story caught the attention of the nation. There was only one problem: it was physiologically impossible to be true.

Six hundred miles away in western Pennsylvania, an emergency medicine doctor and addiction specialist named Ryan Marino saw an incredible news story racing across the internet. He clicked on link after link in baffled disbelief: a police officer claimed that he overdosed on fentanyl from simply touching some powder with his bare hands. *Impossible!* he thought. Yet the media treated the rumor like it had come straight from the FDA.

Marino watched as seemingly every news outlet in the country jumped on the harrowing story. Touch fentanyl and die? Everyone seemed gripped with the fear that they could be next. The officer's brush with fentanyl was recounted everywhere, from the *Washington Post* to CNN; the officer was interviewed on *The Daily,* the number one podcast by the *New York Times*. Dramatic headlines were shared left and right, like this one from the *Washington Post*: "'I Was in Total Shock': Ohio Police Officer Accidentally Overdoses After Traffic Stop."

As he followed Green's account through the many news websites and sources that reported it, Dr. Marino grew increasingly skeptical. As an emergency room doctor, Marino had treated numerous opioid overdoses. He rarely ever needed to use four whole doses of naloxone

to revive someone. Two was usually enough to help people who overdosed on fentanyl from snorting and injecting large amounts of the
drug. Green just briefly touched a few specks of it—and he needed
four Narcan hits? It didn't make sense to Marino. The science of fentanyl was hard to square with all the claims being made in dramatic
news coverage of Green's story.

Could briefly touching fentanyl really cause a healthy grown
man weighing 200 pounds to instantly collapse to the ground? Was
four doses of naloxone really necessary to "bring him back to life"?
Was he really "on the brink of death" from just touching this substance?

Whatever the truth behind Green's story, it was too late. People
were panicking about the spread of fentanyl, the newest opioid on
the scene of America's deadliest drug overdose crisis in recorded
history. A new narrative about fentanyl was being created and spread
in real time.

Chris Green's "near death" experience in 2017 was only one of
the first to make headlines. Years later, who could ignore the man-
made disaster we're living through? The sheer magnitude of overdose
deaths has spawned a hysterical madness that leaks into every aspect
of our lives. Everything is tinged with fear born from misinformation. Some politicians are fighting to label fentanyl a weapon of mass
destruction. Others are trying to authorize the use of military force
against Mexico. Certain judges say that lengthy minimum mandatory sentences don't go far enough for drug convictions. Some of the
grieving public wants swift and certain execution.

The full sweep and force of America's fentanyl crisis, all the fear
and anger and madness it has caused, has yet to be fully accounted
for. I knew I wouldn't feel right until I wrote this book. It felt like I
had no other choice.

In 2022, an average of 300 Americans died from an overdose every single day. That's around 109,680 human souls. One death every

four minutes. People are turned away when they ask for help: according to the National Institutes of Health, only about 20 percent of the roughly 2.5 million people with opioid use disorder (OUD) had received medication treatment in 2021. Why is this getting worse when everyone seems to know it's a problem?

One of the hardest parts of being an advocate is getting people to care about problems that appear distant and far away. It's all too human to perceive a threat as impersonal. When danger strikes, it's always somewhere else. Someone else's family. Someone else's friend. We saw this play out with the COVID-19 pandemic, but we've long seen this same pattern with the overdose crisis in America as well. The federal government didn't declare overdose a "public health emergency" until 2017, when they finally acknowledged the three waves of the crisis—driven by Big Pharma's greed and the widespread availability of pharmaceutical opioids like OxyContin.

Once, I agreed with calling these waves an epidemic. Now I know that they are *endemic*. We might hear a lot of noise about opioids—specifically fentanyl—but the community affected by overdoses has been abandoned. The CDC defines an endemic as "the constant presence and/or usual prevalence of a disease or infectious agent in a population within a geographic area." To put it another way, an endemic is what happens when a life-threatening condition is tolerated. It's become part of daily life. Like the coronavirus, the overdose endemic is consistently present. This is not because we've "won," but because the institutions that are supposed to intervene have given up trying.

I wrote this book because I do not accept the widespread deaths as endemic to our culture. I refuse to normalize it. I can't heartlessly pretend, like so many others, that overdoses are "nature taking its course." Opioid deaths are preventable. They're not natural. They are the consequences of policy failure, combined with misinformation and life-threatening stigma, discrimination, and prejudice. What we don't know is killing us. This book is about what needs to change.

The focus of drug policy right now should be on preventing as many fatal overdoses as possible. People die because that isn't our focus. Instead, America is still fighting a disastrous drug war that focuses on punishment and retribution over the goal of saving lives. Harm reduction and recovery get lip service and a few extra grants. But it's a drop in the bucket compared to the billions poured into criminalizing addiction and punishing sick people. The average overdose prevention or recovery nonprofit operates on a small six-figure budget at best—less than the annual salary of a single Bay Area programmer.

Overdose prevention and recovery support is about access, which means that at the end of the day, survival is about money and community collaboration. When we defund harm reduction and recovery organizations, limit social services and treatment options, close down overdose prevention sites, gentrify historically Black neighborhoods, and price community resource providers out of urban areas, people die. Bigger enforcement and interdiction budgets won't solve the problem. Neither will harsher drug policy.

If we don't correct our current course, we'll be stuck in this vicious cycle of loss, pain, and sickness. Possibly forever.

Understanding this doesn't make it easier to live with. The essential, broad-reaching changes needed to save lives will arrive too late for millions of people. That is, if they arrive at all. I've sat at the table with public officials who are eager to tell CNN how much they "care" about "addicts" as they gut policies that would implement basic recovery and harm-reduction measures in their own jurisdiction. I know from experience that the very politicians who are eager to virtue-signal their way into re-election are not as supportive as they seem.

A few years ago, I had no question about my partisan identity, but I can no longer say that with confidence. I feel like both major parties have left our movement behind—and I find my ideology these days more aligned with independents. Some elected officials on both sides of the aisle offer impactful, meaningful solutions. And on both sides, there are even more people who lean on drug policy that is older—and dustier—than Richard Nixon. More than once, I've met with so-called progressive politicians who are eager to look "woke" on drugs while they sponsor legislation that consigns thousands of my community members to a preventable death.

It's hard not to feel betrayed, especially when I put so much faith in America—its ideals—the principles that were set down to protect our nation from its very first breath.

In this so-called endemic, I am one of the millions of people who are considered disposable because of addiction. Many of my community members are prevented from participating in the electoral process because of draconian laws that say people with drug convictions can't vote. If I need health insurance or medical care, I face discrimination because of my substance use history—even though I've been in recovery for almost a decade. The same is true for housing, employment, and other basic rights. Despite years of trying to bend the arc, people are still not given an equal chance at survival.

At the end of the day, the people I love continue to die—not because nobody cared about them, but because someone's polling points or political positioning was more important than human life. Media outlets that push sensational misinformation and feed on clicks for ad revenue push the narrative that this is hopeless. That the deaths will never stop. Sometimes it's easy to buy into that.

But other times, I know that we can do better.

As you read these pages, know that your long-held beliefs may be challenged. You may feel disheartened. Yet, I hope that this book leads you to the truth, and helps you find your own path. It's not an easy one—I should know. It's one we take turns carrying as we remember to nurture ourselves and one another—to step back when it's needed and honor the moments that sustain us in this long, up-hill battle.

When it's all said and done, I believe that our persistence is what will set this movement apart.

And in the end, I truly believe that history is on our side.

1

MAINSTREAM FEAR

Dr. Ryan Marino likes to sport quirky, thick-framed glasses and Hawaiian shirts. When we first talked on Zoom in 2021, I complimented him on his latest pair of frames: leopard print. Right around the time Chris Green's "fentanyl overdose" went viral in 2017, Marino saw something strange through his fashionable specs: People in the emergency department who presented with all the symptoms of an opioid overdose tested negative for all opioids. No heroin. No oxycodone. No opioids whatsoever showed up in their system. Yet, they were ODing. How could that be?

Marino decided to become a doctor because he was fascinated by science and biology from a young age. As far back as he could remember, he loved to figure out how things worked. He studied medicine at the University of Pittsburgh in Pennsylvania, graduating in 2014; then, he took a position as an assistant professor at Case Western University in Cleveland. Both Ohio and Pennsylvania have overdose death rates far above the national average. And it's not a coincidence that both states are home to small towns like East Liverpool that are reeling from the flight of industry and manufacturing jobs. A study from 2018 by economists at the University of Chicago shows that towns that lost manufacturing jobs saw higher rates of opioid overdose deaths.

Working in Ohio and Pennsylvania guaranteed that Marino would encounter patients from all walks of life, including those suffering from addiction. From the moment he started working on his degree, he'd known medicine would be a hard and demanding job, and he knew he would witness people suffering. But he never would have predicted that his desire to help others would take him to the frontlines of a raging overdose crisis.

In 2021, when I first began interviewing Marino, more than 109,000 people died from drug overdoses, according to estimates by the Centers for Disease Control and Prevention. Overdoses have killed more than one million people since the crisis took off in 1999. And Marino was on the cusp of the wave of medical workers trying to understand why it was happening.

"People who use heroin aren't like what you see in Hollywood movies," Marino told me. "It can really be anyone." Medical schools don't teach a meaningful number of addiction courses, so Marino mostly learned on the job. He had plenty of opportunities to polish his expertise. "At a certain point, addiction started becoming a major part of my clinical work. In an eight-hour shift, I could see the same person twice, and that would not be uncommon."

By 2017, on top of his extra training in addiction medicine, Marino had become a newly minted toxicologist. This is a field of study that tries to understand how the human body interacts with chemicals and medicine. The young doctor was now board-certified in addiction medicine, emergency medicine, and toxicology—a trifecta of expert knowledge about drugs. It seemed like an important but niche combination of skills—until the frenzy over fentanyl began to swirl in the media.

To understand what was happening, Marino had to become something like a drug detective. He used his skills in toxicology to investigate blood and urine samples to try and uncover the culprit behind this rash of overdoses inundating Ohio and Pennsylvania. What was this silent killer's name? Could it be stopped?

Marino eventually realized he was witnessing a dangerous and unprecedented shift in America's drug supply. Epidemiologists and drug experts have come to describe the overdose crisis as playing out in three waves. The first wave, from roughly 1999 to 2010, is the one most people are familiar with. This involved greedy pharmaceutical companies like Purdue Pharma falsely marketing their blockbuster opioid, OxyContin. That drug poured gasoline on America's opioid addiction, including my own. (The death and destruction caused by Purdue, owned by the notorious Sackler family, is well-charted territory, and it's a story I chronicled in my previous two books.)

But a lot has changed since Big Pharma started the first wave.

The second wave began around 2010. The government had cracked down on prescription pain relievers, and the number of prescriptions doctors wrote for opioids fell drastically. But that didn't mean addiction disappeared. The street market adapted. Soon, America was flooded with cheap and high-quality heroin. By 2010, pills like OxyContin were more expensive and became harder to find, and so thousands of people—including me—switched to heroin. Many didn't survive the leap from pills to dope. Between 2010 and 2012, overdose deaths involving heroin more than doubled.

But this second wave wouldn't last for very long. A bigger, more dangerous swell wasn't far behind. Manufacturing enough heroin to meet America's insatiable demand was a costly and resource-heavy enterprise for drug traffickers. Producing heroin at scale requires thousands of acres of farmable land, the right climate, and heavy labor. Farmers must cultivate opium poppies and turn the raw, goopy substance into street-ready heroin. This type of heroin typically comes in the form of sticky black tar or off-white powder—not unlike the grayish powder inside Buckel's Impala.

Around 2014, right as Marino was graduating from medical school, the third, and so far, deadliest, wave of overdoses crashed onto America. Fentanyl entered the scene. And the drug crisis exploded.

Like the first and second waves, the third wave—fentanyl—was very much about making money. Essentially, it was more bang for a drug trafficker's buck. This model worked for the Sackler family, and it worked for El Chapo too. Instead of investing tons of resources into the agricultural production required for heroin, drug cartels switched to synthetic production. Now, the surging demand for opioids in America could be met with only a few basic chemicals and a single rogue chemist. Just like Walter White in the TV show *Breaking Bad,* shady chemists could produce massive amounts of methamphetamine right under everyone's nose—and fentanyl analogues too.

The third wave caught everybody, including Marino, by surprise. So what was going on with Marino's patients who tested negative for all opioids?

It turns out, Marino explained, that standard drug tests used in hospitals and emergency departments simply didn't test for opioids like fentanyl. Instead, they would pick up drugs like oxycodone and heroin. Marino started using high-tech instruments to understand what was happening with his patients. And that's when he discovered that many people were using fentanyl without even realizing it. Before long, the powder people bought on the street had no heroin in it at all. It was something else—a drug from a completely different part of the opioid family. Marino found not only fentanyl in the bodies of people but also strange synthetic cousins of fentanyl, called fentanyl analogues. These versions of fentanyl vary wildly in how strong they are.

Here's an example of the difference. Imagine you're at dinner ordering a glass of your favorite wine. You know it usually contains about 12 percent alcohol, so all you want is enough to feel a nice buzz. Now, imagine that instead of 12 percent alcohol, that glass of red wine was 90 percent alcohol. And you just drank a whole bottle's worth in a single glass without realizing it. That's what happened in America's third wave of the overdose crisis, but on a massive scale.

Witnessing the transition from pills to heroin to fentanyl forced Marino to become an expert in all things fentanyl. He threw himself into learning everything he could about the drug to try and understand the way it interacts with the human body. He was doing all this work to try and save lives, to try and alert people that the heroin they thought they were doing was actually fentanyl, and it was much more lethal.

"I was trying to get awareness out to other people about what was happening," he said. Without intending to, Marino turned into America's Paul Revere. He shouted, "Fentanyl is coming! Fentanyl is coming!" to more than 72,000 followers from his massively popular Twitter account. His popularity online would soon become one of his greatest weapons as the fear around fentanyl morphed into total hysteria.

As more and more stories like Officer Green's went viral, Marino's phone started ringing off the hook with reporters asking him for a quote. All he could tell them was that there's more to this story. It's bigger than you think. And if we don't get ready, a lot of people are going to die.

For Marino, his passion for treating addiction became much bigger than a scientific or theoretical pursuit. Right as the third wave crashed onto America's shores, "I ended up losing someone very close to me to a fentanyl overdose." As he told me this story, his usually energetic and fast-talking tone grew quieter and solemn when he mentioned losing a close friend. For both of us, this heartbreaking loss made the crisis even more personal.

Like me—and many of the people I've met on my journey— Marino was inspired by his grief to help others. He was on a mission to help people with addiction be treated with the dignity and respect they deserve. This wasn't just about a pat on the head or building more rehabs, or even sharing recovery stories in the mainstream. He wanted a total overhaul of the American health-care system.

"In medicine, the treatment of addiction has been lacking, to say the least," he said.

He saw up close how America's health-care system discriminated against people with addiction and treated them like dirt, less than human. But instead of running away from addicted patients, like most of the doctors he trained with did, Marino embraced them.

"When I was in my residency, my colleagues and coworkers would always be like, 'Oh, you just want to take care of the drunks all day?' and things like that really rubbed me the wrong way. Actually, saying that it rubbed me the wrong way is an understatement."

It truly pissed him off.

"I realized that people are getting treated poorly because of all of these misconceptions and biases," Marino said.

If highly trained doctors who take an oath to treat all human beings with respect, to heal their suffering and do no harm—if this is the way they think about addiction—what about everybody else? What do everyday people think about addiction if they've never encountered a loved one with a drug problem? What about the readers of this very book? Do *you* think people who struggle with addiction (or use drugs) should be arrested, locked away, and punished? Is addiction really the individual's fault?

Green and his fellow officers had some harsh words about drug users after the incident where he claimed that touching fentanyl nearly killed him. Of these powerful opioids like fentanyl, he said, "They are not only killing the people willing to shove it into their own veins; now they're killing people like me and my family."

After Green's "exposure" incident, a high-ranking official with the East Liverpool Police Department said to a local news reporter, "It's time our state gets tough on those who peddle this poison and create laws to protect those who protect us."

The story was changing—fast. In this ultra-viral version, people with addictions weren't the victims. Instead, the cops were cast as the ones hurt by fentanyl. Other people's addictions victimized police officers who were caught in the line of fire. While trying to serve and protect, they were exposed to a mysterious chemical weapon that was deadlier than a bullet and more insidious than a criminal network. It was a story straight out of a comic book—and the media ate it up.

If the fentanyl freak-out sounds familiar, it's because it comes from the classic antidrug playbook. This kind of story is very much aligned with the status quo. Black and white, sick and healthy, pure and dirty. America's War on Drugs has always been portrayed as Us (the good guys) versus Them (the drug users, the bad guys). The solution was to punish the bad guys, treat them like supervillains, make them pay, and then banish them—maybe even for life.

Justin Buckel, the 25-year-old who was pulled over by Green on that Friday night in May, was indeed punished.

The state of Ohio threw the book at Buckel. He pleaded guilty to 23 charges stemming from the East Liverpool arrest, including trafficking in heroin, trafficking in cocaine, 13 counts of aggravated possession of drugs, tampering with evidence (for ripping the baggie of powder open and trying to ditch it), and last but not least, "assault on a peace officer."

Buckel was sentenced to six and a half years in prison.

The last charge, "assault on a peace officer," was handed down because Buckel was convicted of "exposing" Green to fentanyl. That assault charge wound up supercharging his punishment. Assault on a police officer is a first-degree felony in Ohio and carries a mandatory minimum sentence of three years in prison and a fine of up to $20,000. Buckel was certainly no cartel leader or drug kingpin. He wasn't a nefarious, cop-killing psycho. He had no intention of harming a cop. He was small potatoes, just a 25-year-old living in the ruins of a hollowed-out manufacturing town, struggling with addiction.

But because he was in possession of fentanyl, Buckel was viewed as a dangerous individual, as someone whose drug use almost led to a police officer dying. He was treated like a terrorist in possession of a chemical weapon.

But what if the police and the news media are wrong about what really happened on that Friday night?

I asked Marino what he thought when he saw Green's "fentanyl overdose" go viral. "I remember that guy was everywhere," Marino said. "He was on the *Today* show and everything. I remember thinking, 'This is ridiculous.'" The broad-shouldered, physically fit, blond-haired, all-American cop was praised as a hero. He looked like a hero too—a superhero.

"At first, I kind of laughed it off," Marino said. "People are desperate to get on TV all the time and will say the craziest things."

As Marino watched Green talk about the harrowing story, he noticed "a bunch of red flags."

Something wasn't adding up.

The most obvious tell for Marino, who witnessed and treated countless overdoses on the job, was that Green's symptoms were not remotely similar to the classic symptoms of an opioid overdose. Usually, an opioid overdose can be spotted because someone has tiny pinpoint pupils. Their breathing is slow and shallow. Their lips begin to turn blue and purple. Losing oxygen, they turn cold and lifeless. People overdosing are completely unconscious until they gradually stop breathing entirely. If they are not given Narcan, they may never wake up.

Green did not show any of these symptoms. Marino examined the story carefully and noticed that Green was never tested at the hospital to see if any drugs were actually in his system. It's extremely unlikely that there would have been because Marino knows from years of medical training and research that fentanyl cannot enter the bloodstream by simply touching it.

"It's impossible," Marino said. "You'd have to be standing in a wind tunnel with fentanyl blowing around everywhere in order to get 'exposed.'"

As Marino investigated, he discovered something that helped explain what really helped fuel the panic. In the months leading up to Green's "exposure," the Drug Enforcement Administration (DEA) began urging local police departments around the US to stock up on protective gear, like masks and gloves, because they thought touching fentanyl could cause an overdose. Police captains relayed this message to all of their officers, telling them that coming into contact with microscopic amounts of fentanyl could be deadly.

This belief turned out to be a powerful force, and became one of the main sources of a massive panic around fentanyl.

At first, Marino wasn't sure what would come from Green's so-called overdose story. Maybe it would just blow away, he thought. Maybe people would forget about it and move on. But soon, he realized how serious a threat this mistaken belief about fentanyl exposure could be.

"I realized this is something that needs to be dealt with head-on," he said. "If not, it's gonna get people killed."

And so, if it wasn't really a fentanyl overdose, what ultimately caused Green to faint and fall to the ground?

"Fear," Marino said. "It's all fear."

2

The bowling ball on my chest is always heaviest at 3 a.m. Its steady pressure pushes me out of sleep most mornings before the sun rises on either coast. I could set my alarm by it, but I don't need to. Wherever I wake up—in hotel rooms, at friends' houses, or in the home I share with my husband—the bowling ball is there, in the pocket right between my ribs and a little bit north of my stomach.

When the weight wakes me up in the morning, it's never for a good reason. Every day, I talk to friends, parents, loved ones, and peer workers as they face yet another unspeakable tragedy. One in ten Americans has lost someone to an overdose, and that number is only rising. An entire generation is dying off, as though killed by a plague that nobody is brave enough to name.

There are no words for these losses—these deaths. What I felt in the beginning—the hot anger and outrage that fueled my advocacy—has faded to a dull ache that sits in my body and never goes away.

It feels like grief. Or maybe, heartbreak.

Years after entering recovery, I need more than my fingers and toes to count the number of people I know who lost their lives to fentanyl. Within the past few years, that number has increased exponentially; it seems like fentanyl was in *everything*, from cocaine to fake prescription pills to bags of heroin. I left the scene at exactly the right moment—and I know that, had I continued to use, I would be dead today. Fentanyl has no discernible taste, smell, or color. The only way to tell if your substances are tainted with it is to test them—how many people living on the streets like I did, or planning to party with their friends, actually do that? I am positive that I would have been a casualty along with many of the people I cared about and used with.

There is no bad time to stop using heroin, but I am positive that I quit at exactly the right moment. In 2014, I was at the tail end of my chaotic drug use. I was more than a little worse for wear. After years of living on and off the streets, I was in bad shape. I injected black tar heroin into every vein that I could find—and they seemed to be shrinking daily, hiding under my skin while I tried to dig them out with the jagged syringe I kept on me at all times. I was the type of IV drug user you see in after-school specials—the kind they tell you to be scared of on the news. I was the addict hiding in a doorway to cook my dope in a battered spoon. I shared needles, slept where I could, and was living, one might say, just to exist.

Heroin didn't even get me high anymore. It just made me feel like I was going to survive.

One of my last using buddies was a guy named Gor. He was close to my age, but, like me, it was hard to tell how old he was. Although he was still in his early thirties, he was battered by countless sleepless nights, never-ending withdrawal, and the anxiety of living minute to minute. His cheeks were carved hollows. His brown eyes darted from side to side. His gums bled from malnutrition, bad dope, and the endless grinding of his jaw. He was Armenian, and his curly black hair was tangled and wild. One side of his head was cropped short, where he'd cut off a matted dreadlock that bothered him. Like mine, his nails were darker and oilier than a mechanic's. We shared the little bit we had, from spare change to the spoon we used as a cooker. We shared needles. Stories. Like me, Gor had a family—a family that loved him. Sometimes, we talked about where we came from, but often, it was just too painful.

The last time I saw Gor, we were dividing a small bag of heroin on South Hill Street in downtown Los Angeles. It was a cold Southern California night shortly after Halloween. We went through our ritual of holding the lighter under our spoon, drawing the foul-looking liquid into our syringe, and painstakingly bringing a vein to the surface of the skin. It was a pathetic amount of dope, hardly enough to take the edge off, but we still split it. Fair was fair.

"I need to get help," I told Gor as I watched him tug his sleeve back.

"That's great, man. You should," he said. The needle found an open lesion on his arm and slid in. I shivered. I had never hated heroin more, or needed it more intensely.

"I'm done with this," I told him, as I had said a hundred times, after every shot.

Little did I know that, this time, I was on my way to speaking the truth.

A few weeks after that score, I finally got into treatment—first, a detox program and then inpatient treatment that would put me on track for sober living and set me up to start getting my life back. I was grateful that I even had a bed. After years of struggling to find the help I needed, I knew how lucky I was. As it turned out, it wasn't a moment too soon.

In my third week of treatment, my counselor finally let me check my email and Facebook under supervision. She watched me while I logged in from her computer and started scrolling through my notifications. Gor and I were Facebook friends, so I clicked on his profile.

"Gone too soon," the posts on his wall said.

I felt the too-familiar bowling ball in my chest. How was this possible?

It was a fentanyl OD. Gor hadn't stood a chance.

At that time, we didn't even know fentanyl was on the streets in Los Angeles. It was a tiny ripple—a hint of the terrible tsunami that was on its way to crush us. I thought of Gor, unknowingly jabbing what would be his last load into his veins. The bag he'd bought was mixed with something else, but he had no way to tell. To him, it probably looked like our usual dose. It killed him.

That could have been me. If I'd been with Gor instead of where I was, it *would* have been. I felt my body turn to ice and start to shake with the realization of what I had just avoided. That bag had my number on it. I sank onto my freshly made bed and hugged myself. I'd dodged a bullet, and I could practically hear it zinging past me.

While heroin was no longer part of my life, it seemed that fentanyl was inescapable. Even in recovery, I couldn't completely avoid it. Seven years into my recovery, I had to have an outpatient medical procedure, and the doctor told me that they'd administer fentanyl as part of my anesthesia. I panicked.

"You can't do that," I sputtered. "I'm in recovery! I could relapse or die."

The doctor tried to reassure me, but I wasn't buying it. I begged for another option, and even asked them to do the procedure without anesthesia, but there was no other way. I was terrified. I reached out to all my support people, told my friends, and hoped for the best. As I was rolled into the operating room, I said a prayer for my recovery. I didn't want to end up like Gor. I didn't want to go back to the misery of shooting up, chasing a high that didn't exist for me anymore. A masked face bent over me and told me to count down from 10.

"Nine, eight," I said. In an instant, the world went dark.

When I woke up, I was shocked by how *normal* I felt. The fentanyl I'd been given was a low pharmaceutical dose. It was administered by an anesthesiologist in a hospital setting where I was monitored. I expected to wake up from surgery foaming at the mouth, pulling out my IV line, and running down the street to find the nearest heroin dealer. Instead, I just felt like myself. (Well, myself plus a little bit of pain.) I'd been given the same fentanyl that is commonly used in epidurals during labor. And I was fine.

Had I been wrong about fentanyl? Was I misinformed? Yes—and no.

———————————

There are a lot of misconceptions swirling around fentanyl. Some law enforcement agencies believe it is a weapon of mass destruction that kills indiscriminately, like poisons or anthrax. Every September and October, like clockwork, Fox News anchors tell viewers that drug dealers are lacing Halloween candy with it. Laypeople have been told not to pick up stray dollar bills off the ground because any bill could have fentanyl on it and cause them to OD. A police department in Arkansas told shoppers to wipe down grocery carts because fentanyl residue might be on the handle. A firefighter once told me he would not give CPR to someone overdosing because he might OD if the victim's sweat got in his mouth.

All of this is complete bullshit.

People believe these sorts of myths and urban legends because they are afraid. Maybe they've lost friends and loved ones to addiction and overdose, and they are grieving. Maybe it's plain old ignorance. But the truth about fentanyl is scary enough without these fantasies and fairy tales. In order to prevent more people from dying, we have to be honest about what we're up against.

That's why it's critically important to reckon with the science and history of fentanyl. Fentanyl is not the boogeyman. It was created by human beings, and we are in the middle of an all-too-human crisis. It's up to us to do something. But first, we have to see the bigger picture.

Like many other drugs today, the story of fentanyl begins with a powerful pharmaceutical company. In 1959, an ambitious chemist named Dr. Paul Janssen first synthesized the pain reliever known as fentanyl while tinkering with the chemical structure of morphine. He was only 33 and worked in a lab given to him by his father, a prominent family doctor in Belgium. In this small lab with just a few scientists, Janssen discovered a medicine that would change the world.

Unlike morphine, which is an opioid derived from the sap of poppy plants, fentanyl is completely synthetic and is made in a laboratory. That means the production of fentanyl requires no farmers, no fields of fragile flower crops, and no perfect growing climate. All it takes to create tons and tons of fentanyl is a chemist, a lab, and the right precursors (the chemicals used in the reaction that produces fentanyl).

The production of fentanyl matters a great deal when it comes to understanding how this drug came to be so widespread and available today. If you've seen any news stories about fentanyl, you've probably heard about how dangerous and potent it is. Fentanyl is at least 100 times more potent than morphine. Whereas drugs like morphine are measured in milligrams, doses of fentanyl are measured in micrograms.

Until Janssen's creation, the world had never seen such a potent opioid. The development of synthetic opioids has marked rapid progress in the field of medicine. It revolutionized surgery. But its legacy is complicated. Like all opioids, fentanyl has a light side and a dark side. The drug has relieved pain and suffering for millions of people and has become a staple of modern medicine, but it has also *caused* profound pain and suffering. A lifesaving medicine in hospitals can also be a life-threatening drug on the street.

That's why fentanyl was called a "good medicine, and a bad drug" at a recent United Nations conference. And something so powerful couldn't be safely isolated for medical use for long. Soon, fentanyl moved out of labs and hospitals and into the hands of shady chemists and drug dealers on the streets of California.

———————————

Paul Janssen, affectionately referred to as "Dr. Paul" by his friends and colleagues, founded the company Janssen Pharmaceuticals in 1953. Young and bright, Janssen's mission was a noble one: create new pharmaceuticals that will treat illnesses, cure diseases, and benefit the world. For Janssen, the mission of medicine was also deeply personal. When he was in high school, his younger sister died of tuberculous and meningitis. He thought better medicine could have saved her. His instincts were right. Today, tuberculosis and meningitis can be managed with antibiotics. Had Janssen's sister been born at a different time, she would have lived.

Janssen's mission brought him instant success. By 1961, Janssen Pharmaceuticals was bought by the health-care giant Johnson & Johnson. "Drugs developed by Dr. Janssen and his company treat a wide range of disorders, including psychoses, chronic pain, and fungal infections," according to a 2003 *New York Times* obituary for Janssen, who died at 77. After a storied career, Janssen held more than 100 patents and authored nearly a thousand scientific papers. One of Janssen's colleagues referred to him as "one of the most productive drug inventors of all time." Today, 11 of Dr. Janssen's discoveries are on the World Health Organization's List of Essential Medicines.

In just one year, working in that small lab given to him by his father, Janssen and his team synthesized five hundred new chemical compounds. Seven of them showed some medical potential to help people. One of those medicines turned out to be a potent and powerful pain reliever that would, in Janssen's own words, "herald a revolution."

Opium and its many chemical cousins have been used to relieve pain and suffering for thousands of years. Around the time Janssen invented fentanyl, medicine was rapidly changing. In the 19th and

20th centuries, morphine was used not only for pain relief, but it was often combined with other drugs to put people to sleep for surgery. The chance of dying during surgery was very high, so surgeons all over the world were looking for better alternatives. Janssen, an avid reader of medical journals, was well aware of morphine's problems. Named after Morpheus, the Greek god of dreams, morphine wasn't suitable for long, complicated surgical procedures. So Janssen set out to invent a better drug.

He began to manipulate the morphine molecule, hoping to invent an opioid that was stronger and safer. The more potent a drug, the lower the dose needed to get an effect. And drugs in lower doses tend to have fewer side effects than drugs that require taking larger amounts. When Janssen first created fentanyl, he had to first test it on animals to see if it actually worked. Back then, there was a popular technique called the hot plate test. The test involved putting a mouse on a heated plate, similar to what's used for keeping coffee mugs warm. The hot plate was surrounded by clear glass so the mouse could be observed and not escape. To keep their paws from overheating, the mice would lick them and jump up to escape the intensifying pain of standing on the burning plate. After dosing the mouse with the drug and turning on the heat, the scientists would start a stopwatch to measure how long it took the mouse to start licking its paws. To prevent any permanent harm to the mice, scientists adopted a 30-second maximum time for the hot plate test.

Mice that were dosed with fentanyl could withstand the heat for much longer than mice dosed with morphine. The higher the dose of fentanyl the mice were given, the longer it took them to start licking their paws and jumping. The hot plate test showed that fentanyl was way, way stronger than morphine—anywhere from 100 to 200 times stronger.

After testing fentanyl on rats and other animals, scientists determined that the drug was safe for humans in controlled and monitored settings. Scientists kept on studying fentanyl, and they learned that it also had a rapid onset, which meant that it kicked in much quicker than other opioids and it didn't last as long. Fentanyl was the fastest acting opioid ever discovered. The rapid onset and short duration of fentanyl is another important property that would have major consequences for America's overdose crisis. It also made surgery much safer. The effects of fentanyl didn't linger around for many hours the way morphine's did, which meant that patients could be put under anesthesia with fentanyl and not have to be monitored for a long time after.

Janssen's discovery began to catch on in the 1960s and 1970s, and fentanyl quickly became the most popular and widely used anesthetic for surgery around the world. In his memoir, Janssen wrote, "Without this [fentanyl] compound and its analogue, sufentanil, open-heart surgery would not be possible." Sufentanil, another synthetic opioid discovered by Janssen, is twice as powerful as fentanyl. Janssen also created carfentanil, which is 10,000 times stronger than morphine, and is primarily used to tranquilize and sedate large animals like elephants.

While fentanyl was being widely used for surgery, it also became a game changer for treating severe pain, especially for cancer patients. By the 1990s, it was being prescribed in the form of patches, fruit-flavored lollipops, and oral sprays to help patients, both young and old, cope with extreme pain at the end of their lives. But the same drug that revolutionized the field of medicine and surgery would also cause hundreds of thousands of overdose deaths in the streets of America, forcing humanity to grapple with the light and dark sides of opioids.

A Series of Close Calls

Just as I had dodged the fentanyl bullet, America has also had many near misses and close calls with the drug over the past 50 years. Long before Purdue Pharma invented OxyContin and sparked a firestorm of addiction and overdoses in the 1990s, and long before fentanyl took over heroin markets in places like Kensington, Philadelphia—actually, only a decade after its initial invention in Belgium—there were at least four reported instances of fentanyl being produced by underground chemists and sold on the street to heroin users in the US.

Most news articles you'll see frame fentanyl like it's something entirely new. And many people are led to believe that America's overdose crisis began with Purdue Pharma and OxyContin in the 1990s. (That's why almost every chart tallying overdose mortality by the Centers for Disease Control begins in 1999.) But the facts and history tell a very different story. It began at least 20 years earlier in California.

A 1991 research article in the prestigious *Journal of the American Medical Association* (*JAMA*) identified a "designer opiate" that caused more than 100 overdose deaths in California in 1979. That "designer opiate" was sold as "China White" on the street. (The name China White is supposed to describe heroin produced in Southeast Asia from countries near the battlefields of Vietnam, which come in the form of a whitish powder. Heroin from Mexico is a sticky substance called "black tar.") But the drug that caused this rash of overdoses in California contained no heroin at all. Researchers nicknamed the mystery drug "bogus China White." It took chemists and toxicologists over one month to identify what this drug actually was. Years later, researchers like Dr. Marino went through the same struggle trying to identify new versions of fentanyl being sold in Pennsylvania in the mid-2010s.

The authorities finally figured it out, and they called the drug 3-methylfentanyl (TMF). It was a close chemical cousin to the original fentanyl invented by Janssen. This version of fentanyl is anywhere from 1,000 to 2,000 times stronger than morphine. Heroin users in the 1970s had no idea how potent fentanyl was, and many inadvertently took doses that were too strong. This led to the first known outbreak of fentanyl overdoses in California. It's also the first documented instance of synthetic opioids and fentanyl analogues being sold on the street as heroin. The *New York Times* ran a short article about the sudden rise in overdose deaths and reported small quantities of synthetic opioids being seized in Riverside, California, where law enforcement suspected that a secret lab was making the drug.

As more heroin was being shipped to America from Southeast Asia, and as more veterans from Vietnam returned home from war having experimented with the drug, America began to experience a small-scale opioid epidemic. But because heroin was coming from so far away, it was a somewhat scarce product. If a shipment of heroin was seized by the DEA, some cities and towns might lose their entire supply. That's where synthetic opioids like fentanyl come into play: with the right ingredients, one chemist anywhere in California can cook up enough fentanyl from scratch to start supplying the whole West Coast.

In 1981, scientists published another paper about the "synthetic heroin" found in California. They titled the article "The Bogus Drug: Three Methyl & Alpha Methyl Fentanyl Sold as 'China White.'" This fascinating study shed urgent light on this early wave of illicitly produced fentanyl. The article detailed the kinds of people in the early 1980s who were using it. The mythical figure we now recognize as a stereotypical drug user—a disheveled, homeless person who lives under a bridge—is far from the reality. Here is the synthetic opioid user the study describes, a man living in California in 1980:

> T.A. is a 33-year-old white male who has completed high school with a diploma. He has lived in the east Contra Costa area all his life and comes from a very wealthy family. He owns his own house, is married, and is the father of two children. He was, up until recently, employed at the local steel mill. Since then he has supported his family by "hustling." One of his "hustles" includes the sales of drugs. He

was introduced to TMF-AMF sometime during the summer of 1980. He says he doesn't like to deal with the drug because there have been complaints from customers and it is difficult to "cut." He claims to have a [fentanyl] habit of at least $100 a day.

Looking back in time, men like T.A. foreshadow the kinds of people who are using opioids across America today. (More on that later.)

This first outbreak of underground fentanyl didn't stop in California. In the late 1980s, opioid overdoses were considered rare in rural Pennsylvania. Suddenly, Allegheny County saw a fourfold increase in drug overdose deaths. From 1986 to 1988, the Allegheny County coroner investigated 99 overdose deaths containing synthetic opioids. Pittsburgh saw as many as 60 nonfatal overdoses in 1988 alone, according to a *New York Times* article with the headline: "Synthetic Heroin Seen As Cause in 18 Deaths." That same year, the very same version of fentanyl—3-methylfentanyl—caused 16 overdose deaths in western Pennsylvania, mostly in small towns outside of Pittsburgh.

The 1988 *Times* article quoted Gary Henderson, then a professor of pharmacology at the University of California–Davis Medical School: "[The death count] is really the first major incident outside of California from a clandestine laboratory putting material on the street. And it's certainly the most fentanyl activity we've seen since 1984."

Law enforcement, public health officials, and epidemiologists were all scrambling to figure out what was going on. Their goal was to find the source of the "synthetic heroin" and put a stop to it before more people died. Writing in a 1991 research article on the western Pennsylvania outbreak, epidemiologists working with the CDC concluded with an eerie warning: "Drug abusers in the northeastern United States should be considered at risk for more 'designer drug' overdose outbreaks in the future."

Decades later, it turned out they were right.

From California to Pennsylvania, these first outbreaks of illicitly made fentanyl being sold as heroin were relatively short-lived. In these early cases, law enforcement investigations quickly uncovered the drug rings responsible for manufacturing and selling fentanyl on the street. The *Times* article reported that the number of deaths caused by synthetic opioids in California peaked at 50 in 1984, largely due to the DEA breaking up the small network of fentanyl producers based in Los Angeles. The Pennsylvania drug ring was also quickly taken down. Seven people, including a professional chemist, were arrested on December 1, 1988, for manufacturing and distributing the synthetic opioids that caused all those overdoses.

But more cases of fentanyl being sold as heroin on the street would keep popping up. The next one came in 1991. Sold on the streets of New York City, bags of heroin stamped with the name of the popular action-comedy movie *Tango and Cash* sent several people to the hospital. These bags turned out to contain heroin mixed with fentanyl. Once again, users had no clue how much of the drug was safe, and many started to overdose. Like the outbreaks before, this one came to an end after law enforcement busted the crew responsible.

After that, things were quiet for over a decade. The next fentanyl outbreak took place between 2005 and 2006, and this one was larger in scale than the previous ones. It was also more complex, and led to many more overdose deaths across America, from Detroit and Chicago to Philadelphia and New Jersey.

Around the country, heroin was being supercharged by dealers who added potent forms of fentanyl into their heroin. One Chicago gang sold their product under ominous names like "Drop Dead," "Flat Line," and "Lethal Injection" to market and brand the enhanced potency of their product. Between April 2005 and December 2006, Chicago saw 342 fentanyl-related deaths, the deadliest overdose outbreak the city had ever seen.

The spikes in fentanyl deaths and emergency room visits from the 1980s and 1990s were mainly traced back to small-scale laboratories that operated within the United States, many of which were in California. But the 2005 and 2006 outbreak was very different. Law enforcement working in the US and Mexico traced the main source of that fentanyl back to a lab in Toluca, Mexico. After Mexican authorities raided and shut down this lab, fentanyl overdoses began to decline in American cities. The supply of fentanyl dried up and eventually returned to heroin.

In total, there were four separate close calls with fentanyl between 1979 and 2006. Each time synthetic opioids and fentanyl analogues popped up in the heroin supply, law enforcement and public health officials acted quickly to figure out what was happening. They contained the danger and shut down the operations before they could spread any further. These quick and effective responses saved many lives. But today's fentanyl crisis is an entirely different beast, and whatever window there might have been to contain and stop the disaster is long gone. Illicit fentanyl has gone global, and there's no stopping it. It's here to stay.

"The Genie Came Out of the Bottle"

The third wave of America's overdose crisis was a perfect storm of horrible events that turned an already bad situation into a nightmare. But unlike weather patterns and hurricanes, this nightmare we're living through is not beyond human influence. What we're dealing with is a man-made catastrophe, the result of decisions made by people and institutions, and federal and local governments.

Overdoses linked to fentanyl in America started to rise again around 2013. Everyone, from the DEA to the CDC to cops and politicians, deployed the weapons they'd used in the 1970s to stop the flow of drugs. First, they made it harder to get OxyContin—which affected everyone, including pain patients. Many people who relied on increasingly hard-to-get Oxy shifted to buying cheap and plentiful heroin. Then, once the government realized heroin deaths were rising and targeted that, the supply shifted to fentanyl. As a result, overdose deaths rose exponentially, killing even more people than previously imaginable.

Californians in 1980 thought 100 overdose deaths from "China White" fentanyl was a massive scandal and a major public health threat. In 2020, California recorded 4,000 fentanyl-related overdose deaths. According to the CDC, it was a 140.5 percent jump from 2019, when 1,675 deaths occurred in the state. The magnitude of this fentanyl outbreak is stunning compared to all the others.

The DEA and law enforcement agencies around the country started to broadcast fentanyl as a new scourge, but doubling down on tactics from the War on Drugs didn't work this time. Banning more drugs, hiring more police officers, turning the border into a political hot potato, and giving drug users longer and harsher prison sentences were not going to stop fentanyl. Breaking up one drug ring in California or Pennsylvania was not going to work either. At the same time, the American government kept framing drug users as a scapegoat for its problems. Cynical politicians and district attorneys vowed to wage a full-on drug war in response to the fear, grief, and panic that was taking hold.

Despite the DEA and the Justice Department's talk about taking millions of doses of fentanyl off the streets, big drug seizures barely made a dent. Massive quantities of fentanyl powders and counterfeit pills are still being sold in big cities and small towns alike because whatever amount the DEA or Border Patrol seizes could almost immediately be replaced, manufactured by a small lab somewhere in Mexico.

In 2013, there were roughly 3,000 overdose deaths linked to fentanyl in the entire country. By 2018, there had been more than 28,000—nearly a tenfold increase in just five years. During this time, experts also say that the official death toll was likely a major undercount since, as Dr. Ryan Marino told me, so few medical examiners and coroners even knew to test for fentanyl during autopsies. Even more problematic, the CDC misclassified many illicit fentanyl deaths as being caused by prescription opioids, creating a situation in which the policy response massively missed its target.

By 2022, the annual death toll surged to more than 71,000, accounting for the vast majority of the more than 111,000 total overdose deaths that year. The synthetic opioid has completely replaced OxyContin and heroin.

That's the story of neighborhoods like Kensington in Philadelphia, where heroin had long been the drug of choice. In 2018, the *New York Times Magazine* dubbed Kensington the "Walmart of Heroin." The feature story paints a depressing and chaotic image of the neighborhood: on a rainy day beneath an underpass on Kensington Avenue, drug users trying to stay dry were injecting in public, nodding off on sidewalks glistening from the rain. But in 2018, fentanyl was already leaking into the heroin supply. Four years later, there was hardly any heroin left in Kensington—it's almost entirely fentanyl. There was no shortage of drug arrests in the area, but somehow the situation kept getting worse and worse.

It's as if the dealers and users were symptoms, not the disease.

"There is truly a sense of desperation," said Jonathan Caulkins, a drug policy researcher at Carnegie Mellon University in Pennsylvania. Caulkins has been studying drug markets for decades and says there has never been a crisis as deadly as the one America is in right now. "The scale of death is ridiculous. And people are clutching at straws."

Caulkins earned his PhD in operations research from the Massachusetts Institute of Technology in 1990, where he learned to analyze complex systems and networks. He explained to me that America's illegal drug supply happens to be one of the most complex, shadowy systems in the world. Illegal drugs are a multibillion-dollar industry, a massive underground market governed by secret networks of criminal organizations. Legend has it that there is so much drug money flowing around the world that, during the 2008 financial crash, the American financial system was largely kept afloat by hundreds of billions in cold hard cash from illegal drug sales. In 2016, Caulkins co-published a paper that found Americans spend nearly $150 billion on cannabis, cocaine, heroin, and methamphetamine in just one year. That's seven billion dollars shy of what we spend on alcohol.

Caulkins is frequently asked to consult on these complex problems for government agencies. What does he tell local and federal governments who wonder what on earth can be done to save lives?

He said, "When I talk to people, we typically go through a conversation where I'll say, '*This* doesn't work that well, and *this* doesn't work that well.' And they'll say, 'OK, Professor Caulkins, smartypants, what should we do?'"

His answer is depressing. "I'm deeply pessimistic of the people who now have opioid use disorder and are purchasing illegal opioids," he said bluntly. "I think if we do everything right, still an awful lot of people are going to die. This is a horrible situation for which we do not really have a fix."

Caulkins told me that when fentanyl arrived—unchecked and untraceable—it was a problem without a solution. He said, "The genie came out of the bottle."

Still, I had to hold out hope that we weren't doomed. There had to be a way out of this. To understand the way forward, I felt like I had to figure out what came before.

3

AMERICA'S LONGEST WAR

Once upon a time, in June 1971, President Richard Nixon changed history by declaring war on "drugs." Most histories trace the origin back to Nixon's statement at a press conference that summer in '71. His exact words were, "Public enemy number one in the United States is drug abuse." He made it sound like drugs—the pills, powders, and pellets that all kinds of people used for all kinds of reasons—were absolutely wreaking havoc on the American public. The solution?

"A new, all-out offensive." With just a few words, America was at war against an invisible—and, as some would later notice, an *imaginary*—enemy.

The War on Drugs is part fact, part fiction, and part fable. At the time I'm writing, 1971 is more than 50 years in the past. Time has a way of muddling the real story, especially when it comes to who did what, and why. The truth about America's drug war is actually much more complicated. The real history dates back way earlier. The version we're told is that drugs are bad, they're new or from other countries, and the government has always opposed them.

That is part of the antidrug fairy tale. In fact, people have *always* used drugs. The government has *always* wrestled with how to respond. Some drugs become legalized and marketed to doctors and patients; voilà, the "drug" becomes "medicine." A drug that is "good" doesn't end up in the government's sights. But, as any drug user or prescriber can tell you, the difference is very much a matter of context.

Some drugs occupy both the "good" and "bad" properties. One example is opioids, which straddle the line between "medicine" and "drug." Opioids are used medically and recreationally. Opioids are used both inside and outside the confines of doctors' offices and hospitals. Try winning a war on that! For over 150 years, various laws, policies, and strategies to deal with drug use and cases of addiction, from prohibition to criminal laws, have failed to come close to stopping addiction or "undesirable" drug use.

Whatever the fairy tale says, the real truth is this: long before Nixon's famous "public enemy" speech, the government had drugs in its crosshairs. Policy constantly negotiated along tenuous lines, deciding which drugs would become illegal and which would become "medicine."

The first ever legislation to so much as mention narcotics was the Chinese Exclusion Act of 1882, which sought to limit Chinese immigration to America, based on fears that migrant workers from China were stealing jobs from white Americans.

One way to control Chinese workers was to regulate their habits. After long days of backbreaking physical labor, Chinese workers smoked opium. The historian David Courtwright described the 1882 Exclusion Act as killing two birds with one stone. According to Courtwright, the law was both "anti-opium as well as anti-Chinese." The 1882 Exclusion Act was the first drug law to limit the use of opium. Did it work? Not really. For almost 150 years, the American government has tried to ban, prohibit, and prevent the use of opiate-based drugs, with little to show for it.

Prohibition creates illegal economies, and the illegal drug trade thrives under the shroud of this darkness. Whenever there's a crackdown, drugs become stronger, cheaper, and more available, both on the street and online. Young people even buy and sell pills on social media platforms. Under prohibition, criminal drug trafficking organizations accumulate enormous amounts of money and power—enough to destabilize entire countries. Despite some of the strictest drug laws on the books and harsh punishments like mandatory minimum sentences in place, America still isn't substance free. Drugs remain staggeringly easy for people to find despite the "all-out offensive" launched in 1971. The approach America stubbornly clings to produces pain and suffering while failing to achieve its most basic goals.

This is just one example of how American drug laws attempting to enforce prohibition have done an incredibly bad job of actually prohibiting drug use. If drug laws don't reduce drug use, then what are they for? What do drug laws actually do? The history of drug laws in America tells a dark story of social and racial control. The drug war is objectively America's longest-running war. So, since it has so obviously failed to stop drug use, make a dent in their availability, stop their import and export, or hurt organized crime—what is the drug war really all about? If the war "failed," why are many of its counterproductive policies still alive and well today? The answer is in the consequences of this assault on drugs. If we redefine the drug war's primary mission and goals, maybe it makes more sense. Maybe it's actually a success.

When Nixon declared a war on drugs, he was really repeating the racist doctrine that inspired laws like the 1882 Exclusion Act. It's impossible to make being Black, Mexican, or Chinese outright illegal, but it *is* possible to criminalize the habits, behaviors, gathering places, and vices of marginalized people. President Nixon is often depicted as one of the main villains and instigators of America's drug war. In certain respects, he's earned that. Here is a shocking confession from one of his most trusted domestic policy advisers, John Ehrlichman:

> You want to know what this was really all about? The Nixon campaign in 1968, and the Nixon White House after that, had two enemies: the antiwar left and black people. You understand what I'm saying? We knew we couldn't make it illegal to be either against the war or black, but by getting the public to associate the hippies with marijuana and blacks with heroin, and then criminalizing both heavily, we could disrupt those communities. We could arrest their leaders, raid their homes, break up their meetings, and vilify them night after night on the evening news. Did we know we were lying about the drugs? Of course we did.

Ehrlichman told this to a journalist named Dan Baum, who quoted the aging Nixon aide in a 2016 story for *Harper's Magazine*. It leaves little doubt that Nixon's drug war was a campaign to oppress the president's enemies and destroy marginalized communities.

Outlawing drugs didn't work, but scapegoating minorities turned out to be a darkly successful drug-war innovation. Politicians realized they could boost their reputations as protectors of America. Those in power could create a false conspiracy that made the War on Drugs seem reasonable—as though America could be destroyed by foreign infiltrators like opium and marijuana—and appeal to bigots as well as anyone concerned about their family's safety.

Don't believe me? In the 1950s, when America was at war with Korea, politicians created a fake story that the Chinese government was using opium to destroy America. (There wasn't a shred of evidence for this, and similar narratives exist around today's fentanyl crisis. Some claim that fentanyl made from chemicals sourced from China is a plot to destroy America, or that Mexican drug cartels are trying to put fentanyl into children's Halloween candy as an act of terrorism.)

It's the same playbook Nixon used, and the decision-makers before him. It's much easier to cast blame on foreign enemies like Mexico and China, while doing little to actually help Americans who are struggling at home. At no point did politicians seem to ask themselves why so many Americans are resorting to drugs to chase a high or ease their pain in the first place.

Defined in this way, is the drug war really a failure? Absolutely not. In the context of a power grab and a deliberate misinformation campaign, it achieves all of its intended outcomes. The series of actions we now understand as the "War on Drugs" laid the groundwork for mass incarceration and numerous racialized backlashes designed to hurt underprivileged and marginalized communities for generations.

If It's Not About Drugs, What Is the Drug War?

A war on drugs is really a war on people. More specifically, a war on drugs is a war on *certain* kinds of people. Mostly Black people, but others too—and those who belong to multiple communities. Homosexuals. Latino people. Indigenous people. Poor people. Sick people. The undesirables. The discarded. The people who aren't "productive" members of society. The same people who fill jails and prisons and who don't count as full participants and citizens in American democracy. Once someone enters the criminal justice system, their likelihood of survival plummets. Research shows that people with opioid addiction who are incarcerated are anywhere from 40 to 120 times more likely to fatally overdose than the general public.

You know who rarely gets in trouble for using drugs? Rich people. If they dabble in drugs and things get out of control, they get sent away to fancy treatment centers in places like sunny Malibu, where they pet horses on ranches and spend their days doing art therapy, while everyone else goes to jail, where their health needs are neglected. (Remember T.A., the hustler? He's the prototype for a privileged opioid user.) A war on drugs is a war on *some* people—I first heard this slogan from activists fighting to end the brutal criminalization of drug users that devastate lives, tear apart families, and destroy communities. If there's one thing the drug war has succeeded in accomplishing, it's been the systematic spread of racism and xenophobia.

Even though white people and Black people use drugs like marijuana at the same rates, Black Americans are 3.6 times more likely to be arrested for pot.[1] Even in states that have legalized weed, Black people are *still* twice as likely to be arrested for cannabis crimes than white people. That doesn't have anything to do with who has it or who's using it but rather who's getting targeted by enforcement policies.

Although they're sometimes held up as "protecting the Black community," strict drug enforcement policies haven't helped folks during the overdose crisis. According to the CDC, fatal overdoses increased by 44 percent among Black people in 2020 compared to 2019—a far higher jump in overdose mortality than other populations have experienced. Among Indigenous (American Indian) and Alaskan Native people, overdoses rose 39 percent during the same window, far surpassing the rate for white people.

It's not because these populations use more drugs than white people, it's because they have fewer recovery resources available to them. One possible explanation for the heightened risk of overdose death in these communities is that their populations are much more likely to be criminalized for using substances, even substances that are legal.

When the drug war is understood as a war on people, the drugs themselves become a secondary concern. While substances from cocaine to heroin do seem to matter to politicians crafting drug laws—and these drugs do cause very real harm—what seems to matter more in the world of policymaking is precisely *who* is using which drug at a given time.

During the modern-day overdose crisis, news coverage of addiction became much more sympathetic to the plight of people addicted to heroin. The people depicted as suffering the most were younger, white, rural, and suburban. A big part of this shift also had to do with the narrative surrounding their addiction. White people weren't depicted as junkies and criminals. Instead, we get another fairy tale: that every white person's addiction started by taking painkillers prescribed by doctors. In other words, it wasn't their fault they got addicted. While this was true for many people (including me), Big Pharma and unethical doctors weren't the only reasons. And focusing on white suffering was just another way to ignore people who were disproportionately harmed.

By contrast, in the 1980s, Black people using crack cocaine received no such sympathy. There was no one to blame—no pharmaceutical company or crack-prescribing doctor. So the media and politicians blamed Black communities for causing their own pain and suffering. Nothing could be further from the truth.

As for Nixon's drug policy agenda in the 1970s, the government said it was concerned for veterans scattered across Europe and Vietnam who started using opium and heroin. The decision on how to treat our veterans became important in determining which kind of drug war Nixon would wage. Would he stick with the harsh criminalization faced by other groups or take a softer, more gentle approach that prioritized research, education, and treatment? Or maybe some combination of both?

For most of the 19th and early 20th centuries, America prioritized supply-side drug enforcement, which often meant punishment for (some) drug users. Shortly after the 1882 Exclusion Act targeting Chinese immigrants, more and more drugs started being classified as illegal. In nearly every case, these drugs were tied to racial minorities, immigrants, and unwieldy populations—like hippies or Black civil rights activists. The substances, like the groups who used them, were deemed a threat to so-called law and order. This pattern goes back more than a century, repeating itself over and over again. Here's how it's played out with some of the most common substances—all of which are still around today.

Cocaine

Drugs like opium and cocaine—an anesthetic that's still used for clinical procedures—came under strict government control in the 1914 Harrison Narcotics Act, which criminalized "non-medical use" of these drugs and relegated them to licensed manufacturers, distributors, and sellers. This helped create the medical and pharmaceutical industry as we know it. Using these drugs outside the realm of medicine was now a crime. Deep-seated fears and panic around racial minorities guided America's earliest drug laws.

The same year the Harrison Narcotics Act passed, the *New York Times* published a story about Black men in the South under this racist headline: "Negro Cocaine 'Fiends' Are a New Southern Menace." Many of these racist narratives were expressed in the way police responded to drugs. For example, sheriffs in southern states believed that cocaine made Black men impervious to .32 caliber, so police departments switched to higher-powered .38-caliber rounds.[2]

Alcohol

After 1914, the government took an increasingly radical stance toward drugs, culminating in the 1920 prohibition of alcohol. Many people seem to forget that alcohol is a drug—and a dangerous one at that. Alcohol causes harm not only to people who drink it, but to society as a whole through drunk driving accidents and alcohol-induced violence. One study concluded that alcohol is the most dangerous drug of them all.[3]

Alcohol prohibition lasted ten disastrous years, during which gang violence tore cities apart as they competed in a thriving illegal market. The government eventually learned that criminalizing a popular drug like alcohol caused many more problems than it solved and overturned prohibition. But it has rarely applied this lesson elsewhere.

Marijuana

In 1937, marijuana became federally prohibited thanks, in part, to another racist panic over immigration. This time, the fear was over migrant workers coming from Mexico. Leading up to the Marihuana Tax Act of 1937, America was awash in anti-marijuana and anti-Mexican "reefer madness"–style propaganda. One local news outlet ran this headline: "Smoking Weed Turns Mexicans Into Wild Beasts." The rhetoric about Mexicans and marijuana sung the same tune as cocaine, giving Black men superhuman strength.

It's not by accident that all of these early drug laws passed while the media widely broadcast blatantly racist propaganda. The goal was to make white people afraid of minorities, and one way to do that was by casting drugs to make them dangerous, violent, and unpredictable. This reinforced the story that was already being told: racial minorities used drugs, and this made them a threat to American society.

Like any war, you can't really paint the War on Drugs with a broad brush. There's a lot more to it than I'm able to fit into these pages. There's the political story of drugs, which is important, but drug use and addiction are also very real issues that any government has to deal with one way or another. And not everyone in Nixon's orbit in the 1970s was a racist crusader who hated Vietnam War protesters, hippies, and Black people. Amid the assaults, there were moments of clarity too. Some of the people Nixon appointed to lead his drug war project actually wanted to help people recover from addiction. For a brief moment, the government tried to examine drugs and addiction through a medical and scientific framework. This angle emphasized treatment instead of punishment. It was a sane, compassionate, and more rational approach to substance regulation.

Ironically, President Nixon's drug war also focused extensively on medicine and public health. In the same famous "public enemy" speech, Nixon said he planned to invest vast sums of money in "rehabilitation, research, and education," and he did. He also pursued a liberal drug policy agenda that precious few policymakers elected today would openly support.

To understand how things have gotten to be so horribly bad today—when drugs are not only cheaper and deadlier than ever but are also swept up in yet another politically motivated backlash—we have to go back to and examine the many twists and turns American drug policy took after Nixon launched today's modern-day drug war.

Here's a hint: Who was standing beside Nixon during his famous "public enemy" speech in 1971? The answer probably isn't whom you think. The president was accompanied by a liberal psychiatrist named Dr. Jerome Jaffe, who was a vocal advocate for treating addiction with medicine instead of police and prisons. Nixon declared a war against drugs, and he decided his top official to lead the charge would be a young liberal doctor studying addiction at the University of Chicago.

On June 18, 1971, just after Nixon's presidential address, the *New York Times* ran a story calling Dr. Jaffe "a drug abuse fighter." Just 37 years old, Dr. Jaffe was appointed director of the Special Action Office for Drug Abuse Prevention.

"Dr. Jaffe will be the man directly responsible. He will report directly to me," Nixon said during his speech. Nixon emphasized that Jaffe's primary responsibilities were research and education, with whatever money and resources were needed. About Dr. Jaffe, the *New York Times* wrote, "Dr. Jaffe is one of a comparatively rare breed of psychopharmacologists and has definite views on the importance of drugs in the treatment of addicts." Dr. Jaffe understood that addiction was a real illness, and like any other illness a doctor confronts, he advocated for the use of medicine.

Nixon's public health opportunity

Dr. Jaffe was part of a small group of doctors trying to figure out the best way to help people who were struggling with heroin addiction. In the 1970s, cocaine and crack cocaine had yet to explode in availability. Research at the time found a high rate of heroin use among Vietnam soldiers—as high as 34 percent, according to some studies.[4] These soldiers were going to need help. In an instance of blowback, heroin use began to rise in urban, largely Black communities, as the drug was being trafficked from war-torn Southeast Asia to America. One trafficking operation hid kilos of heroin in the coffins of dead soldiers being shipped home. The threat of a surge in heroin use sparked a novel approach that hinged on fighting opioid addiction with prescription opioids. In response, Dr. Jaffe was part of a team of doctors who helped establish a nationwide network of methadone treatment programs.

Methadone is a drug in the opioid family. Like its cousins, it carries a lot of cultural baggage and stigma. (Remember medicines prescribed by doctors can be weaponized as potent political tools just as easily as illegal drugs like opium and marijuana.) Methadone may be one of the most heavily regulated and stigmatized medicines in America. All sorts of narratives, fears, and scary stories latch onto it. Just like other opioids, using methadone carries some risks. For instance, it can cause overdoses, especially if it's mixed with other drugs like alcohol and benzodiazepines. But used correctly, methadone is also a lifesaving medicine. In fact, it's one of the most well-researched drugs for the treatment of addiction. Decades of rigorous study show that, for people with moderate to severe opioid addictions, methadone gives them their lives back. More recent research shows that it can reduce a person's risk of a fatal opioid overdose by more than 60 percent.[5] If a cancer drug had this record of success, it would be celebrated as a medical miracle. But addiction is not cancer, and over 150 years of drug wars and propaganda have misled people about what addiction is and how it is best treated. Even today, many people do not support the idea of treating addiction with medicine.

Methadone is just one of the many ironies of Richard Nixon's presidency. On the one hand, Nixon launched a crusade against drugs and nonwhite drug users. On the other hand, the medical doctors he appointed took radical steps to expand addiction treatment where there was hardly any before. Before Dr. Jaffe was tapped to lead Nixon's drug war, more than two-thirds of the government's budget for drug control had gone toward "supply reduction," meaning "eradicating" the drug supply, arresting drug dealers, punishing drug users, and broadly pursuing drugs as a crime.

By 1974, after Jaffe took charge, two-thirds of the federal government's drug budget went toward demand reduction strategies, meaning drug treatment, research, and prevention. Before Nixon's drug war, fewer than 400 patients were prescribed methadone for opioid addiction. By 1976, more than 80,000 people were being treated with it. This rapid expansion of resources for treatment happened under President Nixon's watch because he trusted the instincts of a doctor who was studying addiction and believed in the power of medicine to treat it. All of this sounds unheard of coming from Nixon's White House, but the history doesn't lie.

Methadone was just one part of the newly invigorated "demand-side" drug use prevention strategy established under Nixon. Dr. Jaffe and his team of doctors, policy wonks, and researchers were just as focused on reforming the criminal justice system.

"We also instituted a program in the drug courts called 'treatment alternatives to street crime,' which basically linked treatment with the court system," Dr. Jaffe said. "It was a way of trying to reduce crime by getting people who had been arrested into treatment." Instead of relying on police, prosecutors, and prisons to punish people using drugs, there was a genuine effort to funnel people into treatment. "Lots of the people that we began treating had histories of arrests, and had been in jail," Dr. Jaffe said. "When we did some of the studies on what was happening after treatment, there was a significant reduction in those kinds of behaviors. But totally apart from what we saw statistically, I knew these people personally. I knew their families. And you could see that their lives were dramatically different when they went into treatment."

Between the expansion of methadone and helping people get treatment instead of going to jail, there was a real sense that America was about to take an alternative path to address drugs. There was a fork in the road: Keep treating drug users as criminals, or help them survive addiction and recover by offering everyone quality treatment.

Nixon's medical doctors didn't think all people who used drugs had to be treated like criminals. Medicine, compassion, and treating people with dignity is and always has been the superior approach, both in terms of scientific efficacy and as a matter of morality. It's simply the right thing to do. This compassionate view of addiction was extended to Vietnam soldiers who became addicted during deployment. Under the Code of Military Justice, soldiers who used drugs could be court-martialed. Nixon changed this rule. Soldiers who tested positive for drug use and screened for addiction didn't need to have their honor, dignity, and lives destroyed. Instead, if a veteran tested positive for substances, they would be referred to treatment. This is why *who* is using drugs at any given time matters so much. The government did not want to punish these young soldiers after putting their lives on the line in war.

"There was no point in destroying peoples' lives for that kind of offense," Dr. Jaffe said about addicted soldiers. But the top brass in the military wasn't totally on board with this. Dr. Jaffe said the military viewed this new approach as "mollycoddling" or "being soft on the addicts."

The military's view of drug use and addiction aligned with the dominant view among law enforcement, which highlights an irreconcilable tension between law enforcement on the supply side and

health-care workers on the demand side. Doctors like Jaffe were focused on the demand side. They advocated for treatment; locking
people up in cages was not going to help them recover from addiction. However, the supply-side focus of law enforcement, on trying
to "eradicate" drugs and create "drug-free communities," ultimately
won the day. Nixon ran his campaign on "law and order" and won
the votes of white people.

Doctors like Jaffe could only accomplish so much when police,
prosecutors, and the military viewed addiction treatment as being
"too soft," and even the president who appointed him feared appearing soft on crime and losing his base of white voters. He saw his
medical approach largely cast aside in favor of politics.

Reflecting on his time in the Nixon White House, Dr. Jaffe said:

> I had the feeling, almost from the first day, that the willing-
> ness to look at the demand side, rather than the traditional
> American law enforcement approach might be a transient
> phenomenon—that it might pass, and we would go back
> to our old ways of more and more law enforcement. And
> I was right. We have never had that proportion of federal
> resources devoted to intervention on the demand side. We'd
> never had it before, and we've never had it since. Up to that
> time, we had about 65 years of a law enforcement approach.
> I wasn't certain that the general attitudes of Congress had
> totally changed. It seemed as if every day was an important
> day in getting things done, and putting things into place.
> We really had to move quickly to institutionalize the treat-
> ment system so that it would not just decay and fall apart
> when the current interest in treatment faded.

The interest in expanding treatment over incarceration did indeed fade. In fact, it faded so much that few people even remember
that when it came to drugs, Nixon had many liberal tendencies and

that his administration made the unprecedented move of putting millions of federal funds toward treatment for addiction.

But over time, even the methadone system that Dr. Jaffe helped establish became another tool for law enforcement and punishment. Today, doctors and pharmacies are not even allowed to prescribe methadone to people with OUD. Methadone can only be accessed through a bureaucratic clinic system. (Try holding down a job, taking care of your children, or doing literally anything but wait in line when you rely on these clinics. Methadone patients have to show up at the crack of dawn every day for their dose.) Run down and depressing, methadone clinics are usually only found in poor communities of color.

Crack: The 1980s and 1990s

Once crack cocaine hit the scene in the 1980s and 1990s, the political will and public appetite for compassion and treatment vanished entirely. Drug use was fully viewed as a crime, and drug users, especially Black men and women, were severely punished for their addiction. Robberies, shootings, break-ins, in the public's imagination, could all be traced back to drug use or drug dealing. Drugs became synonymous with crime.

The government's response to the so-called crack epidemic began under President Ronald Reagan and carried all the way into President Bill Clinton's administration. Both political parties vigorously pursued a law enforcement–driven drug war that focused on supply-side approaches rather than investing in social services and health care. Unlike today's opioid crisis, where recovery efforts (and the media) focus on white suburban users, there was no sympathy for crack-cocaine users.

The government's response to crack is yet another sad and brutal case study in how drugs became a symbol for racism and white panic. It's another example of the *who*-factor. Since crack cocaine was associated with urban crime and Black communities, the government had no interest in building a better system of treatment to help people struggling with addiction. Instead, billions of dollars in government resources poured into law enforcement, jails, prisons, and courts. Under President Reagan, this drug strategy culminated in the bipartisan 1986 Anti-Drug Abuse Act. The system for dealing with drugs and addiction became fully punitive under this legislation, outdoing Nixon's drug war.

The approach to cocaine in the 1980s and 1990s devastated Black communities. To this day, thousands upon thousands of families who had a loved one suffer from addiction or be incarcerated have never fully recovered. One law in particular within the 1986 Anti-Drug Abuse Act would prove to be most disastrous: the 100:1 crack versus powder cocaine sentencing.

This law resulted in crack being punished 100 times harsher than powder cocaine, which was still viewed then as a party drug for rich white people. A person caught with just five grams of crack was punished at the same level as someone with 500 grams of powder cocaine, even though the two are the same exact drug. With so many low-level crimes being punished so harshly, the number of people incarcerated in America skyrocketed to unfathomable heights. Black people now make up roughly 13 percent of America's population while being 38 percent of America's jail and prison population. Black people are incarcerated in state prisons at nearly five times the rate of white people. These statistics barely express the horrors of America's drug war.

The scholar Michelle Alexander's words on this subject are sharper and more powerful than anyone else's. Here's how she summarizes the history of racist politics embedded in America's drug war in her book, *The New Jim Crow*:

> In the early years of Jim Crow, conservative white elites competed with each other by passing ever more stringent and oppressive Jim Crow legislation. A century later, politicians in

the early years of the drug war competed with each other to prove who could be tougher on crime by passing ever harsher drug laws—a thinly veiled effort to appeal to poor and working-class whites who, once again, proved they were willing to forego economic and structural reform in exchange for an apparent effort to put blacks back "in their place."

By the 1990s, America was fully entrenched in the logic of a punitive drug war that unleashed mass incarceration on millions of people whose main crime was suffering from untreated drug addiction. It's in this environment that a new and deadlier drug reared its head: opioids.

After crack cocaine, America's drug war in the 21st century would confront its deadliest enemy yet, a new villain more powerful and more potent than the others. And like clockwork, this new villain would become another political weapon wielded to capture the fears of Americans. Panic and fear were soon fueled by misinformation and fantastical stories, generating a ferocious backlash to alternatives to the drug war.

Since 1999, more than one million people have died due to opioid overdoses. The drug war once again shows itself to be a deadly decision made by the government. Despite horrifying levels of preventable and needless deaths, the government clings to this war. And once again, the impulse to punish people who are suffering is entwined with a renewed hunger for ending both mass incarceration and America's longest war. The search continues for a compassionate approach to addiction that prioritizes not just treatment and medicine but also human dignity and the sanctity of every life. This time, the drug war will face opponents who are fierce, organized, and more committed than ever to fighting for what's right.

4

NEWTON'S THIRD LAW

For every action, there is an equal and opposite reaction. That's Newton's third law—true for atoms, and true in life. One thing I've learned is that the universe does not care about good and evil, justice and injustice. It cares about balance.

The border between the United States and Mexico is 1,954 miles long. To the north, the border dividing us from Canada spans 5,525 miles. In 2020, our government allocated around $4.07 billion for its border patrol program. Yet, more than two million people were arrested crossing the southern border that year, and the number of people crossing in Canada has more than tripled.

At the same time, the DEA's annual budget is more than $3 billion. Yet, drugs are cheaper, stronger, and more widely available than ever before. In 2021, the DEA said they seized 50.6 million counterfeit pills containing fentanyl and more than 10,000 pounds of fentanyl powder.[1] These seizures may have prevented some small fraction of people from using fentanyl, but it didn't stop more than 111,000 people dying from overdoses.

The government has tried repeatedly to "eradicate" and stamp out the supply of drugs. This strategy has continuously failed to make a dent in the drug supply. The appearance of fentanyl has created new justifications for harsh strategies—following the flawed logic that to stop fentanyl, all we have to do is stop its flow into the country.

From San Francisco to West Virginia, a more pragmatic approach that focuses on harm reduction, education, and expanding treatment has been met with a fierce and angry backlash. Some grieving parents want to see low level drug dealers charged with murder. They want to send the military to the border to shoot bombs into Mexico. They want to reinforce failed attempts at a border wall. They want police to arrest drug users and subject them to the torture of detoxing inside a jail cell. I don't think it's an accident that Trump's primary pitch for his 2024 presidential run is to finish building his border wall. His other campaign promise? To execute any drug dealer selling fentanyl—just like the Philippines' president Rodrigo "The Punisher" Duterte, who killed 30 suspected drug dealers in his first four days in office. Many heartbroken families are taking the bait. But some are choosing a different path. And that is making all the difference.

On the last day of Bryant Carter's life, his father Gary sensed that something was wrong.

His son's fiancée had come over earlier in the evening on February 22, 2018. When she left, Bryant's normally sunny mood seemed dulled. While he had so much to look forward to—a wedding and a baby on the way—he wasn't smiling when Gary went to say goodnight.

"I knew something was off. He seemed a little down," Gary said. He assumed something happening between Bryant and his fiancée. "There's so many things about that night that kill me," Gary told me later. Years after, each detail still haunted him. Yet, what could he have done differently? Nothing. The facts—and the story's ending—still haven't changed.

From birth, Bryant confronted a series of health challenges.

After he was born, Gary and Tracy had to leave him at the hospital in the infant special care unit. Bryant also had several surgeries on his knees as a toddler, which exposed him to painkillers at a very early age. "We couldn't get the medical records to find out what they'd given him, but he knew there were pills out there that would make him feel better."

The arrival of their son changed life for them. He brought them so much joy, and with it, so much anxiety. Heading into high school, Bryant contracted a serious case of psoriasis, a condition where skin cells stack up on top of one another in painful, unsightly plaques. Bryant was misdiagnosed a few times by primary care providers, and the steroids he was prescribed made the condition worse. Finally, he ended up getting light treatments with a specialist doctor in Boston, who put him on chemotherapy medication—that's how bad it was. He was in terrible pain and felt like the Elephant Man, at a time when young people are desperate to be accepted.

Around that time, Gary's parents' health issues came to a head and Tracy and Gary became their caregivers. Gary's mother had early-onset Alzheimer's and was bedridden, while his father had been suffering from different cancers for more than 20 years. They moved into an in-law apartment in the Carters' house. "That took up more of our focus," Gary said. "We loosened up paying attention to what was going on with the kids."

Gary's parents needed a lot of physical and medical care, and they were both on a lot of medications for their different conditions. His father took 26 pills a day, and both he and Gary's mother needed OxyContin and other forms of oxycodone. Gary and Tracy were conscious of the kids not being able to have access to the pills—or so they thought. They kept all of the medications under lock and key, in a safe. Gary would make up the pill trays, which were kept down in the in-law apartment. Early on in their caregiving roles, health-care providers came to the house during the day so Gary and Tracy could go to work. Sometimes the provider reported a missing dose: "Your father's OxyContin is not in the tray today." It happened enough times that Gary started to get suspicious of the health-care worker and wondered if she was stealing from the cabinet. Finally, Tracy quit her job to stay home during the day so that one of them would be in the house all the time, giving 24/7 care to Gary's parents.

Little did they know that the missing pills weren't being stolen by the health-care provider. It was Bryant. He was going down in the middle of the night when everyone was asleep. Gary said, "He was getting the Oxy because it made him feel better. He was self-medicating from the physical pain and low self-esteem. That's basically how he got hooked on it. Being so focused on my folks, we were blind to it."

Bryant went off for one year of college, during a period when the government was cracking down on pain medications. There were more barriers and more paperwork associated with opioid prescriptions: Gary's parents had to sign a document when they received their medication, acknowledging the legal consequences of losing or sharing the pills. At college, without access to the pain relief he was accustomed to, Bryant began using heroin with his college roommate.

"He finally came to us stating he had a problem," Gary said. "He wanted help. It kills me, because I think he would have been successful." However, because of Bryant's complex medical issues—the chemotherapy infusions he needed to receive for his psoriasis required frequent hospital visits—he couldn't go into a treatment program. Leaving an inpatient program for these visits would never be allowed. Instead, Bryant enrolled in outpatient treatment and used Suboxone. He was doing well and, after some time, began weaning himself off the Suboxone with a doctor's support. He met his fiancée and was excited to plan his wedding with her. Then, it all came crashing down.

Bryant's appendix ruptured, which meant an emergency surgery—a surgery that would require pain medication and anesthesia. Gary and Tracy met him over at the hospital, where their son was being prepped for the operation. He pleaded with them: "They want to give me fentanyl. I told them I'm an addict and I can't have anything." He was so frightened that he said he was willing to go through the surgery with no pain medication at all. He worried about his ability to stay sober, and how his Suboxone medication would interact with any surgically administered drugs. Gary and Tracy talked to the surgeon too, asking about Bryant's other options and explaining the risks to his recovery.

The answer: "Absolutely not." Against his wishes, Bryant was given fentanyl during the surgery. His parents believe it pushed the Suboxone off Bryant's opioid receptors, leaving their son vulnerable to cravings, recurrence of use, and overdose.

Gary said, "It's hard to say what happened. It led to his relapse, where he had a slip and that instance led to more."

In the midst of his relapse, Bryant learned that he was going to be a dad. He was incredibly excited, counting down the weeks until he and his fiancée would find out whether it was a boy or a girl. He was no less enthusiastic about life or the many blessings it held for him. He was never afraid to say "I love you" to his father, or anyone he truly cared about. Even at 25 years old, he'd say it. All through his teens, he'd say it. He didn't care who was around, didn't care about seeming uncool. But this bright, funny, creative young man didn't get a chance to show that love to his future child. The week before their family would learn the sex of the new baby, Bryant accidentally got a dose of illicit fentanyl. It killed him.

On February 22, 2018, Gary said good night to Bryant and went to his own room. Tracy was already curled up in bed. He laid down and closed his eyes, willing his anxiety to go away—it was just the feeling of something being "off." He told himself that everything was fine. It was just another weeknight, with another day ahead for the family. Within a moment, Gary was asleep.

In the middle of the night, Gary said he woke up to hear

Bryant's phone ringing. Answer your phone, he thought to himself. The phone rang, stopped. Rang again. But Gary didn't go down to check on his son. He went back to sleep.

Tracy was the one who found their son the next morning.

She was running late leaving the house and had asked her daughter to make sure Bryant was up for work after she left. For some reason, she changed her mind and went to wake him up herself. She pushed his door open. What she saw stopped her cold in her tracks.

Bryant was by the bed in his pajamas with his head on his Bible. His hands were clasped together. He wasn't breathing. A needle protruded from his arm.

Tracy ran downstairs and found the Narcan and her phone. Without hesitation, she dialed 911 and alerted her family. She did everything she could—everything anyone could have done. When she tried to roll her son's body to one side, he had already stiffened—rigor mortis, making it impossible to get the overdose-reversing medication to his nose.

While she waited for emergency services, she sensed it was already too late. Years later, she told me that she wonders why she didn't scream. Her actions were instant, practical. After all, she'd been practicing for this—going to naloxone trainings and watching her son's recovery like a hawk. They had Narcan in the house. They were as ready to cope with the situation as they could be. In the moment of crisis, she took every step to save her son's life. Yet, she asks herself why her story wasn't like some other parents'. She said, "In the movies, in stories, it's always the same. How come I didn't let out a bloodcurdling scream? Why didn't I hold him like it was the last time? I never had that screaming, disastrous moment."

It didn't make the loss any less painful. Six months after Bryant's death on February 23, 2018, she wrote about her grief on Facebook:

At 7:30 a.m. it will be 6 months. 6 months ago that I found Bryant, on his knees with his head on his Bible. Gone. On his knees praying for strength. On his knees praying for peace. On his knees praying. And while I'm grateful he found Jesus and I know he is at peace, my broken heart wishes he asked ME for strength that day. 6 months.

From the moment Bryant was born, Gary and Tracy loved him. They protected him, fussed over him, taught him how to be a man. Although they were aware of his addiction and supported his recovery, they could not have prepared themselves for the shock and devastation of losing Bryant. No parent can. Many of the families I've talked to are just like Gary and Tracy. For years after their loss, they ask themselves: Did I do something wrong? Could I have done more? Was I a bad parent?

Grief is love with nowhere to go. Bryant was on the cusp of so many good things. Like many others, he was excited for what was ahead. He was thrilled to be marrying his sweetheart and raising their son together. When he passed, his parents were left wondering—now what? They could have given up on life, become bitter, or veered into reactionary politics, seeking to blame someone for Bryant's death. They could have allowed the media to paint Bryant as a sensational casualty. (One article portrayed Bryant as a pill thief, completely overwriting his complex medical issues, pain management needs, and early exposure to painkillers. He was memorialized not as a person, but as a stereotype.)

Instead, Gary and Tracy both devoted themselves to helping other parents who were coping with the same loss. Their grief became a powerful tool—finding solutions, public health activism, and educating other families. They continue to honor their son's life by carrying his memory forward and sharing it with others. Instead of tucking Bryant away, they carried him into the light. They found a way to connect to their son and through him to touch others. Bryant's hands—the hands that had clasped in prayer—were now answering the prayers of others.

For many grieving parents, the pain of loss fuels a battle about fighting fentanyl and getting revenge, and that's an understandable impulse. But in reality, the fight pits them against reformers who want a new, innovative approach to drug policy. On one side, we have commonsense solutions that center on public health. On the other side, we have people who want to return to a more muscular, more punitive, and harsher drug war than ever.

Making matters worse are the many cynical politicians who play on Americans' fears about fentanyl. They have an unfailing instinct for what gets people heated—and there is palpable rage among people on all sides of the fentanyl issue. Frontline workers are exhausted, burned-out, and frustrated that their work isn't being funded or supported at the scale it needs to be. Right-wing news outlets shout from the rooftops that the Biden administration is distributing free crack pipes. The families who've lost their teenage and young adult children to fentanyl are furious that the government hasn't helped them.

All of this anger is finding expression in a new toxic form of politics. Many people are looking for leaders who are going to act on their behalf and make their rage a reality.

Perhaps the angriest and most cynical politician on this front is J. D. Vance, a Republican senator from Ohio elected during the 2022 midterms. On the campaign trail, Vance spewed horrifying and conspiratorial rhetoric that was almost identical to racist comments made a century ago about Chinese or Mexican migrants who were scapegoated for opium and marijuana. In an interview with the right-wing conspiracy outlet Gateway Pundit, J. D. Vance said this about President Biden's drug policy:[2]

> If you wanted to kill a bunch of MAGA voters in the middle of the heartland, how better than to target them and their kids with this deadly fentanyl? . . . It does look intentional. It's like Joe Biden wants to punish the people who didn't vote for him, and opening up the floodgates to the border is one way to do it.

This is a new spin on the old version of racist antidrug rhetoric. Senator Vance suggested that Democrats are intentionally trying to kill Republican voters in the "heartland" by flooding the country with fentanyl. It's a shocking thing to say, and it feeds into fringe talking points that blame Mexico for all of America's problems.

A few years ago, the lines between the political parties were much clearer. Fentanyl has blurred those lines. Republicans want to send the military to Trump's border wall and put an end to immigration from Mexico and Latin America. However, they're not the only ones talking about incarceration instead of expanding treatment. Democrats in big cities like San Francisco are also calling for a return to harsh drug enforcement. New York City's Mayor Eric Adams implemented a policy that would force unhoused and mentally ill people into institutions that they can't leave.

Of course, none of these policies will stop the flow of fentanyl or the subsequent overdose deaths. But politicians are good at tapping into the resentment that people feel when they're afraid and powerless, regardless of party affiliation. And the overdose crisis has left thousands of grieving families feeling very, very angry.

It wasn't always this way. Instead of a joint war against drugs, with both major political parties trying to look the toughest and meanest and strongest, many politicians instead said they supported the expansion of treatment. Like Nixon in the 1970s, policymakers once invested time and budgets to eradicate addiction as a public health issue, and listened to experts.

Politicians and police started vocally supporting treatment instead of jail. Public enemy number one was Big Pharma, represented by rich businessmen like Richard Sackler.

During the 2016 election, presidential candidates from both major parties called for empathy. Candidates Jeb Bush and Carly Fiorina told stories of family members who struggled with addiction; Hillary Clinton hosted town halls and forums in rural states like New Hampshire that were hard hit by the crisis. There was a glimmer of hope that we were on the brink of meaningful change.

Then, four short years later, COVID-19 came to America.

It was a recipe for disaster on so many levels. It wasn't just coronavirus. Isolation is fuel for drug use. Many of us know from personal experience that our own heads are like bad neighborhoods—dangerous places to hang out alone. Being shut inside could help prevent a deadly virus from spreading, but it would also create fertile ground for a different kind of disease to fester.

My worst fears about the toll of mental health quickly became real. And those of us who've struggled with addiction became collateral damage of the pandemic.

During the first year of COVID-19, more than 100,000 people died from drug overdoses for the first time in American history. A 28.5 percent spike in overdose deaths from the year prior; overdose mortality had never topped six figures since recordkeeping began.[3] In just two months during 2020 after the pandemic lockdowns, 13,400 people died from overdoses.[4] Fentanyl was implicated in the majority of them. According to the CDC, synthetic opioid–involved death rates increased by over 56 percent from 2019 to 2020 and accounted for over 82 percent of all opioid-involved deaths in 2020. Deaths didn't decline after society opened back up after the pandemic: in a 12-month window from 2021 to 2022, more than 111,000 people died from overdoses.

While it may seem easy to point the finger at fentanyl alone, I think the pandemic proved that the overdose crisis was about more than opioids—arguably, it was never just about them. Over the past five years, a diverse array of synthetic drugs has entered the mainstream, from opioids to methamphetamine and obscure tranquilizers used by veterinarians like xylazine to new sedatives that have never even been tested on human beings. As the global supply chain melted down during the pandemic, causing shortages of goods and medicines, the supply of illicit, black-market, and street drugs drastically shifted. This pool of substances became more and more deadly; without regulation, accessible test strips, overdose prevention sites, or treatment touchpoints, anyone using illicit substances was at a heightened risk of overdose.

The pandemic laid bare just how vulnerable Americans are. It also exposed what a massive failure American drug policy has been, and how unprepared and ill-equipped the health-care system is to treat addiction at scale. Gun-blazing policies only made existing problems worse. Intercepting one shipment of drugs meant that hundreds more passed by undetected. The border enforcement budgets may have been worth billions of dollars, but what were we actually getting for that money? Singularly focusing on immigration wasn't going to stop people from dying—or killing themselves.

In reality, I think it's more complex than that. During the pandemic, America's decades-long overdose crisis collided head-on with COVID, fueling unprecedented levels of stress and loneliness. On top of that, almost everyone experienced some degree of job and financial insecurity. Overwhelmed hospitals meant that patients seeking help faced even more barriers to accessing quality treatment and health care. During the pandemic, over 54 percent of behavioral health programs had to shut their doors. Sixty-five percent had to turn patients away. Over 1,000 addiction treatment providers shut down completely. Struggling people were left alone for too many hours of the day, out of sight of friends, family, and social support.

Folks more sophisticated than I have called addiction a "disease of loneliness." Some experts claim that there's a correlation between rising opioid use rates and a sense of isolation, hopelessness, and struggle. The ever-popular observation that "the opposite of addiction is connection" became gospel during the pandemic. Many people say that they became addicted as a response to isolation or trauma. This may be true, but it doesn't answer the questions of fentanyl. If someone overdoses on fentanyl—unintentionally—can you claim it was loneliness that killed them?

I was definitely in the at-risk pool during the height of COVID. To cope, I threw myself into work, which (for the majority of the pandemic) included participation in the Purdue Pharma bankruptcy. I spent as many as 14 hours a day in my home office listening to conference calls or participating in video meetings while I tried to piece together the sordid tale of how the Sacklers netted billions while addicting countless Americans. I was under a colossal amount of pressure. The TV seemed to bring nothing but bad news—more deaths, ventilator shortages, anti-vax rallies, super-spreader events. Like many other people, I hardly left the house and had to set a reminder on my calendar to shower. Between meetings, I went into the backyard to watch my dog sniff around and clicked into Zoom support groups for my mental health and recovery. I wasn't the only one struggling.

Every one of the groups where I sought support was full of people who were worse off than me. They were coping with relapses, the deaths of loved ones, and isolation. It was a collective nightmare. While opioids were taking the spotlight, other substances were just as lethal—add loneliness, stir, and chill.

While the media couldn't stop talking about fentanyl, alcohol was also a huge problem. During the pandemic, people drank more to cope with stress. Deaths from alcohol, ranging from liver disease to accidents, rose to 99,017 in 2020, up from 78,927 in 2019, a 25 percent spike.[5] Alcohol-related deaths rose sharply for everybody—among people from just about every racial and ethnic group. Younger folks saw a 40 percent increase in alcohol-related deaths, the biggest rise of any demographic. Among adults younger than 65, deaths from alcohol actually outnumbered deaths from COVID-19, the *New York Times* reported.[6]

Whatever the numbers and statistics say, they simply cannot capture the impact of this much loss and suffering, or the anger that has followed it. Over 20 years, more than a million Americans died from drug overdoses—and that number is only accelerating. That's too many grieving families. Too much rage. Too much pain. The overdose crisis has begun to feel intractable, like it'll never end.

As a result, people are angry. They're resentful. The drug war's dark history is now playing on repeat, and the old tensions between law and order and public health are being inflamed once again. The intensified drug war, which focuses on fentanyl, is only making things worse.

It's not just the misinformation about fentanyl that creates problems—it's how the crisis itself is talked about. Many people view this crisis as a static event. In reality, it should be treated like a public health crisis or a natural disaster—an avalanche of overdoses. While the average person probably still thinks the Sacklers and opioids like OxyContin are to blame, there is more to it. A *lot* more.

The story we know about the overdose crisis usually begins in 1995 when the FDA approved the now infamous painkiller Oxy-Contin.[7] The innovation with OxyContin was that, instead of dosing every 4 to 6 hours, this new "time-release" formula of oxycodone could be taken once every 12 hours, for "all day relief."[8] One pill during the day and one pill at night could replace the half a dozen or so pills one would normally need. Infrequent dosing and the "controlled release" of the opioid also supposedly lowered the risk for addiction. The FDA bought Purdue's marketing strategy—partially because key FDA staff were bought by Purdue Pharma. Also, Purdue criminally misstated the number of people who would become addicted to OxyContin. The company put the risk at less than 1 percent, when the true risk is closer to 8 percent.[9]

And just like that, the FDA and the DEA let Purdue Pharma's drug right into America's loosely regulated pharmaceutical markets.

After OxyContin was approved by the government, the Sackler family made billions of dollars in profits based on false marketing, which was dressed up as rigorous science. That they have never seen the inside of a criminal court is in itself criminal. Yet, while they unquestionably caused pain, suffering, and death for millions of innocent people—they are not solely to blame for the opioid epidemic. While it's true that some people began their opioid misuse with a prescription, prescription drugs have not been the main contributor to addiction and overdose for at least 15 years. (This is long before the CDC's changes to opioid prescribing.)

A 2019 study found only 1.3 percent of people in Massachusetts who died from an overdose between 2013 and 2015 had a doctor's prescription for the drugs that killed them.[10] The vast majority of overdose deaths involve multiple drugs—not the kind that are prescribed.

The number of deaths involving prescription opioids like oxycodone has been nowhere near as high as deaths from synthetic opioids like fentanyl. More than four times as many people died from fentanyl in 2021 than from prescription opioids, which only account for a small fraction of annual overdose deaths.[11] In my book *Unsettled*, I exposed how the Sacklers were absolutely guilty in the public eye, but my main point was that they did not act alone. Big Pharma was enabled by a corrupt system that, instead of protecting ordinary Americans, shields the wealthy and powerful from the consequences of their illegal actions. Corporations have the freedom to break the law, cause grave harm to society, and profit from it. Meanwhile, a person caught with a gram of anything illicit could spend days, weeks, or months in jail. The system is corrupt and broken, which is why singularly blaming OxyContin, the Sacklers, and Big Pharma for the overdose crisis obscures the bigger picture.

What if someone's addiction didn't begin with a doctor's prescription? Are they any less deserving of help and sympathy?

Meanwhile, the government set out to aggressively reduce what they saw as the oversupply of opioid pain relievers, even though the majority of overdoses were happening on the street markets. The medical industry felt the pressure and clamped down. In 2010, the FDA forced Purdue to take their original OxyContin formula off the market and replace it with what was called an "abuse-deterrent" formula, which would be more difficult to crush, snort, and inject. The new pills encased the strong dose of oxycodone in a polyethylene oxide matrix that hardened the tablets. They hit the market in August of 2010, and the FDA quickly stopped shipments of the old formula that was so popular on the streets. (In 2013, the very day Purdue's patent on its original OxyContin expired, the FDA decided that it would not approve any generic versions of the drug.[12] This is a common patent practice in the pharmaceutical industry known as "evergreening," which means a company adds additional protections to a patent and artificially extends its length and therefore its dominance in the painkiller market without having to compete with companies selling a cheaper generic product.)

In 2010, there were roughly 3,000 deaths related to heroin in America. By 2013, this number had jumped to more than 8,000. While deaths caused by pharmaceutical opioids began to steady and slow down, the death rate from heroin tripled in another three years.[13] From 2010 to 2021, the number of opioid deaths involving prescription opioids like oxycodone stayed flat and low, while the number of deaths involving street opioids skyrocketed.

Now, this was all *before* fentanyl began making a serious impact on public health. At the time, people (including me) blamed Purdue Pharma and corporate greed. Other parts of the narrative were different too. The early waves of the overdose crisis largely impacted older white people in rural areas and younger whites in suburban enclaves—so, instead of demonizing opioid users, solutions focused on expanding treatment.

When it came to white users, police officers and police chiefs around the country said, "We cannot arrest our way out of this." Police officers even admitted that they stopped arresting the kids they busted for heroin. The cops knew these young people were struggling with addiction and didn't want to ruin their lives with a drug charge. In that context, law enforcement was more than willing to try a public health approach that didn't rely on punishment and incarceration.

Compared to the crack epidemic, this was night and day. Black youth in the 1980s and 1990s were punished through a bipartisan drug war. But for white youth swept up in the opioid crisis? Not so much. In 2015, the *New York Times* published a story about the modern-day overdose crisis with this headline: "In Heroin Crisis, White Families Seek Gentler War on Drugs." The *Times* wrote:

> When the nation's long-running war against drugs was de-fined by the crack epidemic and based in poor, predomi-nantly black urban areas, the public response was defined by zero tolerance and stiff prison sentences. But today's her-oin crisis is different. While heroin use has climbed among all demographic groups, it has skyrocketed among whites; nearly 90 percent of those who tried heroin for the first time in the last decade were white.[14]
>
> And the growing army of families of those lost to heroin—many of them in the suburbs and small towns—are now using their influence, anger and grief to cushion the country's approach to drugs, from altering the language around addiction to prodding government to treat it not as a crime, but as a disease.

The *Times* concluded that "punishment is out and compassion is in," thanks to the white families advocating for treatment instead of a police crackdown on drug users.

So, did that new approach mean the crisis was over? No, not even close. The War on Drugs merely shifted and took on a new form. White families who told the *New York Times* they wanted a gentler drug war wouldn't get it. Many families, in fact, would soon begin to advocate for an even harsher war against drugs.

Feeling like their children's deaths have slipped under the political radar, these families have organized numerous events to grab attention and turn up the heat on politicians. In June 2021, hundreds of family members protested in front of the headquarters of a social media company called Snapchat.[15] (Multiple police investigations have traced the overdoses of young people back to purchases made on the platform.) In attendance was Steve Filson, who lost his 29-year-old daughter Jessica to a fentanyl overdose in January 2020. He wore a dark black-and-gray suit and walked solemnly on the sidewalk carrying a sign that read "Forever 29," with the words "victim of a drug-induced homicide poisoned by fentanyl." Other parents held yellow signs with a picture of their deceased child that read "Snapchat is an accomplice to my murder" in big, bold black letters. Their posters advertised a website for a group called Drug Induced Homicide.

This group, formed by grieving parents, blames dealers for overdoses: "Why are drug dealers getting away with murder?" The group advertises a service from a company called Second Peek Investigations that says its mission is to "bring justice to your loved ones" by conducting a "deep dive into the provided digital devices to gather the evidence you need to seek a fair and just due process."[16] By investigating cell phones and social media accounts, the families hope to convict the person who gave their child drugs, for homicide.

The next year, many of the same parents rallied in front of the White House in September 2022. These families were angry at President Biden's administration for what they saw as his inaction on the issue of overdose deaths. One of their demands was—you guessed it—to get the government to increase drug enforcement at the US–

Mexico border to disrupt the flow of drugs. Some parents carried signs that blamed Biden's "open border" policy for fentanyl. Others carried signs that read, "China's synthetic drugs are a weapon of mass destruction." Some compared fentanyl to anthrax.

They said their children weren't addicted to drugs but were poisoned and deceived. One of the dads in the crowd shouted into a megaphone, urging President Biden to "wake up" and do something about overdose deaths. The families built a symbolic wall nearly 400 feet long and decorated it with portraits of 3,500 people who died from fentanyl overdoses, many of whom were younger than 25 years old. Some of the posters listed the birth and death dates of the deceased with the words "Forever 19" or "Forever 21."

They said the government should not be focusing on harm reduction, and claimed the more important and urgent solution was stopping the flow of fentanyl by cutting off the drug supply. These families, to be sure, did not speak for everyone who lost a family member or loved one to addiction. But they spoke loudly. They wanted what they perceived as justice, as though out to hunt the beast, bring it down, and get revenge. They wanted to build a wall—but to stop what? Fentanyl doesn't have any villain's name or face attached to it. There is no Sackler family in charge of fentanyl production. While fentanyl is a critical medicine used safely in hospitals and by pain patients every day, there are no corporations or government agencies that regulate the *illicit* versions of fentanyl sold on the street that are responsible for so many deaths today.

The nature of fentanyl—its potency, portability, and ubiquity—makes it nearly impossible to trace. The drug is a moving target that evades well-meaning policy. It is the ideal viral news subject—a monster that is always lurking under the bed. It stokes panic and misinformation.

The solution is to find balance. A commonsense, informed approach to curtailing the overdose crisis will save lives—and contend with a daunting reality. The reality is that no barrier is high enough and no budget hefty enough to stop fentanyl. The answer isn't more prisons or bigger guns. The answer is a dramatic reimagining of how to fight fentanyl. The first step to getting there? Getting honest with ourselves.

5

SADISTIC ARITHMETIC

"You sold dope to somebody, who sold it to somebody who died. That's a Class X felony."

Two hours into the police interrogation in the Multnomah County Justice Center, Todd Schmidt felt his last shot of heroin trickle out of his bloodstream. His guts bubbled and growled as his system clenched, preparing for the all-too-familiar shock of opioid withdrawal. He'd felt this familiar misery often enough—but this was the first time it had hit him while he was in handcuffs. Todd shut his eyes, which were suddenly burning with tears. The single bulb in the ceiling of the interrogation room whined at a frequency that only Todd seemed to hear. The two plainclothes cops who'd brought him in grinned at him.

"You ready to give us a name yet?" the one with the black mustache said.

"It's you or him," said the blond one. "Come on, Schmidt. One of you's got to do the time."

With his belly full of the heroin baggies he had swallowed and his brain screaming for more dope, Todd squirmed in his seat and scraped his metal chair against the cement floor. His palms were sweating. The nausea that dogged him everywhere—from his first waking moments to the brutal hours between dime bags when he held a sign at an intersection and begged for change—crept into the corners of his consciousness. In a little while, he was going to be very, very sick. The backpack the police confiscated contained only a *Street Roots* newspaper, some food wrappers, and a dented deodorant tube that was stuffed with 17 baggies of dope. If that was found, Todd was in a world of trouble.

His stomach growled again. He hadn't eaten since the day before; the double-wrapped baggies were the only thing inside him. Each one held a marble-size dab of heroin, cut with God-knows-what, and packed in a couple layers of plastic. Todd hoped they were sealed tight. If several of the baggies were to break, it would flood his system with the substance he was addicted to. That would be it—an instant overdose. *Pop. Dead.*

Yet, at the same time, he wished they would. What were these cops saying? That Todd was liable for delivering drugs that resulted in death—a drug-induced homicide? He tried to focus on the dented gray table in front of him.

"I won't say anything else without my lawyer," he finally spat out.

The cops glanced at one another.

"We'll take you to make a call," the blond cop said. "But I'll tell you what. When you get someone to pick up, ask him if he knows who Len Bias is."

In 2012, Leonard Kevin "Len" Bias had been dead for 26 years. However, he was as present in the interrogation room as the cops. Bias—once hailed as the greatest baller of all time, even better than Michael Jordan—died of a cocaine overdose two days after being selected by the Boston Celtics, with the second overall pick in the 1986 NBA draft. Bias and his friends went out to celebrate.

The two teammates who used cocaine with Len the night of his fatal overdose, Terry Long and David Gregg, were suspended from the team. They were charged with possession of cocaine and obstruction of justice. Brian Tribble, the person who provided the cocaine, was indicted for possession of cocaine and possession of cocaine with intent to distribute. All three defendants pleaded not guilty, but two months later, Long and Gregg cut a deal with the prosecution. They both cooperated, providing testimony that convicted Tribble in exchange for getting their own charges dropped. This added three more indictments to Tribble's sheet: one count of conspiracy to obstruct justice and two counts of obstruction of justice. Each of these counts was punishable by up to five years in federal prison, plus a steep fine.

A year after Len's death, a jury acquitted Tribble of all charges related to the Bias case on June 3, 1987. However, this wasn't the end of the story.

As you may recall, the mid-80s was prime time for the war against drugs. First Lady Nancy Reagan was ramping up her "Just Say No" campaign, while President Ronald Reagan and Congress were hell-bent on implementing severe punishments for drug convictions in the form of long, mandatory minimum sentences for even the most minor drug offense.

Looking tough on drugs was a new priority for many politicians and policymakers, and Len Bias's overdose—the death of a young, handsome, gifted, and incredibly promising athlete—put the issue squarely in the public eye. According to the *New York Times,* Bias's death "created a media frenzy amid a national panic over crack, a cheap, smokable form of cocaine that was alarming drug abuse experts and fueling a wave of violent crime in American cities, especially Black neighborhoods." Congressional committees, including those led by future president Joe Biden, began writing antidrug legislation only weeks after Bias's death. The same year, Reagan signed the Anti-Drug Abuse Act of 1986 on October 27. This law, known as the "Len Bias Law," provided a mandatory minimum prison term of 20 years, plus a fine of up to $2 million for cases of drug distribution that led to the death or serious injury of a person.

The Len Bias Law wasn't a state law. It's federal—which means a grand jury trial and judge with no leeway in their options for sentencing. The state could still pile on charges for possession and delivery, which were about five years each. In Oregon, where Todd was arrested, drug court judges used a sentencing matrix to assess someone's criminal history and sentence them using a grid pattern. But Len Bias was a different ball game.

Three thousand miles and many years away from where Len Bias took his last breaths, Todd Schmidt (who was born and raised in Portland, Oregon, and a lifelong Portland Trail Blazers fan) was feeling the iron grip of the old federal law.

Todd had never met the person who had been killed by the heroin he allegedly sold. The odds were good he had never crossed paths with that person or even seen his face. Most deals, in his experience, were anonymous. When the police urged him to divulge the name of his customer, or of the small-fish dealer who paid Todd in dope to distribute drugs and collect cash, Todd came up empty. He was no Tony Montana. He slept on a friend's floor at the Yards at Union Station, where he could hear the trains running every hour of the night. His shoes had holes in them. He wasn't getting rich off heroin, and neither was the guy he worked for, a dude named Ranchero, who rented a run-down room by the hour at the Super Discount Lodge off the freeway exit. When Todd sold dope, he got a call with a pay phone caller ID on his disposable gas station cell, met the caller on a corner, and traded a baggie for a few bills. His customers were strangers in black hoodies. They had names like Peanut Butter, Scraggle Steve, Noble, and Stayton Scottie. They all looked the same to Todd, and if pressed, he couldn't have picked one of them out of a lineup.

But the police said he had to, or he was looking at two decades in prison. But if Todd did name his dealer, or tell the cops where to find him, Todd was putting his life at risk. (Yes, "Todd Schmidt" is a pseudonym.) For all its pretensions to culture, Portland, Oregon, is a small town. The entire downtown can be crossed on foot in under an hour. Street people, unhoused folks, and drug dealers tend to know each other by sight, if not by their chosen name. A loose association of distributors runs through every single-use bathroom between the 405 corridor to the Willamette River, bounded on both sides by neighborhoods that do everything they can to keep *those people* out. Todd had been running these few city blocks for years. If he pointed the finger, he would be immediately known as a rat—and maybe murdered, shanked in prison, or given a dirty shot of dope. He didn't want to die.

At the same time, he didn't want to live behind bars. As he dialed the county court's municipal phone with shaking hands, he hoped that there was a public defender on the call list who might be able to take his case. It's not like he really had his own lawyer. He knew from other people's stories that public defenders were overburdened, inexperienced, and incapable of mounting a strong defense, hence why district attorneys have such high conviction rates. In a case like Todd's, which he described as "one junkie's word against another," a public defender was likely to urge Todd to just cut a deal. But that deal meant federal prison—or else retaliation from the bigger fish the police were trying to catch.

"The Len Bias Law is valuable because it gives the criminal justice system leverage," Todd said. "It doesn't matter where you are in the food chain. The police pressure the user to give up their dealer. They're looking for the bigger fish, who's connected to a bigger fish, who's working for the shark."

Todd was a minnow; he didn't know any sharks. And in this case, there was nobody bigger to catch. The dealer Todd worked for, Ranchero, disappeared; he simply checked out of his hourly motel as soon as he heard Todd was busted. The mid-level dealer a notch above Ranchero was someone Todd had never heard of and couldn't name. But that didn't convince the DA. They piled on the pressure, threatening Todd with a life sentence and every possible punishment the

law could produce. No matter what Todd did, they only wanted
more. His arrest turned him into a pawn, stuck in the middle between upstream dealers and the justice system. The Len Bias Law
was one of many sharp sticks the DA could use to goad Todd into
cooperating in a sting, naming other users, or anything they wanted.
Todd was stuck. Even with legal representation, he knew he couldn't
escape the Len Bias mandatory minimum—and he knew it had an
85 percent conviction rate. Those were very bad odds. He decided
to play the game and take the way out that the courts offered him.

"The fact is, I sold dope that probably killed a few people. By
2012, there was fentanyl in the system. Even a small town like Portland was getting fire dope, and it was impossible to get naloxone unless
you took a class with the county, and who was going to do that? Back
then, you took your shot and hoped you'd get lucky."

Later, in his case, Todd requested a copy of the toxicology report
of the person who died. The man was homeless, with no family. He'd
overdosed in the bathroom of a Denny's on Martin Luther King Jr.
Blvd. There was alcohol in his system. He was an infrequent user
with a low tolerance and no safeguards in place. The dope that killed
him went from Todd to a frequent user, to an infrequent user who
was drunk when he used it. The stranger died. (That's three degrees
of separation.) The victim never had the chance to access recovery, as
Todd did. Now over a decade in recovery, Todd works with the mental health and behavioral health administration in Oregon, trying to
ensure that the systems in place to help people have low barriers to
access. He sees it as his service—an act of restitution for the many
lives he harmed when he was dealing and in active addiction. His
experience being homeless, with drug dealing, make him a special
kind of expert on these matters.

"Whose fault was the overdose death?" Todd asked. "I think
it's complicated. We aren't criminal masterminds. Most of us are on
the receiving end of the threat. I think it's wrong to give someone
20 years just for being a low-bottom user. The system needs a funda-

mental change, but they'll never repeal Len Bias. It gives prosecutors too much power, and at a time when dope is cheaper and more potent than ever, the outcomes are disastrous."

The overdose crisis isn't new at all—it's just accelerating. Since I wrote *American Fix* in 2018, overdose death rates have continued to skyrocket. So have drug arrests and incarceration rates, with more than one million people arrested for drugs every year. That was no coincidence. The *Seattle Times* shared a Pew Report from 2023 that said, "While about 2 percent of the US population has a co-occurring disorder (both a mental illness and substance use), people with both diagnoses made up a disproportionate 15 percent of arrests."

To better understand the perspective of those who actually enforce the law, I reached out to my friend Sheriff Karl Leonard of Chesterfield, Virginia, to talk more about fentanyl and the criminal justice system. Sheriff Leonard has worked on the front lines of the drug epidemic for more than four decades. Now retired from the Coast Guard, Sheriff Leonard is dedicated to law enforcement in his community. (Did I mention he's a Republican?)

In 2016, he launched a unique program at Chesterfield County Jail. Helping Addicts Recover Progressively (HARP) offers recovery-centered programs for people who want to pursue recovery while they're incarcerated. During the day, the jail is open to visitors, families, and community resources. After leaving jail, people are supported with a network that helps them stay connected, from a safe ride home from the rural jail location to job opportunities and sober housing. The HARP program is said to have a higher rate of success than private rehabs. Sheriff Leonard credits this to an unconventional program that is based on the lived experiences of people in recovery and the realities of addiction in an era when fentanyl is king.

"Harsher sentences are not a deterrent," he said. "When someone uses, they're not thinking of the consequences. That's the power of the disease. Active addiction is not rational."

He also pointed out that, while it was once easier to identify drug dealers and distribution networks, the triangle-shaped "corporation" model is quickly becoming a thing of the past. Earlier in the War on Drugs, law enforcement focused on tracing dealers up a chain of command to a kingpin or primary distributor. Each level of the organization was linked to the one above it, so catching a street dealer (like Todd Schmidt) who was willing to talk could potentially bust a much larger operation. However, fentanyl has blurred the line between "dealer" and "user." Nowadays, drug markets are much more fractured, and high-level suppliers are rarely ever caught handling drugs themselves; thus, they are insulated from prosecution, while low-level dealers like Todd take on all the risk.

The high percentage of fentanyl in the street drug supply makes it possible for one person to cut their substance multiple times and still retain enough potency to make it worth using. Mixing fentanyl with heroin means that dealers can turn higher profits—and that users can share their drugs too. In other words, fentanyl has created a lower barrier to entry into the drug business.

"The line is muddy," Sheriff Leonard said. "The dealer used to be the person who was bringing drugs into the country, not an individual with three grams of heroin. Now, it's more common for people to use together. One person will buy the substance and cut it to recoup the costs. They might also cut it to make more product."

Now, it's much more likely that someone is not buying heroin from a shady *Scarface*-type dealer. They're getting it from a person they already know and trust—a family member, schoolmate, colleague, or friend. That person may not know how much fentanyl is in their supply, either because they trust the person who gave them the substance or because they don't have access to resources such as drug-checking technology, or overdose prevention sites where drugs are tested by professionals on the spot. When someone overdoses, it isn't an act of murder—it's a mistake, and a bad one.

Overdoses are common in the substance use community. Most of us have overdosed at least once, just as most people who drink have overdone it from time to time. The difference between alcohol and a drug like fentanyl is that there's much less room for error. When an overdose turns fatal, it has a wide ripple effect, affecting everyone from loved ones to the friend who split the bag with them.

Yet, try explaining that to the politicians on both sides of the aisle who are stumping for tougher crackdowns and higher mandatory minimum sentences. The same politicians who view drug dealers as predatory monsters, rather than the much more nuanced truth that there are "dealers" like Todd, who live hard lives and aren't getting rich selling drugs, but nursing their own traumas by self-medication. Instead of putting efforts into overdose prevention, paying for resources that support long-term wellness and reduce recidivism, and seeking realistic solutions to fentanyl, these policymakers will go to any length to make it seem they're doing something to stop overdose deaths—even if that means the policies they pursue are misguided and destroy more lives.

From coast to coast, during the fentanyl epidemic, new laws are being passed that repeat the same mistakes of the 1980s crack epidemic. Starting with the 2016 campaign promises to curb the opioid epidemic, state leaders have been urged to double down on targeting fentanyl. Former attorney general Jeff Sessions said in Concord, New Hampshire, on July 12, 2018, "We are not going to accept the status quo. We will not allow this to continue. We can weaken these networks, reduce fentanyl availability, and save lives." He ordered federal prosecutors in Ohio, Tennessee, Kentucky, West Virginia, Maine, California, and Pennsylvania, as well as in New Hampshire, to harshly prosecute anyone suspected of fentanyl dealing.

A few years later, policymakers from both political parties are still taking this mandate seriously. Senator Marco Rubio (R-Florida) and his colleagues reintroduced the Felony Murder for Deadly Fentanyl Distribution Act in 2023. The bill makes the distribution of fentanyl, resulting in death, punishable by federal felony murder charges. Senator Rubio said this was a "commonsense step" to protect communities. "We need to stop the flow of fentanyl and punish those responsible for poisoning our communities. If the illicit sale of this drug results in death, then the seller should be charged with felony murder." The senators apparently haven't thought through the many consequences of this law, such as people being afraid to dial 911 for help during an overdose if they fear they will be charged with murder.

In 2023, legislative bodies in 46 states introduced hundreds of bills targeting fentanyl and fentanyl users. Virginia lawmakers described fentanyl as "a weapon of terrorism," while Arkansas and Texas joined more than 30 other states in adding drug-induced homicide statutes for lethal fentanyl overdoses, even if the substance was shared between friends. A new Iowa law punishes the "sale or manufacture" of up to five grams of fentanyl with a ten-year prison sentence. In Arizona, where first-degree murder is punishable by life in prison or the death penalty, overdoses traced back to a specific individual might become murders under House Bill 2779, punishable by 25 years in prison. In a separate Arizona bill, SB 1029 would expand the state's first-degree murder statutes to include deaths caused by fentanyl, which even includes cases of "accidental" death.

Is all this really the best answer? Not at all. Jennifer Carroll, a medical anthropologist at North Carolina State University, told the *New York Times* that these types of laws were counterproductive. She said, "We are falling back on these really comfy, straightforward law-and-order solutions even though they didn't work before, they're not working now, and there's growing evidence telling us they're making things worse."

This isn't a purely academic opinion. Sheriff Leonard, a Republican himself, said that harsher penalties and longer sentences do not work as deterrents. That's what the scientific literature shows as well: more imprisonment does not correlate with reduced drug use or overdoses. Yet, American lawmakers are stuck on a carousel of incarceration.

History has shown that more severe consequences for low-level drug crimes haven't done anything to prevent overdose deaths. Nor have raids, border seizures, or regulatory crackdowns slowed the distribution of fentanyl.

Harsher drug laws not only don't stop overdoses, but they also increase the likelihood that someone will die. I know this sounds counterintuitive to most laypeople, but many of the best ideas to treat addiction and prevent overdoses are counterintuitive. For instance, in prior chapters, I discussed how prescribing opioids to people with opioid addiction is a safe, effective treatment that saves lives. Similarly, harsher drug laws and disrupting drug markets can actually lead to worse outcomes, like more fatal and nonfatal overdoses. Research even shows that the more police seize drugs, the more overdoses there are. Instead of focusing so much on the drug supply and arresting dealers like Todd, lawmakers must focus on strategies that actually help people survive their addictions and find recovery.

Take New Jersey, for example, where Republicans called for tougher sentencing rules for fentanyl possession, and recovery advocates and overdose survivors pushed back. Caitlin O'Neill, co-director of the New Jersey Harm Reduction Coalition, said, "The demand for the street drug market is not going away, and it has not gone away in the 50-plus years of harsher drug war enforcement. What these bills will do is destroy the people who use drugs and the people who live in neighborhoods targeted by the drug overdose laws."

Overdose rates continue to rise, and policymakers seem happier throwing the book at sick people instead of addressing the systemic issues that prevent them from getting help.

Sheriff Leonard said, "We've spent untold trillions on the drug war. Is it working? Just look at the results, which are more drugs, more deaths, and more access than before. This is not a problem that the government can solve. It must be a community effort."

As a dedicated community leader, Leonard is personally and profoundly involved in recovery efforts in Chesterfield. He remembers sitting with a mother while her son was taken off life support—another person killed by a fentanyl overdose. Leonard said that the experience was eye-opening for him. Supporting a devastated family member taught him about the intense grief that follows this kind of loss, as well as the pain of unanswered questions. This pain is compounded by the severe stigma of addiction, which keeps people isolated, ashamed, and hurting. The more we stigmatize addiction, the harder it is for people to come forward and ask for help. The more people hide their addiction, the more dangerous it becomes.

"Families go through addiction together," he said. "So many parents go into isolation during their child's addiction, and the truth is so many struggle with the deep shame of that. They may blame themselves or feel like they could have done more to help. Much of the focus of both laws and solutions is on the sick person, but the parent needs help as well. That person is suffering too."

He said that family groups, an opportunity to share feelings, and better education about addiction could help change how grieving parents respond to overdose losses. The focus on retribution might shift toward healing. It might also mean that people like Todd Schmidt don't spend years of their lives in prison but reenter society with a sincere desire to get healthy and help support others in their recovery. What good is it for society for someone like Todd to spend his life in prison? It's a waste of so much human potential.

But for some people, that change can't come quickly enough. As you read this, tens of thousands of people are stuck behind bars—waiting for substance use treatment, waiting for their sentencing, waiting to serve a mandatory minimum, waiting for a fresh start, waiting for a second chance. One of those people who is stuck waiting is a young woman named Emma Semler.

What does a drug dealer look like? Pop culture offers plenty of images to choose from. Over the decades, the archetype of the dealer has shifted, both in antidrug propaganda and in the media. Many of these images are now iconic, from Elvira Hancock (played by Michelle Pfeiffer) hoovering a miniature pyramid of cocaine in *Scarface* to the tender-hearted crack dealer Juan in *Moonlight* to the dreadlocked, grill-wearing pimp Drexl Spivey in *True Romance*.

Most of the time, drug dealers are portrayed as outsiders—people already living on the fringes of society and doing what they must to survive. In the media, dealers tend to be dangerous men who put their self-interest ahead of the safety of the people they deal to. Dead customer? Too bad. To these characters, money matters more than human life.

When I say "drug dealer," most people don't imagine young suburban white women. They certainly don't envision somebody like Emma Semler.

Emma looked more like a sorority sister than a drug dealer. With beach-blond curls and a broad smile framed by charming dimples, she looked bubbly and friendly—the last person on earth to know anything about heroin. However, Emma was all too familiar with opioids. In her teens, she developed an addiction to heroin and sought treatment in her home state of Pennsylvania. At the rehab, she met another young woman named Jennifer Rose Werstler. The two became friends. Jenny Rose and Emma recovered together, relapsed together after treatment, and used heroin together. At the height of her addiction, Emma was using up to 10 bags of heroin a day.

But who was counting at that point? In active addiction, days and years melt together. The only unit of time that matters is the bag of dope, which, in the fentanyl era, lasts just a couple of short hours.

When its effects start to wear off, time starts up—and it aches until you use again, and again, and again. Addiction traps people in time.

However, May 9, 2014, was a big day because Jenny Rose was turning 20. Although Jenny Rose was newly in recovery again, with 60 days off opioids, she was eager to use. She hit Emma up and messaged her, asking her to score enough for all of them. Emma, her younger sister Sarah, and Jenny Rose celebrated with a bag—as they'd agreed. They met up in their Philadelphia neighborhood, divided a bag of heroin, and went to the bathroom of a KFC to get high. Since it was her birthday, Jenny Rose got an extra dose. As soon as she injected, she began to OD. She collapsed and was unresponsive.

Emma and her sister panicked, grabbed the remaining heroin and syringe, and ran, leaving Jenny Rose behind. Later, a KFC employee found Jenny Rose in the bathroom and called 911. When the paramedics came, they weren't able to revive her. It was too late—and on her birthday, Jenny Rose lost her life to an overdose.

Jenny Rose's mother, Margaret Werstler, remembers her daughter as "a young, beautiful girl who lost her life to heroin overdose." She said, "Jenny Rose's addiction affected our relationship as a mother and daughter. It affected my marriage, with countless arguments and sleepless nights. We, as parents, have now fallen victim to heroin. It took the life of our only child."

Margaret blamed inadequate treatment for Jenny's death, saying that she came back home too soon from the sober living in Florida, where she'd been staying after rehab. Margaret said that Jenny "came home from treatment only because her lawyer wanted her to close her court case. We, her parents, were telling the lawyer, 'Don't bring her home yet, she's not ready.' Something is seriously wrong with our current system—it doesn't take care of or care about people struggling with addiction."

Once again, a brush with the criminal justice system massively harmed a person's recovery. What if Jenny didn't have a case hanging over her recovery? What if she could just focus on getting health care and getting better? What if she didn't have to be home, in a triggering environment, waiting for a court date?

Emma didn't hear the news about Jenny until the next morning. She was devastated. To quell her anxiety and fear, she promptly used the rest of the heroin that had killed her friend. But Emma's nightmare was just beginning.

Thanks to new, tough-on-drugs policies, Emma wasn't seen as a grieving friend in the eyes of the law. She wasn't allowed to mourn her friend Jenny. She wasn't viewed as a young girl, scared and addicted. Instead, Emma was a criminal—and slapped by a federal prosecutor with a 21-year mandatory minimum prison sentence for her friend's overdose. It was sadistic arithmetic, designed to add to Emma's suffering and exact retribution for the death of her friend.

How could a prosecutor stretch the definition of a dealer beyond recognition?

Because Jenny had messaged Emma on Facebook to ask her to help buy heroin, Emma was now designated a "drug dealer."

Because Emma loaned Jenny the cash for the drugs, Emma was seen as responsible for the purity, quality, and safety of those drugs.

Because Emma had paid for the baggie and provided a syringe, she could be charged with possession of narcotics with intention to distribute.

Because the KFC bathroom where the three women used was within 1,000 feet of a school, she would face a more severe punishment that included another mandatory minimum sentence. (School zone enhancements were also part of the 1986 drug law.)

Because Emma shared the heroin with two other people—her younger sister and her friend—she could be charged with "distribution of drugs."

Because Emma ran instead of staying to help Jenny Rose, and because Jenny lost her life, Emma could be charged with drug-induced homicide, staring down two decades in prison.

As soon as the three girls stepped into that restroom, Emma was subject to the same laws designed to target drug kingpins like El Chapo. They were the same laws that the Multnomah County DA used to extort Todd Schmidt into a deal, putting his life at risk and forcing him to cooperate or end up in federal prison. However, unlike Todd, Emma wasn't so lucky. She had no one to point the DA toward, and so she ended up feeling the full brunt of the federal and state legal systems.

In the end, Emma was sentenced to 21 years in prison for drug-induced homicide. The fact that this whole tragedy was an accident—and avoidable—was not part of the story. Jenny Rose's early exit from treatment wasn't part of it either. Nor was her mother's feeling that her daughter needed more time with her support systems.

To hear the prosecution tell it, 18-year-old Emma may as well have deliberately and maliciously plotted to murder Jenny Rose by poisoning her. The US Attorney's Office, Eastern District of Pennsylvania, threw the book at Emma, as though she wanted her friend dead. Her age, friendship with Jenny, and willingness to enter recovery were not considered. She was given the mandatory minimum sentence of 20 years, plus another year for good measure.

Despite Margaret's earlier statements, Jenny's family agreed with the harsh sentencing. They seemed to see the mandatory minimum as retribution for their daughter's death. When US District Judge Gene E. K. Pratter heard the case, she also dismissed any appeals for mercy. She told Emma that she wasn't taking the case seriously enough and that she had yet to hear her apologize to Werstler's family. (This is common in cases that involve serious injury, damages, or loss of life. Apologizing can be interpreted as admitting fault, so defense lawyers often recommend not saying "I'm sorry" until after judgment.)

After hearing Judge Pratter's comments, Emma turned to

Jenny's family members, who were sitting in the courtroom. She mouthed the words, "I'm sorry."

Her apology wasn't acceptable to Jenny's family. Jenny's mother, Margaret Werstler, responded, "You're only sorry for yourself." She later stated to the court that she saw Emma as responsible for Jenny's death—directly or indirectly, it was on Emma's shoulders (even though it was Jenny, wanting to score, who first messaged Emma on Facebook).

Margaret said, "For almost five years, I have been asking myself and God, 'Why? Why my baby? Why did my only child die? Why did you leave my child alone during the most important time in her life when she needed help the most? Why didn't you help save her life?'"

Yet, what could they have done? Two scared teenagers, without naloxone, in a state that wouldn't pass Good Samaritan laws protecting them for several more months—it's hard to say that Emma was acting irrationally. Her decisions were driven by the logic of America's drug war.

Even if she had stayed to help Jenny, she might still have the same mandatory sentence. Punished for doing the right thing! The drug war is a lose-lose scenario. Emma is damned if she does, damned if she doesn't.

That doesn't make an ounce of sense. Attorneys Leo Beletsky and Jeremiah Goulka of the Northeastern University School of Law pointed out that ultra-harsh rulings that went outside the scope of Drug Distribution Resulting in Death (DDRD) laws were counter-effective. Severe and mandatory maximum sentences actually encourage people to run—instead of staying to save a life. Beletsky and Goulka wrote, "Rather than deterring drug trafficking, such prosecutions deter help-seeking during overdose events and interfere with overdose prevention measures. This cuts at cross purposes to overdose crisis response, leading to more, not fewer, deaths." Good

Samaritan laws passed in all 50 states, but not at the federal level, also help protect people who stay to help overdosing friends.

Drug-induced homicide laws functionally destroy over a decade of work putting Good Samaritan protections in place. By turning overdoses into murders, these "homicide" rules turn public health problems into criminal justice problems. It's yet another instance where law enforcement undermines the so-called public health approach to addiction. Drug-induced homicide laws not only stretch the definition of a drug dealer beyond recognition, but they also ignore the basic facts of any accident—including the fact that people who are scared to be charged as killers simply won't call 911 when their friend is in danger.

So, it seems that many forces conspired to end Jenny Rose's life. Emma Semler didn't plan to be present for her friend's final, fatal injection. She was just as vulnerable as Jenny Rose, and had been failed by the same systems that had set her friend up to die. Jenny's mother, Margaret, once said, "So many people tried to help Jenny, but in the end, she wasn't ready to cut her treatment short—and it killed her. Our lives will never be the same. I hate this disease, and heroin is the devil."

During the trial, it seems her anger shifted to Emma—a young woman just as sick as Jenny, and just as powerless to leave her addiction behind.

The prosecution lawyers honed in on Emma's choice to run, framing it as cold-blooded and calculated rather than a snap decision in the moment. Jonathan Wilson, special agent in charge of the DEA's Philadelphia field office, pointed out that had Emma tried to help her friend, Jenny might still be alive. Emma, he said, had the opportunity to save Jenny—and chose to abandon her.

"The fact that Semler left the victim alone as she was overdosing is particularly disturbing, as she most likely could have been aided by first responders," Wilson said.

First Assistant US Attorney Jennifer Arbittier Williams agreed in her own statement: "This defendant acted with complete disregard for another human life, the life of a supposed friend."

This wasn't the end of the road for Emma. She appealed her sentence, making national headlines when the Third Circuit Court decided to overturn her conviction. She was issued a new jury trial, but rather than try for a "not guilty" verdict, she chose to plead guilty—this time to a lesser charge. This lesser charge has a sentencing guideline range of 7–10 years in prison, according to the US Attorney's Office for the Eastern District of Pennsylvania.

And yes, the prosecution planned to get every single one of those 120 months out of Emma.

They said a full 10-year sentence was the only way to get justice for Jenny's death. A memorandum written by Assistant US Attorneys Everett Witherell and Kelly Harrell said that the maximum sentence was an "appropriate and just resolution to this case that reflects the seriousness of the defendant's conduct, provides finality, takes into account . . . individual circumstances of this defendant and this case, and is the sentence that is sufficient but not greater than necessary to achieve the goals of sentencing."

The memorandum also commented on the "magnitude of this tragedy," which was brought about by a "series of devastating choices made by the defendant." Witherell and Harrell wrote that "one life was lost and another was permanently scarred by this unimaginable tragedy."

Anyone can tell you that permanent scars—the scars of loss, grief, and self-hatred that come with losing a friend or loved one—don't heal quickly. If ever. They certainly don't heal behind bars. When the prosecution said Emma's life was "permanently scarred," they seemed to take no responsibility for deepening her pain. An eye for an eye blinds the world; in this case, Emma was punished for a tragedy that involved her but wasn't necessarily her fault.

There must be a better way—which is why understanding fentanyl and how people use substances are key to reforming our criminal justice system. Relying on barbaric, cruel laws, these relics of Reagan's drug war put people like Emma Semler behind bars instead of into treatment or other community support programs. In most cases, providing a fatal dose of opioids is not deliberate. It is not premeditated. It is not like in the movies. It is a tragedy, but not a murder. Someone decides to use drugs. And they ask someone for the drugs. The transaction takes two people, at a minimum. The logic of the drug war is twisted. Had Jenny been caught in possession of that dose of heroin that killed her, the government would not have viewed her as a victim. She would have been in violation of her probation—and incarcerated. Only because she died did the government view her as a victim. While she was alive and using, she was a criminal, just like Emma.

When Todd Schmidt was released from jail, the first thing he did was get high again. He was on pretrial release, pending the mandatory minimum the DA's office had threatened. The stress was unbearable—get used by the dope dealers, get used by the cops, get a hot shot, get shanked, get ratted out, get fucked up. For Todd, it was lose–lose. He had whiplash from being yo-yoed between the opposing worlds of the court system and the streets. The cops never found the 17 baggies of dope hidden in his deodorant tube. He used them all in no time. When the rinse on his last bag failed to dull his dope sickness, Todd limped down to the corner and made a call from the pay phone.

"Hello?" the voice at the other end said.

They met at the corner of Sixth and Morrison. The dealer was a young woman slinging bags for some dude named Ranchero. Todd bought a dime from his very own replacement—a girl in a black hoodie. She took his cash without smiling, her head down. She was gone in an instant.

Todd didn't catch her name.

6

IN SEARCH OF A NEW MODEL

By the time Justin DeLong died of an opioid overdose on March 28, 2014, he had been through the wringer more times than his best friend, Morgan Godvin, could count. Morgan and his mom had seen Justin dragged out of his bed, brutalized by cops, and subjected to violence by the state. Addiction made Justin an easy victim for a jail-happy court system. Everyone around him, Morgan said, was collateral damage. Oregon is last in the nation for access to addiction recovery services, so the state dealt with Justin's death the way it dealt with any drug-related incident.

They turned it into a crime scene. A terrible accident was being investigated as murder.

Although she was practically Justin's sister, Morgan was one of the last people to know that he'd passed. She got the news, not from her friends or even Justin's family, whom she was close with. She heard it from the police who broke into her home the next day, put her in handcuffs, and said she was being arrested under a federal law, "delivery resulting in death," for Justin's overdose. She had sold Justin the baggie of black tar heroin he had used on the day of his death. While it was not cut with fentanyl—which wouldn't saturate Portland's heroin supply until 2020—the black tar caused respiratory failure. No one with naloxone was around to revive him, and he died.

"Until the moment of his death," Morgan said, "Justin was used by the state. In death, he was treated as a victim and a pawn."

She was investigated by the DEA in connection with Justin's fatal overdose. Just like Todd Schmidt, Morgan was threatened with a 20-year mandatory minimum sentence. After her previous convictions—one for felony possession of heroin, and one felony for "heroin residue" found during an illegal search of her car—Morgan was in a frightening situation. A federal drug delivery charge is treated like manslaughter. It's called "death by delivery" and places blame on the person who shared, sold, or traded a substance to the person who used it and died. The person blamed often had zero intent to kill; in fact, just the opposite: the person blamed is often a friend or a lover.

"The investigation was the kind of thing that gives the DEA wet dreams," Morgan said. "I didn't even need to cooperate with them because my roommate was who I bought my dope from. Through texts, they could prove I sold Justin the fatal gram, and then they arrested my roommate with several ounces and worked up that chain."

Morgan and her four co-defendants got a combined 60-year sentence. Morgan was able to get a plea deal and was prosecuted on a lesser charge: "conspiracy to distribute heroin." She was given five years. "But it didn't stop anything. Nobody in Portland went dopesick the day we were arrested," Morgan said. "The DEA wasn't bringing down kingpins. They were sending five so-called junkies and a couple cogs in the wheel to prison where they thought we belonged."

She was 24, her mother had died of a prescription overdose three months earlier, and now her best friend was gone. Morgan felt like her life was crumbling. She entered the meat grinder of the prison system, scared, alone, and overwhelmed. After nine months in Multnomah County's Inverness Jail, a year at Columbia County Jail, and two years at Dublin's Federal Correctional Institution in the Bay Area of California, Morgan was transferred to a federal halfway house. She became a student at Portland State University, earning a double major in public health and Spanish. Though she used heroin for the first year of her incarceration, Morgan was able to claw her own way to recovery despite an utter lack of recovery resources and mental health counseling. In January 2019, she was released from house arrest and transferred to what's called "supervised release."

By then, fentanyl had reared its ugly head in Portland—and once again, Morgan's friends were dying. Morgan left prison with a profound desire to change the system. Relieved from active heroin addiction, she found a new focus in drug policy reform—the same policies that had made her and Justin's existence a living hell, while at the same time offering zero support. She couldn't ignore the fact that the DEA was using the same incompetent playbook for fentanyl as it did for heroin. The results would be just as deadly.

"They're acting like fentanyl is a weapon of mass destruction, like nothing that has ever come before," Morgan said. "It's as if people are not consensually using fentanyl or other opioids. There are situations where fentanyl is not used with consent, when people overdose because they don't know what's in the substance they're using. But Justin and I were consenting. We used to joke about dying and the life-and-death nature of heroin addiction. It was part of the way we lived. We had basic risk tolerance. It was kind of accepted that if you used, you would eventually OD."

Morgan has been quick to name her white middle-class privilege in helping her build a meaningful life after incarceration. She's written that if she were Black, she would likely still be in prison, citing a 2014 University of Michigan Law School study that shows Black defendants are 75 percent likelier to receive a mandatory minimum sentence than white ones who committed the same crime. She points out that her life today—with positions on state policy committees, a voice in the advocacy community, and long-term recovery—is the result not just of her talents but her identity. She is living proof of the benefits that come with being white, female, and suburban. Because of the identity she was born with, Morgan was able to get past many of the barriers that Black, Indigenous, and People of Color (BIPOC) people face. Morgan managed to recover not because of the draconian drug war, but, rather, in spite of it.

"Because I'm white and middle class, I'm not in prison," she says. "I speak institutions' language, and I share new perspectives with people in power in a way that resonates with them, because they can identify with me. It's cultural specificity, the 'privileged white people' edition."

The privilege inherent in these systems couldn't be more obvious than in Denzel Hilton's family. Fentanyl killed his brother, Horatio, a Black man who had more than 18 years of recovery at the time of his death. Fentanyl nearly killed Denzel's daughter Cleo, a young Black nonbinary person who survived addiction and has been sober for more than five years. And fentanyl is currently ravaging Cleo's mother, Jodie—a white woman who is going through the spin-dry cycle of short-term detoxes that I experienced myself. (Out of respect, aliases are being used for these individuals.)

Denzel's entire family is haunted by fentanyl. It is a constant presence. Sitting in his posh West Hills home, wearing an Armani zip-up, with a new Mercedes sedan parked by the curb, Denzel is still painfully aware of his proximity to addiction. It lives in the house with him, sleeps next to him in his king-size bed, and shares his evening meals. He says that 45 years is nothing to addiction.

"I'm still counting days," he said. "I've been sober for 16,500 days, and what I know is that all I've got is today. My wife is good when she's not using, but we are literally in the middle of an epidemic. Fentanyl kills everybody."

Denzel survived the crack epidemic of the 1980s by sticking with heroin. He speaks about his time on the streets with dry wit, the levity of a true survivor.

"I'm old enough to know how this shit works," he said. "You can do anything you want when your addiction is talking to you. In my era, you could sociably shoot heroin, smoke dope, and drink, and not do yourself too much harm. Now, it's all needles and caps, and people who can't even think straight, much less think about treatment. Folks are stuck outside."

"The crack epidemic was the turning point," he said. In the 1970s, when he ripped and ran down the length of I-5, things were fairly mellow. He transported pounds of heroin from California to the Pacific Northwest. Still, Portland wasn't his favorite place. Denzel spent most of his time in Berkeley; before gentrification, it was the hood, not the hippie-crunchy tech district it is now. That's where he encountered crack for the first time and its nasty little cousin, speed. Both are produced by boiling powdered cocaine or other substances in a mixture of water and ammonia or baking soda. Both will make you completely sick.

"I wore out my nose," he says. "I got a bag of what I thought was coke and ended up counting cars all night. It was white, but it was tweak. I could tell from my behavior that there was something in it."

After that, he stuck with heroin and cocaine that he tested himself—and as a high-level distributor in the region, he had access to the cleanest drugs in the network.

"The perk of being a dealer at that level is that you always know what you're getting. My guy paid me in China White heroin and the purest and prettiest coke I've ever seen. I tested it in a tall glass of bleach to make sure it wasn't cut with anything, and it would float down like fish scales," he said.

He was aware that it wasn't the same for everybody. Around him, people were vanishing left and right. At the Black-owned nightclubs, where folks used to dance and hang out, the well-dressed people grabbing a drink and a bump on the weekends were switching from coke to something harder.

"Places like Geneva's, Burger Barn, Upstairs Downstairs over on MLK and Union—the vibe changed. Suddenly, you were see-ing people in the alleys. The burning trash barrels, people running around all crazy. Shit all of a sudden changed. The Black neighbor-hoods used to be quiet and safe for the most part. Then, for the first time, we had shootings. Crack brought in the guns and the police. I remember being shocked by the boldness of it."

The options for Black people, especially Black crack users, were few and far between. Denzel witnessed the transition from the druggy 1970s to the harsh drug war of the 1980s. As crack began to generate a fierce government backlash, mass incarceration soared to new heights. It swept up Denzel, along with many others. In 1978, when Denzel entered recovery through the prison system, he had no idea what was available to him.

"My cellmate at the jail told me I would get an easier sentence if I just told them I wanted to quit. I never even heard of that. And now, [well into the overdose crisis of the 2020s,] you've got Oregon governor Tina Kotek on the TV saying she's going to pass a $200 million bill for addiction services. Hell, in 1978, I didn't even know detox existed."

Without diversion programs or state-funded treatment, Denzel had no other options. It was either live on the street and be killed, or be locked in a cage.

Denzel's wife Jodie—who is white and middle class, like Morgan Godvin—knows all about detox. For decades, she had been a se-cret opioid user who snuck prescription pills and other substances behind her sober husband's back. Because of the sweeping changes to recovery policy in the last five years, she was well aware of the treatment and recovery support options that were available to her, and she didn't need to go to jail to get them.

Denzel said. "When I came into the rooms, you could cut the cigarette smoke with a knife. The brothers in those groups told me that when someone dies, someone else gets a seat."

Jodie's experience couldn't be more different. She picked one of the 30-odd detox clinics in her area, called them, and was admitted the next day. She was believed, and she was encouraged to work on herself in these short-term programs. After a medically supported detox, she was given the option to transition to a 28-day or even 90-day program at a residential treatment center. All of this was covered by her private insurance. Still, her first three attempts weren't completely successful. Jodie lasted less than a month between detoxes—a common experience, since relapse rates are extremely high for people who leave treatment without adequate support.

Still, Jodie was able to access not one, but five different treatment centers. She was given the grace and tolerance that everyone deserves, but that most folks—including me—are denied for one reason or another. She was able to take months away from working and domestic responsibilities while her husband supported her, paid for her health care, and took her to recovery meetings so she could connect with other women dealing with similar struggles. With her pretty face, tearstained cheeks, and blond hair, Jodie's crash landing was comparatively very, very soft. For her, it was still hell—just with nicer upholstery.

"Treatment is like a vacation for her," Jodie and Denzel's daughter Cleo said bitterly. Now in their early twenties, Cleo lives with their partner a few miles from their parents. They visit every few days to spend time with Denzel, watch TV, and play with their parents' tattered-ear cats. "She isn't sleeping on a busted mattress or sharing a group shower. That doesn't make it easier, but it sure doesn't make it harder."

Cleo's substance use started in their teens, much earlier in life than either of their folks. As a trauma survivor and one of the only Black students in their entire school system, they felt chronically out of place. Knowing that they were nonbinary and queer created even more separation. They turned to drugs to cope with the unbearable feeling of living on the wrong planet, speaking a language nobody else could hear. Their first exposure to fentanyl was in high school when a friend offered to share a fentanyl inhaler. Cleo was already a binge drinker and used other substances, but fentanyl was like throwing gas on a barbecue.

"I will never forget that feeling," they said. "It was a sense of sudden connection. After so much pain and isolation, I felt like I was coming home."

Within a year of fentanyl use, Cleo's golden skin had turned gray, and their once-glossy curls were dull frizz. They tried needles once, liked it too much, and got scared—they realized how entrenched their addiction was and how far it had progressed. Barely 19, Cleo had few options. They couldn't even get a credit card, much less figure out how to pay for a 28-day treatment program.

Fortunately, Cleo was able to access the tools they'd seen their father use for years. It might not have been a luxurious Malibu "day spa" rehab, but it worked. Cleo was able to detox and find recovery in the same spaces that Denzel frequented, rooms full of seasoned and sober Black men who welcomed Cleo with the warm words, "Come on in, kid. We've been saving you a chair."

Within a few years of recovery, Cleo began a career as a peer recovery support specialist, focusing on the experiences of young people in recovery. Cleo's experience benefits many, many others—some of whom stay in touch to let Cleo know that their words and actions have had a lasting effect.

"You can do anything you want when your addiction is arrested," Denzel explained. "Cleo turned their life around. The changes came good and fast. But again, I think that's a heroin thing. If it had been crack for any of us, it would be a different story."

There is something uniquely American about Denzel, Jodie, and Cleo's recovery story. Even in an interracial family, there is a severe disparity in access to recovery services. Jodie visited almost half a dozen facilities in her search for sobriety. Denzel, a Black man, arrived through the court system. And Cleo detoxed on their own. The Surgeon General's report from 2016 notes that definitions of recovery vary starkly between racial groups. More than 80 percent of the Black people surveyed for the report said that total abstinence was what defined recovery. Overwhelmingly, Black folks found support in zero-cost recovery groups such as Narcotics Anonymous.

White people, on the other hand, tended to have a much broader definition—what I would call a *non*definition—of recovery. They were more likely to acknowledge that there are many paths to recovery. They were also more likely to access medical care for their addiction issues. Considering that only 10 percent of people ever receive any medical support of any kind for substance use, that's significant. More and more people are like Cleo—shoved out of an exclusive system that doesn't acknowledge their existence or offer culturally competent care.

But other countries seem to have found a solution that works better, and works in a surprising and broad-reaching way. While this type of approach is still considered "radical" in the United States, it's been the gold standard for more than two decades in Europe, and drug-related deaths on the continent have become far less common as a result.

When it comes to the most tolerant drug policy, you'll often hear rumblings of the "Portugal model." This model has become synonymous with drug decriminalization, but that is just one of its many features. In 2001, Portugal completely transformed its drug policy, pivoting away from crime and punishment toward a health-centered approach. Portugal's model involved a massive nationwide overhaul, including education, policing, culture, politics, and the law.

"It's a total package," said Dr. João Goulão, the soft-spoken Portuguese physician who is credited as the architect of Portugal's drug policy. Dr. Goulão often emphasizes that decriminalization alone cannot explain Portugal's success. "The biggest effect has been to allow stigma to fall, to let people speak clearly, and to pursue professional help without fear."

Portugal's policy is rooted in harm reduction, mobilizing public resources to offer low-barrier support for drug users of all kinds. The key words here are "public resources," a host of them, ranging from counseling, health care, and policing to education. The Portugal model works by creating robust infrastructure that encourages people to seek help if they need it, and for not punishing them for the impact drugs have on their lives. Just as importantly, if drugs aren't interfering in someone's day-to-day life, their drug case is suspended. The vast majority of drug cases in Portugal are suspended because a person's substance use is deemed to be low risk and nonproblematic. That means funding and resources are not wasted on people who don't need help, and the focus can be on helping those who are actually struggling. All of these elements are part of the "total package," with an array of institutions and communities working in tandem to save people from unnecessary punishment and to help those in need. When all of these components are clicking together and well funded, the Portugal model lives up to its own high ideals. But its success didn't happen overnight, and to this day, Portugal is still a work in progress.

What prompted Portugal to transform its policy? Overdose deaths and HIV infections were spiking, resulting in the small nation having the highest rates in the European Union. While fentanyl hadn't made its appearance (yet), the country was awash in Afghan-sourced heroin. To address this, the Portuguese government refashioned its drug policy away from zero tolerance and incarceration and toward health care and compassion. A major part of Portugal's project was addressing the social fact of drugs as a taboo and the ostracization of drug users. Rather than punishing and pushing people who use drugs out of society, the goal was to bring them in closer.

But the part of the Portugal model that gets the most attention is its decriminalization of personal possession of all drugs—yes, even heroin. This means that possessing drugs for personal use in Portugal does not result in a criminal record or the stigma that comes with being incarcerated. A person may be fined or required to do community service—but they won't see the inside of a jail cell simply because they suffer from addiction. Dr. Goulão said his primary goal was to create a space for drug users to reflect on the role drugs play in their lives with caring professionals. The hope is that people with problematic drug use will eventually want to enter a process of change of their own volition.

In this model, the essential ingredients of success are all the things we lack in the United States: compassionate care accessible in people's communities; no low-level and petty drug convictions; frequent and nonpunitive touchpoints with drug users; open conversations about drugs that destigmatize; low-barrier, zero-cost, on-demand treatment; and freely offered harm reduction services and supplies, including clean syringes, naloxone, and medication treatment options like buprenorphine and methadone. The US is starting to implement some of these measures, but mostly in a chaotic patchwork fashion that many people struggle to access.

Portugal has blazed a trail for drug policy that other nations around the world have started to emulate. Transform Drug Policy Foundation reported in 2021 that the Portugal model was holding strong 20 years after its initiation:

- Drug-related deaths have remained below the EU average since 2001.
- The proportion of prisoners sentenced for drugs has fallen from 40 percent to 15 percent.
- Rates of drug use have remained consistently below the EU average.

For years, I've explored whether Portugal's model, or something like it, could ever work in the US. Can we reverse so many decades of punishment and cruelty and change course?

The *Surgeon General's 2016 Report on Alcohol, Drugs, and Health,* authored by Dr. Vivek Murthy (who was handpicked by President Obama), suggests that Portugal's dream is possible here. According to the 2016 report on addiction, the first ever of its kind by the US Surgeon General, many of the elements of the Portugal model would reduce overdose death rates in the US. Here are some of the key findings of the report (and yes, they're all direct quotes):

- "Effective integration of prevention, treatment, and recovery services across health-care systems is key to addressing substance misuse and its consequences."
- "The shame and discrimination that prevents many individuals from seeking help must be vigorously combated."
- "Access to high-quality treatment is a human right, although recovery is more than treatment."
- "Harm reduction programs provide public health-oriented, evidence-based, and cost-effective services to prevent and reduce substance use-related risks among those actively using substances, and substantial evidence supports their effectiveness."
- "Evidence-based behavioral and medication-assisted treatments applied using a chronic-illness-management approach have been shown to facilitate recovery from substance use disorders, prevent relapse, and improve other outcomes, such as reducing criminal behavior and the spread of infectious diseases."
- "Access to recovery support services can help former substance users achieve and sustain long-term wellness."

- "Embedding prevention, treatment, and recovery services into the larger health-care system will increase access to care, improve quality of services, and produce improved outcomes for countless Americans."

These points reflect the basic concepts behind the Portugal model. Making recovery services as helpful as possible and universally available, eliminating the shame of being sick or asking for help, and focusing on harm reduction rather than only abstinence and incarceration are all working in Portugal. The US Surgeon General's report points to the same north star. But asking America to adopt the Portugal model is like stepping through the looking glass. This approach is an inverted image of what we have in America. So how can we get there?

Harm reduction is unquestionably an evidence-based path to saving lives and helping people get healthy. However, it has to be more than an idea. It has to have the foundation of solid, committed funding and infrastructure that supports meaningful cultural and systemic change. In July 2023, the *Washington Post* reported that "Portugal was once hailed for decriminalizing drugs," but 20 years later, the country is having "doubts" about its drug policy. Heavily implied in the *Washington Post*'s reporting is the notion that the Portugal model is no longer as successful: "Police are less motivated to register people who misuse drugs and there are year-long waits for state-funded rehabilitation treatment even as the number of people seeking help has fallen dramatically." Police complain of "fatigue" and say that "urban visibility of the drug problem . . . is at its worst point in decades."

On top of that, overdose rates almost doubled in Lisbon from 2019 to 2023, hitting their highest rate in 12 years. Is the model the problem? No. And it's not the policy either. It's what happens when resources are stripped and funding is taken away. The Portugal model could soon become a shell of its former self.

Buried deep in the *Washington Post*'s article about Portugal is the fact that funding for public services has been slashed. Funding for addiction treatment was cut by 79 percent while the oversight of many drug services was decentralized and handed off to several nonprofits. All those ingredients that blended together to create a delicate balance have been changed and modified, tearing Portugal's "total package" into small parts. The *Washington Post* reported, "A funding drop from 76 million euros ($82.7 million) to 16 million euros ($17.4 million) forced Portugal's main institution to outsource work previously done by the state to nonprofit groups, including the street teams that engage with people who use drugs." The long fallout from defunding the program resulted in (surprise, surprise) rising overdose rates, fewer people making it into recovery programs, and less direct support.

You can't defund a complex infrastructure—especially one that works across multiple systems, such as health care, criminal justice, and housing—and expect it not to collapse. *New York Times* opinion writer Maia Szalavitz sprayed a fire hose of criticism in response to the lopsided coverage of Portugal's drug policy in outlets like the *Washington Post*.

"The data in zero cases favors criminalization of possession," Szalavitz wrote. For example, states and countries with more drug arrests and higher incarceration rates don't have less drug use. "Think about it for a minute: if criminalization is so great at reducing drug problems, how come cutting the medical supply doesn't stop [people] from turning to street drugs when pill mills close? How did cutting medical supply in half DOUBLE the [overdose] death rate?"

All the facts point to Portugal's model remaining viable, so long as the methods and funding that made it work in the first place aren't rolled back by political pressure and doubt. Drugs are still too often a magnet for toxic politics that feed into punitive measures. Instead, we must commit to what works in spite of the political noise. Since implementing many of Portugal's findings on a smaller scale and following the Surgeon General's recommendations, we know the same ideas can work in the United States too. It isn't just about an accepting attitude toward people who struggle with substance use. To save lives, we have to put our money where our mouths are.

Reading and rereading the many articles, reports, and research papers about Portugal's drug policy, I would say that what used to sound radical and innovative only a few years ago now sounds more like common sense: People who struggle with addiction are often deeply ashamed, and they're afraid of judgment and punishment, which keeps them in the dark and out of reach of whatever help is available to them. The Portugal model was dead set on disrupting that shame spiral, while the American model does the opposite: piling on even more shame and fear. It just doesn't make sense. Why kick people when they're already so far down? If addiction is a brain disease, and if people use drugs *despite* negative consequences, why does the American government, no matter who the president is or what party is in power, keep throwing negative consequences on people who use drugs?

When you treat people with dignity and kindness, and give them the support they need, they get healthy sooner and stay that way longer. They're also less likely to die. The research proves that, as in Europe, lower barriers to care increase life expectancy. Safer use options, along with naloxone, fentanyl test strips, overdose prevention sites, and clean supplies, all reduce the risk that someone will overdose or contract hepatitis C or HIV while using. And people are more likely to seek and access help when they know where to find it, they don't have to wait to get it, and they don't feel ashamed or belittled for needing it. That's not just my opinion—it's the facts. And that means we must fight for funding programs that work. Sadly, funding for vital programs in the US has been off to a rocky start.

In 2023, *The Intercept* reported that the CDC's National Harm Reduction Technical Assistance Center, or TA Center for short, imploded and left programs offering critical services across the country in the lurch. What happened turned out to be a very Washington type of scandal. The TA Center partnered with a specific coalition of harm reduction groups that had deep expertise and experience doing harm reduction across America. These groups collaborated with the CDC's bureaucracy to ensure programs preventing overdose and blood-borne infections received the right funding and support from the government. This is how the process worked since its founding in 2019. But that whole process blew up when the CDC changed how the TA Center operated. Instead of a partnership and collaboration with harm reduction groups, the TA Center would serve as a federal contract, which was awarded to a Florida-based firm called H2 PCI, a contractor with close ties to the defense industry and almost zero public health and harm reduction experience. What happened next? Layoffs, resignations, and harm reduction organizations scrambling to find alternative revenue streams to keep their operations going.

In prison, Morgan Godvin experienced the full brunt of the American model. She wrote, "The Bureau of Prisons ran a drug treatment program, but it focused on criminal thinking patterns instead of the root causes of addiction, such as trauma." The treatment program labeled her thinking as criminally selfish and antisocial. She found it totally useless. In a prison of 1,400 inmates, 1 in 3 came out of the foster care system. Almost everyone was a survivor of sexual trauma. It was brutal, lonely, and miserable—in fact, the purpose of prison seemed to be to traumatize the inmates even more.

Instead of receiving sympathy and understanding, Morgan was shamed for her addiction. While she had the support of her friend Justin's family, the rest of the world saw her as a criminal and a junkie. Morgan wasn't given an opportunity to heal from the experiences that would have caused her to keep using. Even basic medical care was hard to come by. She wasn't asking for special treatment. Any treatment was better than the nothing she had. She wasn't exactly sleeping on a tufted mattress and eating a Little Gem Lettuce salad with every meal.

To study the Portugal model, Morgan visited the capital, Lisbon, in the summer of 2022. She learned Portuguese, embedded herself with users, and worked with the government to make sure she saw every inch of the drug network. What she observed while she was there was truly earthshaking. The first thing she noticed was the near absence of unhoused people. She said that Portugal treated their heroin addiction issue so effectively that she had to walk around Lisbon for 15 days before she saw evidence of IV drug use. (This directly contradicts the *Washington Post*'s descriptions of dangerous or seedy open-air drug markets and the increasing visibility of drug use.)

Thanks to Portugal's universal health-care access, Portugal has residential, outpatient, and other kinds of treatment that are free for anyone to use—subsidized by the government. This includes specialized care for complex and severely ill people. Morgan explained that what shows up in Portuguese data as "treatment" is actually one-on-one talk therapy. In the US, addiction treatment instead relies heavily on group therapy and programs rooted in self-help, which research shows are not as effective as individualized therapy. There is a national cultural respect for individual mental health treatment that is missing in the US, as well as an approach Morgan calls "medicalization, not legalization."

Walking the narrow streets of Lisbon, vibrating with life and sound, and trolleys, street vendors, and musicians, Morgan recalled a scene that stuck out to her: she observed a man experiencing homelessness who had woken up in a doorway. He was agitated, deciding whether he would use heroin or take his dose of methadone. He took the methadone out of his pocket. Morgan watched him make his decision. He picked the medication—thanks to Portugal's free mobile methadone service, this wasn't a hard decision at all—and went back to sleep.

"Whatever petty nonsense he was going to do: averted," she said. "It was cool. There were shelters; people were housed. The homelessness that we now see here in Portland only happens when property and rents increase in the absence of government subsidies."

The concept of having a delivery van or a mobile peer support service also made a strong impression on Morgan. She said, "So many days in my addiction, I didn't want to go on a mission. There's so much chasing, 12–14 hours a day of chasing. If I could walk somewhere and get a dose, that might have completely changed my story. The night Justin died, he didn't have an alternative. He had to rely on his social network to procure the drug he was addicted to."

The Portugal model was designed to reduce HIV infections and heroin overdoses. And it achieved both of those goals—when it was fully funded—for the population of people who used opioids, including fentanyl. But crack was becoming prevalent in Portugal when Morgan visited, and because crack is a stimulant, it requires a different response.

Morgan said, "They're having a resurgence of crack cocaine. They can't get a handle on crack. They said it was easier to respond to heroin. For heroin, there are very effective medications. But meth and crack have stretched the limits of their treatment system."

Heroin is not a drug that makes the average person get busy. (I think they should call it an *inactive* addiction, honestly.) When someone is using, or when they've just used, they nod off. They sleep. They kind of droop in place like a wilting flower. Overall, I think of heroin as a passive drug. Aside from the daily quest to buy and use heroin, people don't get up to a whole lot. Heroin and other opiates are the opposite of crack, which produces a buzzing, compulsive energy.

Denzel described crack as a "schizoid" substance. "Crack makes you crazy," he said. "The worst part is, it's tough to get someone in treatment for it. Most of the Black guys I knew who used it in the '80s are dead now because of the nature of that drug. In a Black neighborhood, you take the survivors from that epidemic, and it's maybe a handful of people. Mostly men. But I know white men like my dude Snickers and my dude Kermit, who tore it up for decades and got out without a single conviction. You can't tell me it's not about Black and white. If a cop looks over and sees a Black man short-circuiting, brother, he's going to jail."

In Portugal, the challenge of addressing crack with a model designed for heroin—especially a model in the midst of being defunded—is based on a few things. First, crack causes a different set of behaviors than heroin. People using crack tend to have a harder time following up with peer support and showing up for appointments. Medical treatment for crack is also stuck in the Stone Age. There is no "crack agonist" medication. People who are addicted to opioids have a number of options for medication-assisted treatment, including buprenorphine, methadone, and naltrexone. For crack, there's no FDA-approved medicine.

"It's hard to imagine safer use when it comes to crack," Morgan said. "Fundamentally, it's a housing issue first in the US. There's something about getting sleep and safety and some human contact every one to three days that makes a difference. When you raise the bottom just a little bit, there's less far to fall for everyone."

Morgan noticed that in Portugal, the mental health of people who used crack was substantially better than that of people who used stimulants in the US. In Lisbon, unhoused people were able to sleep in a €20 hostel room or go to a shelter a few times a week. At these places, folks could get their clothes washed, rest, and be fed every day. In Portland or San Francisco, there are hardly any cheap rooms available anymore, let alone places where people can drop in for showers, laundry, and rest. The cost of living in West Coast cities is sky-high, and soaring rents and mass evictions during the COVID-19 pandemic have led to more and more people stuck living outside. Compared to other countries, the American model is exceptionally cruel.

Morgan's hometown of Portland is on a downward spiral. But unlike so many commentators and pundits, Morgan does not blame the deteriorating conditions on decriminalization.

"Within the last three years, people lost their reprieve in Portland," she said. "They're swinging machetes in the street because they don't have a moment's reprieve from the vigilance homelessness requires: seven nights a week, spent in the frigid cold with one or both eyes open. People step in front of my car in psychosis."

It's a losing battle, she says. And she doesn't want to bury any more friends.

I realize we cannot simply cut-and-paste Portugal's drug policy into the American context. But we can, and I believe we must, try to adapt many of its features. The $50 billion (yes, that's "billion" with a "B") settlement that came out of the 2020–2021 opioid litigation was supposed to be earmarked to curb the addiction and overdose crisis. Namely, billions of dollars from Big Pharma ought to be going toward building a public health and treatment infrastructure tailored to people who use drugs and those seeking recovery.

During Purdue Pharma's bankruptcy, it became very clear to me that selfishness, ignorance, and infighting were working against the victims of the crisis and putting money into states' pockets instead. The money represented a huge opportunity to change the way the United States addressed substance use and addiction. Yet, instead of being released to recovery community organizations, creating and funding new treatment facilities, and supporting folks who work on the front lines of the epidemic, much of it is being squandered. Many of those billions are more likely to go toward public golf courses and to filling budget holes and potholes than to help people who use drugs. Lawyers and professional firms made out like bandits, while the rest of us got shafted.

For example, Mendocino County in Northern California has reported the highest rate of overdose deaths in the state. The rural coastal county's board of supervisors decided to use some of its share of the opioid settlement funds to help fill a budget shortfall. They spent more than $63,000 on their "general" fund. This represents nearly 7 percent of their opioid settlement distribution. They chose to pay their bills instead of using the money for its intended purpose, which was to address the overdose crisis.

What really troubles me is the absence of oversight. As the billions of dollars from the opioid settlements are finally released to the states, there is no "opioid crisis accountability coordinator" assigned to track spending or disbursement. According to NPR, as of April 2023, "The [White House] Office of National Drug Control Policy has not released public statements about the settlements in over a year. And the settlement funds are mentioned just twice in a 150-page national strategy to reduce drug trafficking and overdose deaths." All this time, energy, and anger directed at Big Pharma successfully extracted $50 billion—for what?

Who can trust that this money is going to help any of us? While the federal government isn't legally obligated to take part in the conversation between Big Pharma and the states, its silence seems to drive home the lesson I learned in *Unsettled*: There is a vast difference between what is legal and what is right and just. President Biden's 2020 campaign promises included oversight of how this money will be spent. Now, the promise has melted like chocolate chip ice cream in July.

As *Kaiser Health News (KHN)* points out, $50 billion is double NASA's budget and five times the revenue of an NBA season. It's enough to change millions of people's lives. So, where is the money going? The biggest failure of the opioid litigation is that we aren't spending the settlement—or are we? *KHN* investigated and found that only 12 states (including Oregon) have committed to detailed public reporting of all their spending. Aneri Pattani wrote in *KHN*, "Most of the settlements stipulate that states must spend at least 85 percent of the money they will receive over the next 15 years on addiction treatment and prevention. But defining those concepts depends on stakeholders' views—and state politics. To some, it might mean opening more treatment sites. To others, it means building more jails and prisons and buying police cruisers." Opioid settlement funds, much like the billions gained from Big Tobacco companies, have become a quick infusion of cash for budget-starved states.

West Virginia was one of the first states to settle with Purdue Pharma in 2004, and what did the hardest-hit state in the nation do with that money? They built a gym for cops.[1] In Greene County, Tennessee, which has collected more than $2.7 million in settlement money, they've put $2.4 million of it toward paying the county's debt. Astonishingly, they even appropriated $50,000 from settlement funds to buy a pickup truck, which will drive incarcerated people around to pick up trash on roads around the county—nothing to do with abating the overdose crisis.

People are being kept in the dark as to where all these billions of dollars are going. Unlike Portugal or Oregon, which commit to making their budgets and decisions available to the public, the United States defaults to hiding its billions in piggy banks scattered across the country. Portugal has a 96/100 freedom rating. That's higher than the US's 83/100, according to Freedom in the World, a research group that assigns a freedom score and status to 210 countries and territories and makes policy recommendations for improvement.

Financial transparency, public services, freedom of expression, and political and civil rights are all part of that score. The methodology behind these scores asks, "Is the budget-making process subject to meaningful legislative review and public scrutiny?" and "Has partisan polarization or obstructionism seriously impaired basic executive or legislative functions, such as approving a budget or filling important vacancies?" The answers for our own country do not bode well for the opioid settlement funds.

Yet, we have the resources—and the means—to truly transform the landscape in the US. We can create our own version of the Portugal model.

A 2023 report released by Rand Corp called *America's Opioid Ecosystem: How Leveraging System Interactions Can Help Curb Ad-*

diction, Overdose, and Other Harms suggests that the Portugal model *is* possible in the US. That is, if we can get over partisanship, political infighting, and stigma and change the narrative of addiction.

I think we, like Portugal, need to take a multi-decade view of our efforts. For the past 70 years, America has waged an all-out drug war. That's 70 years of historical force that isn't easy to stop on a dime. It's only been a few years since states like Oregon decided to try something different, and it will take time to unravel decades of incompetence and mismanagement.

I believe that a better future is possible, as long as we accept the truth about drug use and how carceral solutions undermine our nation's goals of helping people stay healthy, safe, and alive. We can't just attack a broken system; we have to offer a vision of a better one. The science, data, and evidence are on our side. The Rand report's extensive study of American opioid manufacturing, distributing, and user networks showed the following:

1. *The evidence base for supply control and reduction interventions is limited.* Supply control is usually shorthand for law enforcement and the DEA's drug war model. This means that trying to follow a trail of fentanyl crumbs up the supply chain in order to catch bigger and bigger distributors doesn't work. The way Denzel used drugs—as a high-level distributor in a pyramid of dealers organized in a global economic system, from the most powerful at the top to street-level hustlers at the bottom—is a relic of the 1970s. Now, people use drugs the way Morgan and Cleo did. They get their substances from friends, roommates, and folks they trust. The distribution model has flattened, going from a pyramid to a pancake.

2. *There is limited evidence of elevated prices resulting from increases in the risk of arrest, incarceration, or seizure.*

Meaning, we can't arrest our way out of an overdose crisis. Addiction is not a moral failing. It isn't solved by a long, hard think in prison. Taking one so-called dealer off the street does not actually limit the drug supply, not even to a particular neighborhood or community. Nor does it drive prices up.

3. *Drug war tactics make the crisis worse.* In fact, raiding trap houses and busting local dealers creates even more volatility in the drug supply, and has been linked to more fatal and nonfatal overdoses. One emergency medical services physician said that he knows he must stock up on naloxone every time the police celebrate taking "drugs off the street" in a press conference. Their bust signals that there is going to be a spate of overdoses coming. Fentanyl has also made old-school drug enforcement tactics entirely moot. The synthetic drug supply is unlimited and universal. Because drugs no longer flow through one local dealer, they can be obtained anywhere and everywhere, in spaces that are difficult to reach, including the mail and internet.

4. *There is very little evidence to suggest that increasing prison sentences for street-level dealers in mature markets will have any lasting effect on supply or purity-adjusted prices.* Mandatory minimum sentences do nothing to "scare people straight." (As if!) The people whom the government identifies as street-level dealers are usually just normal people. They deal to support their families, or because they can split their drugs with their friends. They are not silk suit–wearing El Chapo clones who travel with AK-47s in private helicopters. They are normal-looking, everyday people. And arresting people

like that only ensures that they will sit behind bars for a long time and emerge years later, irreversibly damaged, with a criminal record that makes it impossible to re-enter society.

5. *Supply reduction in the form of domestic drug law enforcement aimed at users and street-level dealers has been found to generate harms and excesses of its own.* Surprise, surprise. Law enforcement sometimes does more harm than good when they try to round up the usual suspects. Terrorizing a population of people without real cause or real solutions only makes the problem worse, and it doesn't decrease the supply.

The Rand report is not a piece of activist speculation; it's a document with hundreds of citations and a rigorous analysis of the empirical literature. It's the most careful look to date at what works and what doesn't in a specifically American context. We do not suffer from a lack of knowledge. We know what we need to do. However, the sanest, most rational, and efficacious policy does not automatically win any debate. We have to be smart, strategic, and, most crucially, persuasive. Applying the findings from the Rand report is no easy feat.

The Politics of Oregon

On Voting Day 2020 in Oregon, more than 1 million voters over-whelmingly and enthusiastically passed Measure 110. Officially called the Drug Addiction Treatment and Recovery Act, the state ballot measure was touted as a revolutionary and sweeping change to drug policy and law. The main idea behind Measure 110 entailed shifting substance use out of the realm of law enforcement and into the compassionate hands of public health and health care.

The new law had two main features. First, it stripped criminal penalties for personal drug possession. Instead of misdemeanors or felonies, possessing a small amount of drugs was reduced to a non-criminal $100 citation—no more serious than a speeding ticket. The fine could be waived if the person cited agreed to a free health assessment conducted by a licensed counselor. Measure 110 would build an entire network of assessment hubs that would then transfer people with addiction and other health problems to treatment.

The second aspect to Measure 110 involved financing the necessary health care infrastructure. Oregon consistently has one of the nation's highest rates of untreated addiction, and also consistently ranks dead last in treatment access. To tackle this gap, Measure 110 redirected tens of millions of dollars in cannabis tax revenue, in addition to using savings from reduced spending on arrests, courts, and incarceration, all going toward more services and treatment. (Weed was legalized in Oregon on July 1, 2015. The annual revenue generated by marijuana was more than $178 million in 2021; a 2023 state report found $37 million in savings by reducing the number of people in jails and prison.[2])

Proponents of the bill hailed Measure 110 as a Portugal-style approach to dealing with substance use. That was how Measure 110 was supposed to work. At least, in theory. As rubber met the road, problems quickly arose.

Measure 110 was being implemented right as a storm of chaos swept through America, and this storm hit Oregon in unique ways. The state just had the deadliest season of wildfires in its history. Police officers were dealing with civil unrest and protests against police brutality stemming from the murder of George Floyd. The COVID-19 pandemic turned society upside down, creating new forms of social isolation, mental illness, and complex health problems. On top of all that, a tsunami of fentanyl just hit the West Coast, accelerating the rate of overdose deaths and creating more severe addiction on the streets.

In the midst of all of this, Oregon was tasked with implementing Measure 110, which meant a complete overhaul to the state's approach to treating substance use and preventing overdose. Like so many issues in America, Measure 110 was swallowed by fierce political division and deeply polarized opinion.

Four years since Measure 110 was voted into law, everyone wants to know: Well, did it work?

The outcomes from Measure 110 are about as clear as muddy water. While there is some evidence showing that more people are accessing treatment under the law, it's also the case that overdoses have risen since it went into effect. Critics of Measure 110 blame higher overdose deaths on the law. Supporters of Measure 110 blame the volatile drug supply, a society wrestling with civil unrest, and an overall lack of governmental and political leadership to help steer the historic change.

Meanwhile, Oregon's drug policy became a political lightning rod and a national flashpoint in America's debate over how to respond to the ever-worsening overdose crisis and the multitude of problems—like homelessness—plaguing major cities, especially along the West Coast. City blocks have been overrun by tent encampments and public drug use, creating tension among city residents. Despite enforcement efforts and more drug seizures, there appears to be limitless quantities of cheap and ultra-potent synthetic drugs, like meth and fentanyl, on the street. In cities like Portland, fentanyl pills are sold for as little as $3. The situation is a hot mess.

Measure 110 was best by political division and polarization from the very beginning. Law enforcement, prosecutors, and sheriffs all thought removing criminal penalties for drug possession was a terrible idea. People in the recovery community supported more treatment, but were skeptical of how it would all work. However, many agreed that the drug war had not made things better. Hence, the ballot's overwhelming support in November 2020.

The division over Measure 110 converged into a bona fide backlash.

In January 2024, state officials, public health experts, and epidemiologists studying Measure 110 convened a symposium in Salem, Oregon, to share their research and organize a concerted push against the law's critics, which they accused of marinating in "bad vibes" over a dispassionate assessment of the evidence.

Dr. Ricky Bluthenthal, a professor at University of Southern California's Keck School of Medicine, gave the opening remarks and presented his take. Bluthenthal compared ending the drug war to the long fight to end racial segregation in America. The 1960s wave of civil rights legislation enshrined the right for Black people to vote while prohibiting racial segregation and discrimination. "So, did we all start living together after that?" Bluthenthal asked the crowd. No. "But, we're still working on that project 80 years later." Just because it's not perfect doesn't mean we should stop, he said. His point is that change takes time. Five decades of bad drug policy will not turn on a dime. Bluthenthal thinks Measure 110 is worth the effort, and wants to see it succeed.

Critics, like Stanford psychology professor Keith Humphreys, argue that Oregon's experiment is not only misguided, but that it has already failed. By removing arrests for drug crimes, Humphreys says that Measure 110 also removed a crucial form of legal pressure that spur people into getting treatment. "On the one hand, we have highly rewarding drugs which are widely available, and on the other hand, little or no pressure to stop using them." Humphreys added, "Under these conditions, we should expect to see exactly what Oregon is experiencing: Extensive drug use, extensive addiction and not much treatment seeking."

The debate has caused fractures among Oregon lawmakers. Some want to amend Measure 110 and add criminal penalties back to drug possession and criminalize public drug use more harshly. Others want to give the law more time, and do not want to be seen as reversing the people's support for the law. Remember, voters passed it overwhelmingly.

Only time will tell what Oregon decides to do. But Measure 110 gets to the heart of a much broader debate over how to deal with substance use in the 21st century, as synthetic drugs take over the new world we're all living in. If so many people believe that the drug war has failed, then what comes after? What replaces the drug war? Even the most conservative lawmakers in Oregon recognize that Measure 110 did not *cause* the state's fentanyl crisis. And it's very much an open debate as to whether the law made things worse or not. In a state with a population of 4 million people, it's not easy to identify a law's cause and effect in real time.

It's also difficult to parse out everyone's agenda and personal political motivation from the reality on the ground. What really happened remains unclear.

For starters, the law was beyond ambitious, and its implementation involved tight deadlines. Basically, an entire state needed to radically change decades of law and build a massive new public health system from scratch—all during a historic pandemic and societal breakdown. The law's main action was the construction of a new on-ramp to treatment through police encounters, through citations and tickets instead of arrests and jail. The idea was that those who were ticketed would call a hotline, get assessed, and then receive help if they needed it.

In reality, things haven't worked that way. An investigation by Oregon Public Broadcasting quoted police officers frustrated by the lack of results. The officer tells the person to call the number and the $100 fine goes away. The problem is: Very few people are making that phone call. The ticket goes unpaid. Nothing changes. Oregon Public Broadcasting quoted a Portland Police Sergeant who said the bike squad wrote more than 700 tickets "and got absolutely nowhere with it." Before Measure 110, police made 9,500 arrests each year. After Measure 110, police only gave out about 2,500 tickets per year. Seeing the futility in the new ticketing system, many police officers simply stopped issuing them.

The OPB investigation placed much of the blame on a failure of leadership. For example, Oregon's new governor proposed funding to train police about the new law through an online course. Officers would be given explicit instruction on how to effectively approach those they were citing. Lawmakers, inexplicably, decided not to fund the training course. In another instance, a Senate committee tasked with oversight of Measure 110 heard testimony from experts that the ticketing system was not working as the on-ramp to treatment many imagined it to be. After the testimony, the committee took no action to fix it.

"The combined result of all the legislative efforts on Measure 110 was to leave Oregon with no carrot and no stick to steer people into treatment," the OPB investigation concluded.

Morgan Godvin says it's hard for her to hear all this criticism. She started on the state's Alcohol and Drug Policy Commission as part of the group overseeing how Oregon chose to deal with people coping with addiction. Then, she was appointed to the Measure 110 Oversight and Accountability Committee, a body that would decide how to fund treatment programs and services across the state. Morgan has worked tirelessly to try and bring the bickering factions together and make the law work as best as it can.

"I have personally voted on hundreds of millions of dollars in hard action funds and policy," Morgan said. "I do everything I can— everything I can think of. People say 'you have to pick,' but I see it as synergy. It has to be, because what we're dealing with is so complex." She added, "The solution is a little bit of everything. It's academic research, public policy, direct policy, journalism, and social media. I make those things work. It's never enough."

The law can change. The policy can change. But that isn't the end of the work. It's only the beginning.

In *The Washington Post*, the author Michael Clune reiterated Humphreys's point, about the connection between arrest and recovery. "For me and for nearly every other person I know recovering from addiction, it took arrest and prosecution," Clune wrote. "I believe that arrest saved my life." And this is why he thinks the idea to strip drugs of criminal penalties, like the way Oregon did, is a grave mistake. "Through a court-mandated treatment program, I began my road to recovery. I recently celebrated 21 years of being clean."

Even though my own recovery story is quite different, I still understand why someone like Clune thinks policing and the courts are necessary.

And then I remember Denzel Hilton. After 15 years of hard drug use and 45 years of recovery, he saw the change in Oregon and saw himself and his family finally recognized with dignity. Watching TV one day, Denzel heard about the Measure 110 Committee that Morgan is part of. He felt like things were finally changing; he's finally seeing the doors open for people like him to access the help they need. Instead of being pushed into a cage, scolded by judges, folks who need health care, treatment, and support are finally getting it. Through it all, he knows in his bones that a better life is possible. He has to believe in that.

"I didn't get sober and become a saint," he said. "The shit one does! All those years, I was shortchanging myself. I knew our system was fucked up, and I didn't trust it to help me. I was right not to, back then. This might be the change we need. But it's a day at a time, right? I guess we'll know when we get there."

No one really knows if Oregon is on the right path to getting there. As Morgan said, the problem is endlessly complex and deeply interconnected. States like Oregon that did change drug laws saw a rise in overdoses. States right next door to Oregon that didn't change drug laws also saw overdoses jump. Meanwhile, unrelenting waves of fentanyl keep crashing down. The supply is deadly and limitless.

Everyone ultimately wants the same result: to save lives, to improve quality of life, to help people recover, and to help people live a life of dignity and meaning.

I understand the criticisms. However, I also know plenty of

people, including myself, who found recovery without the threat of jail looming over them. Then again, if people committed crimes beyond just using drugs, of course there should be consequences. I still recognize the need for positive incentives to help get more folks into treatment.

Morgan continued, "There's no easy answer. And it's this uncertainty about the future and the right path forward that has generated so much of the political fighting, tension, and disagreement. The solution is a little bit of everything. It's academic research, public policy, direct policy, journalism, and social media. I make those things work. It's never enough."

Morgan has learned that just because something is hard, it doesn't mean you wave the white flag. What we've learned from Portugal and Oregon is that change takes time. The law can change, policy can change—but that isn't the end of the work. It's only the beginning.

The lesson from Portugal is that in addition to changing laws and policy, there must also be a change in culture. To save lives, we have to stop pushing drug users away. "Out of sight and out of mind" is an attitude that kills people. What Portugal did instead was invite people in, invest in their lives, and—with words and actions—show them they matter. The results speak for themselves: the model works if it's given a fair shot and the funding it deserves.

It took Denzel 15 years of hard drug use and 45 years of recovery to see himself and his family finally recognized with the dignity they deserve. Watching TV one day, Denzel heard about the Measure 110 Committee that Morgan is part of. He felt like things were changing; he's finally seeing the doors open for people to access the help they need. Instead of being pushed into a cage by a judge, folks who need help may one day be able to get into treatment when they need it—like Denzel's wife, but not his daughter. Through it all, he knows in his bones that a better life is possible.

"I didn't get sober and become a saint," he said. "The shit one does! All those years, I was shortchanging myself. I knew our system was fucked up, and I didn't trust it to help me. I was right not to, back then. This might be the change we need. But it's a day at a time, right? I guess we'll know when we get there."

7

"I FORGIVE YOU"

When you begin a journey of revenge, start by digging two graves: one for your enemy, and one for yourself.

—UNKNOWN

Christie Barker-Cummings stood outside her home in a sparse North Carolina suburb with spotty cell service. She was holding one of her most prized and meaningful possessions: a portrait of her 18-year-old son, Kevin. The portrait's background was a blend of bright yellows bleeding into darker greens, and a few chaotic strokes of blue. Kevin smiled in the foreground, exposing dimples on the left side of his face. His dark brown hair was disheveled. He looked like what he was: a teenager who had just woken up after sleeping in until noon on the weekend. Christie said the abstract portrait of her son was stunningly accurate, uncanny in the way it captured Kevin's "intense" personality.

"It's a really strange painting," Christie told me. "If you look at the eyes, if you zoom in, they're entirely black. There's no color. There's no differentiation between his iris and pupil. There is no light in his actual eyes. But somehow, there's an illusion of light—something vibrant and alive about him."

On October 4, 2022, Christie decided that she would bring Kevin's portrait with her to the Hillsborough, North Carolina, courtroom, where the man who sold the mixture of heroin and fentanyl that led to her son's fatal overdose in 2018 was being sentenced by the judge. Word of the second-degree murder case spread far beyond this quiet North Carolina town. Local news covered every twist and turn, and even made a documentary about Christie and other grieving families. The trial became a huge focus, leaving many torn and divided over whether suspected dealers should really be charged with murder.

"I can bring a big photo to court," Christie thought. "But this portrait would really stand out." She wanted something big, something moving, something that could visually communicate the unspeakable.

"When your child dies," Christie said, "you feel like the entire world should stop."

Four long years after losing her son, Christie was having her day in court confronting the man who provided the fatal dose of drugs.

After Kevin's death, the town's district attorney, Jeff Nieman, took up the cause of prosecuting people who sell drugs that result in fatal overdoses as murderers. Between 2019 and 2023, North Carolina prosecutors have filed more than 140 "death by distribution" cases throughout the state.[1] It hasn't seemed to slow things down much; in fact, between 2019 and 2021, the latest year for which reliable data are available, overdose deaths jumped by 70 percent in the state.

The North Carolina counties that filed the most drug-homicide charges have also seen the highest increase in overdose deaths, while deaths declined in counties that haven't filed any "death by distribution" cases.

The case of Kevin's "murder" illustrates why these prosecutions are not having their intended effect.

In the case of Kevin's death, the person who found himself in the crosshairs of the law was 44-year-old Nathan Windham, a working-class construction worker who had lived in North Carolina all of his life. The local district attorney had made up his mind that Nathan would face the wrath of the law. It was playing out just like Morgan Godvin's case. Just like Todd Schmidt's case. Just like Emma Semler's. Just like those of so many people who find themselves ensnared in America's never-ending drug war.

On that breezy fall day in court, Nathan's eyes looked tired and red from all the crying he'd been doing. For his role in Kevin's death, Nathan was facing a 26-year prison sentence. Like so many others who catch a drug-induced homicide charge, Nathan was a drug user himself. Calling him a "drug dealer" would render the term virtually meaningless. He was no kingpin. He was not wealthy. He had worked a physically demanding job for decades of his life, and he struggled with physical and emotional pain. As all the legal research and policy analysis makes painfully clear, putting Nathan in prison would not change the composition of North Carolina's drug market in any measurable way whatsoever. Putting him in prison would not "choke off the supply" or "send a message" to other dealers the way prosecutors imagine. What would 20 years in prison for Nathan really accomplish?

What is the point of prosecution?

It's best to think of these cases in the realm of emotion, not logic. As a prosecutor once bluntly stated as to why he charges "dealers" with murder: "You owe me for that dead kid."[2] His answer is aligned with the results of a study of North Carolina prosecutors, which sought to understand what motivates them to pursue these cases.[3] Of the 24 prosecutors who responded, all of them ranked drug-induced homicide prosecutions as "highly likely to serve justice for the deceased and obtain justice or closure for the family of the deceased." In their eyes, they see themselves as carrying out the wishes of the victim's family. (Conveniently, prosecutors ignore the families who do not want to pursue the dealer.)

Earlier in this book, I analyzed how these severe punishments impact people who use, sell, and share drugs, and how they punish people like Morgan and Todd and Emma and so many others who are already suffering from their own addictions. Dozens of studies have also analyzed how these punitive laws have consistently failed to make a dent in the number of people who use or sell drugs—dating all the way back to the 1980s. But how does this appetite for prosecution affect the American family? The answer is in the stories of grieving parents like Christie, who find themselves at the center of our nation's fentanyl crisis.

A Bitter Divide

Across the country, grieving parents are bitterly divided over what to do when their child dies from an overdose. They disagree not only about whom, or what, to blame, but also the very core meaning of their child's death. Many congregate in massive Facebook groups, stoking each other's anger. The ones who believe that their child was "poisoned" by a nefarious and deceptive drug dealer sometimes say they hope the military and law enforcement steps in with the full force of the state. Or, if they think their child "overdosed," they characterize the loss as a preventable death that could have been avoided with better education and better drug policy rooted in public health and harm reduction.

Ultimately, grief is what places these bereaved parents on opposite sides of the War on Drugs. The chasm between the "poisoning" and "overdose" factions has grown wide, sparking intense ideological battles that play out in politics, communities, and online. Drug-induced homicide cases are where the two camps diverge most dramatically today. One side of the debate views murder convictions as their ticket to justice, and the other portrays prosecution and incarceration as yet another failed tactic that causes more harm than good.

Whichever side they choose, the power of grieving parents is undoubtedly a force to be reckoned with. Moms and dads—often white suburban parents with significant resources at their disposal—have played an influential role in advocating for drug laws. Seemingly every decade in America has brought about a new "drug epidemic," causing fresh waves of fear followed by new rounds of punitive legislation. Often, parent movements are fueled by a combination of pain and agony.

What it comes down to is simple. Every parent wants their child's life and death to mean something. After a loss that is unimaginably painful, they're left trying to find meaning and make sense out of the senseless.

"Grief is not something you overcome or cure," said Laura Vargas, a therapist who specializes in counseling parents who've lost a child to an overdose. "It's something you carry with you your whole life. One of the biggest opportunities to process it is to find meaning. Some parents really struggle with this. Sometimes the meaning they make is, 'I'm going to get justice.'"

Justice can mean different things to different families. Some pursue their child's dealer, vigilante-style. Other parents pour their energy into public health and harm reduction activism, and dedicate their lives to preventing as many fatal overdoses as possible. Some stick stubbornly to the narrative that their child's overdose was an intentional "poisoning." Others accept that their child kept secrets, used substances, and had unfair consequences for their choices. Whatever meaning these parents choose affects all of us.

"I feel like a lot of parents want to put the blame on fentanyl," Christie, Kevin's mom, told me. "Like, it suddenly becomes, 'My child would be here and have no issues if they didn't accidentally get poisoned by fentanyl.' I don't think that's true for a majority of cases."

So few parents actually get justice or the redemption they deserve. That experience is rarely, if ever, delivered by the courts.

The day of Nathan Windham's trial brought together two families: Kevin's and Nathan's. The October air in the dreary courtroom was thick with unexpressed emotions. During the hearing, both families sat nervously in the gallery, stewing in their personal pressure cookers. Four years of pain and patience crescendoed in this one moment.

Christie, sitting next to Kevin's big portrait on a wooden pew, prepared to read her victim's impact statement. Nathan had also written a statement that he was anxious to read aloud. Nathan Windham's wife, Laura, also sat in the gallery that day, her face beet red, wiping away tears. During one moment, Christie and Laura locked eyes, and Laura, not making any sound, mouthed the words, "I'm so sorry." So much was at stake for Laura too. Her husband could go behind bars for decades. Her life, Nathan's, and the future of their marriage all hung in the balance.

Finally, the judge told Christie it was her turn on the stand. Wearing a white blazer and a black blouse, Christie sat in the witness box. Holding the bright yellow portrait of Kevin, she began to tell the story of her son's life and death. However, her intention wasn't to accuse Nathan or demand that he be punished to the fullest extent of the law. She didn't want revenge or to make Nathan out to be a bad guy. She didn't want to deploy the narrative so many other parents repeated in their grief groups. Instead, she decided she was not going to sugarcoat anything. At that moment, she wanted Kevin's death to mean something more than sending a man to prison for two decades. And the only way to do that was to own up to Kevin's role, not Nathan's.

Sitting on the stand, Christie started to describe her son. He was funny, athletic, and brilliantly cerebral. He scored a 1,400 on his SAT, and he was offered multiple academic scholarships for college. Christie called Kevin her "shooting star" because he burned so fast and so bright. "He was born six weeks early, but by nine months, he was speaking in phrases," she said. "His first word was *light*." But there was also a moody darkness and intensity to Kevin. He'd sometimes say things that made his mom worry.

One time, Kevin was sitting on his mom's bed while she was getting ready to go out. Out of nowhere, Kevin looked somber. "Mom," he said, "when I look into the future, I don't see anything."

"What do you mean?" Christie asked.

"I try to imagine the future, and I don't see anything," he repeated.

Christie thought Kevin meant that he was confused, the way a lot of teenagers are. Overwhelmed about high school ending. Unsure about which direction to take in life. Questioning his identity, who he was, and who he wanted to become.

"No," he said. "That's not what I mean, Mom. When I look into the future ahead, I see nothing. I see black."

The scene still stuck out to Christie years later. It was as though Kevin was adrift at sea with nothing to anchor him. He felt like there was nothing tangible in life he could grab on to, nothing there to keep him from floating farther and farther into the void. In the two years before Kevin died, he had struggled mightily with both anxiety and addiction. His drug of choice was prescription: Xanax, not opioids. He liked to take benzodiazepines, a class of antianxiety drugs that slow down the central nervous system. They provide a soothing balm for high-strung and anxious people like Kevin. The pills numbed his emotional pain, perhaps helping him cope with the vast emptiness he felt.

Christie also described the litany of measures she took as a mother to try and help. She tried anything and everything in her power. An Ivy League–trained epidemiologist, Christie is sharp and fast-talking. "I'm a scientist," she said. "I tend to be very practical and logical." Being steeped in the scientific literature on chronic diseases, Christie understood that Kevin needed medical attention. On several occasions before Kevin turned 18, Christie had him involuntarily committed to the University of North Carolina's adolescent psychiatric unit. But forcing him to get help never stuck. He would sober up briefly, only to return to the exact same life that generated his pain and his pursuit of numbness.

During one of Kevin's binges, he was spiraling out and acting erratically. Christie asked Kevin to leave the house because his younger brothers were home, and she didn't want him around in the mind-altered state he was in. Kevin grew furious and started vandalizing the house. He poured milk and maple syrup on the furniture and all over the walls and floor. He crushed a bag of Cheetos, grinding them into orange dust, and poured out the bag on Christie's hair.

Christie was at a complete loss. Out of desperation, she called the police. When they arrived, she explained the situation. She told the police that she had already committed Kevin before. He'd been in therapy and treatment. He broke every boundary she'd set. Nothing was working.

The officers on the scene asked Christie if she wanted to try going a different route this time. They explained that the vandalism—and the Cheeto incident—were intended to provoke and arouse fear, which met the legal criteria for simple assault, and they offered to press charges on Kevin for his actions.

It was a drastic measure, something Christie hadn't ever done before. It's not like she wanted Kevin to rot in a jail cell; she just wanted the chaos to end. She needed to protect her other children and her own sanity. So she agreed to press charges. She reasoned that maybe consequences this serious would somehow jolt Kevin.

The police arrested Kevin right there on the spot. And what unfolded next would prove to be a pivotal event leading up to his death. It's what helped Christie realize that the problems she and her son faced were bigger than any single person.

After being booked and processed, Kevin stood in front of a judge who admonished him for the way he was acting. The judge told Kevin, who was 17 at the time and had no criminal record, that she was treating him as an adult. Rather than release him right away on a fine and a misdemeanor charge, which she would normally do in such circumstances, Kevin was punished with what the judge described as "a wake-up call." Kevin was sentenced with a one-two punch. First, he was ordered to attend inpatient addiction treatment. Second, and more acutely, he would spend the next 10 days in county lockup with adults convicted of more serious crimes.

Christie paused on this point to emphasize its magnitude—how one decision can change everything.

"That's where Kevin met Nathan," Christie said.

While Kevin was in jail for simple assault, Nathan was in jail for driving while intoxicated. Inside, the two got along, and they exchanged phone numbers. Then, months later, when Kevin was turning 18, they reconnected on the outside. Kevin wanted to celebrate his birthday by buying drugs. Kevin repeatedly texted Nathan, asking him if he could sell him anything. Nathan had heroin—he was a habitual user. But Nathan was reluctant to sell heroin to Kevin. Nathan said no several times. Text messages between the two show that Kevin wouldn't let up. He kept on asking and asking.

"Kevin is a very persistent person," Christie said. "Like, he could drive you insane."

Windham eventually caved. But he was adamant that he would not sell Kevin heroin—for lots of reasons. He was not a heroin dealer. He wasn't trying to make money. He wasn't trying to profit and prey on Kevin's desire for drugs. It was Kevin who was soliciting Nathan, not the other way around. So they decided to make a trade: Kevin would trade Nathan marijuana in exchange for heroin. What neither of them knew at the time was that the heroin had fentanyl in it. They had no idea that America's drug market was being rapidly contaminated by ultra-potent forms of synthetic fentanyl. In 2018, few were prepared for the transition from prescription pills to heroin to fentanyl. The quickly changing drug supply, more than anything else, is responsible for the huge and horrifying waves of deaths.

Kevin's fatal overdose was preventable—but it didn't start or end with the drugs he got. It all started with his introduction to serious users in jail. Looking back, Christie commented on how putting a 17-year-old in lockup with adults was wildly inappropriate. Instead of scaring Kevin away from doing drugs, jail taught him where to find more. Carceral punishment hadn't solved the problem. If anything, it made the situation indescribably worse.

The experience helped Christie realize that demonizing a drug like fentanyl is a dead end. It's what helped her shift her perspective, that relying on policing and punishment doesn't help either. "We're all a part of this social epidemic," Christie said. "It's man-made."

The circumstances leading up to Kevin's death also throw a wrench in the simple, cut-and-dry narrative that prosecutors tend to rely on when they argue for drug-induced homicide cases. When two people are addicted, it's not so clear who the bad guy is. Proving that either person had any intent to harm the other is impossible, along with whether either of them actually knew about the drugs they were using, sharing, trading, or selling. (After all, it's not as if drugs are bought or sold with a list of ingredients or proof by volume, the way alcohol is.)

And yet, in murder cases, prosecutors must prove something called "malice aforethought." In legal terms, "malice" means conscious intent to cause death or great bodily harm. If you're into true-crime shows, you've probably heard malice referred to as "premeditation." Proving that Nathan had intent to harm Kevin would be a high bar for any prosecutor to clear. The evidence of the case showed that, rather than malice, the true cause of Kevin's death was closer to ignorance.

Still, none of the facts or legal technicalities change the ultimate outcome. Kevin snorted some of a fentanyl-heroin mixture.

Because he had little tolerance for opioids, he overdosed and died. Physiologically, that's what all overdoses are: a discrepancy between the dose of a drug and somebody's tolerance for it.

We also know how to prevent these deaths. And yet, so little is being done to do so. Instead, America continues to cling to the same reactionary impulses.

On the witness stand, Christie tried to articulate how her entire world shattered in the moment she learned Kevin had died. When she got the call from her ex-husband, who yelled into the phone, "Kevin's dead! Kevin's dead!" Christie remembers being in her car and racing to the house. She remembers screaming at the top of her lungs and thinking, "This cannot be happening!" She remembers arriving at the house and screaming more at the police officers who blocked her from going inside the room where Kevin took his last breaths. But she overpowered them, and they relented. She remembers the guttural, raging screams that seemed to tear out of her body, so primal that she did not recognize the animal pain and fury as coming from her own mouth.

By the time Christie finished her statement, there wasn't a dry eye in the courtroom. She stood up, still holding Kevin's yellow portrait, and sat down in the gallery beside her family. Now, it was the defense's turn. Fighting back tears, Nathan's defense attorney spoke to the judge. He said that in nearly 50 years of practicing defense law, he'd never spoken directly to a family on the opposite side of a contentious case. But this time, Nathan Windham's attorney felt compelled to say something.

"Addiction is a terrible thing," he said. "Addiction lives in a lot of lives." The defense attorney shared that his own family had also been touched by addiction.

The mood in the courtroom was shifting. It was like Christie switched open an emotional valve, and suddenly, everyone's steaming hot pain came rushing out. The pressure cooker was wide open.

The boiling tension that had been building all these years began to dissipate little by little, as everybody in the trial, but for the judge, spoke openly about their own pain.

Before it was Nathan's turn to speak, his defense attorney shared some revealing and relevant details about Nathan's life and the kind of man he is. When Nathan learned that Kevin had died, he turned himself in right away. There was no need for a lengthy murder investigation. Nathan admitted to his role instantly. And then, after leaving jail on bond, Nathan and his wife Laura eventually found recovery for their own addictions to meth and heroin. They'd both gotten sober together, even with a 26-year prison sentence hanging over their relationship. Nathan and Laura became active in the local recovery community, and they shared their story of redemption at church groups on Sunday mornings. Whatever was about to happen, Kevin's death had already changed the two of them forever.

Now it was Nathan's turn to talk. Through sobs and tears, Nathan read his letter to Kevin's family.

"We both had something in common," Nathan said about himself and Kevin, "addiction and mental health issues." He added, "I realize a lot of people have been hurt, and lives have been forever changed by my actions."

Nathan expressed how guilty he felt. How sorry he was. He told the court how he prayed every day, hoping that somehow he could be forgiven. Then, something happened that nobody in the courtroom expected. As he stepped off the stand, and walked back to the defense's table, Christie and Nathan embraced each other.

Christie said, "It just occurred to me that I have that power to forgive him. I'm holding that power. How cruel to make him hang in the balance." As Christie hugged Nathan in court, she told him, "I don't blame you. I forgive you."

And just like that, Christie said that she was released from a prison of her own. All the labels fell apart. Instead of a victim and defendant squaring off, they encountered each other as fully human.

If Christie believed her son had a mental illness that impaired his ability to control his own behavior and actions, then didn't the same logic apply to Nathan, who was also struggling? Christie felt that if given the chance, Nathan would gladly switch places with Kevin. But he couldn't. And Nathan would live with that burden and carry that weight for his entire life.

By forgiving Nathan, Christie freed herself. With the agreement of Kevin's family, the prosecutor offered Nathan a plea deal for a reduced sentence. Instead of 26 years, Nathan would serve only two years at the most. District Attorney Nieman told WRAL, a local news outlet, that he could count on one hand the number of times he cried in court. And this case was one of those rare moments.

"I had never seen, in my experience, a man who had just pleaded guilty to a homicide hug the mother of the person he's now been convicted of killing," District Attorney Nieman said.

Perhaps that's because cases like these are not normal homicides. When Kevin died, something terrible happened—yes—but nobody wanted it to happen.

From inside prison, Nathan said there's not a day goes by that he doesn't think about Kevin and his family. "I'm just, so—sorry," he said.

After the trial, Christie found herself at the center of a contentious debate swirling around her: Should Nathan, who sold her son heroin and fentanyl, actually be sent to prison for two decades instead of only two years? Can she blame him for Kevin's death? What role did Kevin play in all this? Which side was more culpable? Though she still grieves, she's comfortable with where she landed on these hard questions.

Christie's case is painful, but there are so many lessons we can learn from it. Her own outlook and understanding of her son's death have ramifications for American drug policy, the criminal justice system, and what punishment and redemption look like in the fentanyl era, when people don't know what they've gotten themselves into before it's too late. But more than anything else, the case of Christie's son is about the journey of grief, and how entire communities are affected by the decisions and actions of bereaved parents. Should they seek vengeance or forgiveness?

When I spoke with her, Christie told me she was glad that Nathan was being held accountable for Kevin's death. After all, Nathan was much older than Kevin, more than twice his age. As an adult, Nathan should've known better than to sell heroin to an 18-year-old. It was a reckless move, she thought. But she also saw Kevin's role. She couldn't pretend that he wasn't a participant as well; she had no reason to rewrite his story after his death.

However, she didn't come to this conclusion overnight; Nathan Windham's murder trial was delayed for four years. During that time, Christie's grief changed and evolved, thanks in part to grief support groups. She credits them with helping her see through the hazy fog of grief.

"I met the mothers who had formed the group," Christie said. "And it was really life-changing for me because suddenly I saw, 'Wow, Kevin's not unique. This is happening all over the place.'" She heard the stories of other young people like Kevin, who also struggled with social anxiety and depression, felt existentially lost, and self-medicated with drugs. Bonding with other parents helped Christie find a way to live with her grief, rather than be dominated and enraged by it.

By the time the trial took place, she no longer felt that Nathan was to blame. She didn't think a murder charge made sense anymore. Sending Nathan away for 26 years would not bring Kevin back. It wouldn't help anybody's situation.

As an epidemiologist, Christie viewed her son's struggle through a medical lens. She thought about how his mental health and addiction were related to his biology and genetics. She thought Kevin's addiction had deeply affected his ability to control himself. If Nathan hadn't sold him drugs that day, he would've kept on looking until he found someone who could offer him something else. That's what addiction is. It's compulsive behavior—a raging forest fire inside the brain that no amount of water can put out.

Not every parent shares the same beliefs as Christie. Her story serves as a stark contrast to other parents who find themselves in her shoes. They cannot, or will not, forgive whomever sold their child drugs. Rather than forgiveness, this faction of parents advocates for maximum penalties. They demand that the courts show no mercy. These parents start Facebook groups and nonprofits and make alliances with politicians, police, prosecutors, and federal agencies like the DEA. Some even have a "memorandum of agreements" with the DEA, where they form a cooperative partnership with one another because their respective agendas overlap. In wanting to wage a war on drugs, these parents are also at war against other grieving parents—parents like Christie, who think differently and want to seek a different outcome.

"There are a couple of really, really militant anti-fentanyl groups," Christie explained. "They go march on Washington, and it starts to feel like a lynching, like a scapegoating. And it's not something productive. I feel like that extremism turns off the majority and impairs our ability to make real change."

Just as America is beset by toxic politics and partisan division, I've witnessed the same sharp and bitter divide play out between grieving parents who view the drug war through very different lenses. This grief divide was clearly illustrated in a story for the *New Republic* which chronicled the legislative battle in California over Senate Bill 44, known as "Alexandra's Law." Parents fought against one another over this bill, which was written to make it easier for prosecutors to charge drug dealers with murder. Once again, these parents were locked in a battle over drug-induced homicide. Democrats in California voted down the bill, leaving an army of grieving parents outraged. Alexandra's father, Matt Capelouto, stormed out of the hearing, furious. He accused Democrats of supporting drug dealers, the kind he believes Alexandra was "poisoned" by. The dealer who sold his daughter a fake pill is spending nine years in federal prison for it, but Capelouto feels that is insufficient. He will not stop trying to pass even tougher drug laws.

Aimee Dunkle, who is a board member of Grief Recovery After Substance Passing (GRASP), testified against "Alexandra's Law." Her own son Ben died from a heroin overdose because the friends he was with were too afraid to dial 911. (One of them already had a criminal record and feared prosecution for helping his friend.) Aimee thinks these drug-induced homicide laws undermine the protections of Good Samaritan laws that grant immunity to people who dial 911 during an overdose. Dunkle fought a long, hard battle to pass Good Samaritan laws in California. She thinks drug-induced homicide laws make more people afraid of calling for help. As a result of her testimony, she faced horrific comments, and even threats, from the other parents trying to pass Alexandra's Law. Some of them wrote to Dunkle: "How dare you compare your son's 'overdose' to my child's 'poisoning.'"

Moms like Dunkle take offense to the "poisoning" narrative that's emerged. "It's voiced in this way," Dunkle explained. "'My kid was a good kid,' which means that *my* kid was not." She added, "My kid was a beautiful and wonderful kid, and he did not deserve to die."

Nobody deserves it. Whether someone was injecting heroin or taking a counterfeit pill, they should not die from it. Opioid overdoses are preventable, and we know from decades of experience that punitive drug laws simply do not prevent deaths or reduce harm. Instead, what evidence we do have shows that the drug war is a project of harm maximization. That's why, in her spare time, Dunkle hands out naloxone kits in her Orange County hometown. Since her son died, she's distributed tens of thousands of doses. She rests easy at night knowing that the anti-overdose medication is being put to use and saving people from suffering the same fate as her son.

Dr. Tamara Olt is an OB-GYN in Peoria, Illinois, who lost her own son to a heroin overdose when he was just 16 years old. She said she feels like the parents who are adamant their child was "poisoned" are attempting to rewrite the story of responsibility. She told me that it seemed like folks who lean into this narrative are trying to find someone or something external to blame.

Instead, she said, "I put the blame on myself. I put the blame on Josh." It took years of grief support through GRASP to help Dr. Olt unravel her pain and the shame of losing a child to an overdose. Today, she runs a harm reduction organization that distributes naloxone, sterile syringes, and fentanyl test strips. She also prescribes buprenorphine to pregnant women who struggle with opioid addiction. Like the other families of loss dedicated to stopping overdoses, her goal is to save as many lives as possible.

Jeff Johnston, who founded the Living Undeterred Project after his oldest son Seth's fentanyl overdose, believes that connecting with other parents can be transformative. He raises awareness, hosts a podcast, and hosted events in 38 states on his own dime, without corporate sponsorship. The effort keeps him moving forward. He said a part of him died and part of him was reborn when he learned of Seth's passing. He tries to see his family's loss as an opportunity to serve others—his Twelfth Step, as he puts it, is his son's grave site. Rather than follow "a road of despair," he encourages other families to seek "a road of inspiration."

"I blame the system," said Sue Ousterman, whose son died in 2020. Sue said that grief support programs like Philly HEALs also helped her work through her pain. Rather than pursue revenge and retribution, Sue has sought other outlets to work through her loss. She started grief counseling with therapist Laura Vargas in Philadelphia. (The city offers free grief support to every parent whose child dies from an overdose.) The grief therapist said, "It's time to throw out the five stages of grief. There's no such thing as the five stages of grief."

Vargas said her work in Philly focuses on helping families integrate grief into the fabric of their lives. "It's helping them understand what that means for them, for their history, for their person's legacy, and how they're going to keep living with it. That is the process," Vargas said, adding that it's messy beyond description. "People are back and forth and all over the place. And yes, they might experience elements of the stages of grief, but it's not just checking off a box and moving on to the next one."

For Sue, her goal is to find a way to bring light and color and beauty into a world clouded by darkness. It makes her think of gardening, which she loves to do, and finds to be healing.

All the families I have spoken to share the same loss. Many of them feel saddened by the division within their community. Individually, in some alternate universe, they might all have been friends and worked together to change the world. But in reality, they can't help but vehemently disagree with each other. Their dramatic division hit me one night in the spring of 2023 while I was watching TV with my dog Quincy. I turned on CNN, and a *Town Hall* titled "America Addicted: The Fentanyl Crisis" had just started. Anderson Cooper was hosting, and he said that everybody in the room was in some way impacted by America's deadliest drug crisis in recorded history.

On stage, Cooper was interviewing two grieving families. Both of them said they carry naloxone everywhere they go now, and that they support the nationwide push to make the lifesaving drug available everywhere. I nodded along, thinking, *Finally, harm reduction is mainstream and normalized—so normal that it's being supported on national TV by grieving parents.*

Then, Cooper asked the two families, "What do you want to see changed? What can be done?" A mom and son responded that they want more awareness and education around fentanyl, but they also support "tougher laws" and "more prosecution on the dealers." Another mom chimed in, and said she wants the country to embrace the distinction between an "overdose" and a "poisoning." She explained how, in her opinion, the latter is a serious crime that ought to be prosecuted.

"Poisoning is different," she said. "If you put something in somebody's drink, and they die from it, that's poisoning—they didn't know they took what they took." I sighed loudly to myself. It's not like somebody taking heroin knows what's in the baggie, or somebody buying cocaine knows what's cut into their eight ball. Buying illegal drugs is highly dangerous and risky for everybody, quite different from ordering a martini at a bar. The "poisoning" story felt like it was trying to create a new class of victimhood.

What parents decide to do with their pain matters. Its impact is just as powerful as the overdose death that created it. And right now, the biggest result of this pain may be the drumbeat of the "poisoning" narrative. Here it was being broadcast to millions of people on CNN! I'm not one to tell a grieving parent what to do with their grief. But I can't help but be alarmed by a simple and overly reductive narrative being created to add fuel to the drug war. The implication of the "fentanyl poisoning" story is that there are bad guys and villains responsible for all these young people dying. It's not that simple.

Later in the segment, Anderson Cooper interviewed Anne Milgram, the director of the DEA. She sounded scripted and was incredibly careful with her words, the way federal bureaucrats tend to be. She amplified the "fentanyl poisoning" phrase, and discussed the DEA's ongoing efforts to prosecute drug dealers. (This was without so much of a mention that this agenda has continued to fail for decades. More on that later.) Nevertheless, Milgram vowed to bring justice to the surviving families of "fentanyl poisoning victims."

And then, inexplicably, Cooper invited Senator Lindsey Graham to speak on the fentanyl crisis. The bombastic South Carolina Republican was given the stage to spew his absurd fairy-tale agenda. He called for the US military to invade Mexico, wage an overt war on "drug cartels," and bomb their drug manufacturing laboratories.

"We're not going to solve the problem until the cost of poisoning Americans goes up," Senator Graham said—once again, there was the word *poison*. "The fentanyl drug dealers will go into a different line of business if they start getting killed and going to jail."

I finally shouted at the TV, waking Quincy up from his nap. *They want to wage an actual war? They want to kill and arrest more people? As though that's ever worked.* Every four minutes an American was dying from an overdose. And it felt like everybody's slogan seemed to be Bomb Mexico! Execute Drug Dealers! I felt like I was underwater, as though all of the progress we've made expanding health care, harm reduction, recovery support services, and spreading a more compassionate response to addiction was sinking to the bottom of a black ocean. Where were the moms like Christie and Sue, who would push back against calls for more crime and punishment? Why didn't CNN invite *them* on? Instead of compassion, everybody was calling for blood.

By the time I calmed down (and Quincy went back to sleep), the microphone was handed to a fiery woman named Dita Bhargava. Cooper introduced Dita as a mom whose 26-year-old son died from "fentanyl poisoning." Not to have anyone putting words in her mouth, Dita asked Senator Graham this question on live TV (emphasis mine):

> Senator Graham, anyone who has lost someone they know to *overdose* would turn back time to provide a safe place for their loved one to take their drug and save their life— potentially, 100,000 precious lives saved per year, with an opportunity to educate about treatment and recovery provided, especially with the scourge of dangerous and lethal fentanyl. All the data from Europe, Canada, and a couple of facilities in the U.S. show that safe injection facilities work, prevent people from dying, and give them an opportunity to learn that recovery is real. Senator Graham, would you

support legalizing and funding safe injection facilities to
save precious lives?

Dita's face looked pained as she confronted one of the most
powerful people in America. Senator Graham tried to maintain his
unflappable political poker face while Dita spoke favorably of harm
reduction, but he couldn't help squirming in his seat. Finally, he said,
"I don't really understand the question. We're not talking about injections here; we're talking about people taking a pill thinking it was
Percocet and wound up being fentanyl. The bottom line—"

Dita interrupted the senator. "They could take the pill in the
safe injection site," she shot back. The senator stammered. And Dita
kept pressing her point:

> The whole point is that they would not die if they were do-
> ing it safely where people could help them with Narcan and
> watch over them. My son died because there was nobody
> there to help him. He had Narcan all around him, and no-
> body knew he was overdosing, but if he knew there was a
> safe place to take his drug of choice, he would be alive today
> because he wanted nothing more than to be on a path of
> recovery and enjoy the love of his friends and his family.

Damn. How was Senator Graham, who obviously doesn't support
consumption sites (also known as overdose prevention sites), going to
respond? "To be honest with you, ma'am, no. I don't think that's a very
good idea at all. I don't think there is a 'safe' place to do this."

Graham can believe whatever he wants to, but it was obvious he
was ignoring Dita, not to mention the decades of research into overdose prevention. Dita held the microphone to her mouth, her brown
eyes sharp as daggers. She said, "That's too bad, Senator: 100,000
people is a lot of people in our country who could be alive if they
were given a safe place to use."

Senator Graham's voice softened. He mewed again, "I don't think that's the answer." Their exchange ended, and the room erupted in applause—not for the senator, but for Dita, who wasn't afraid to confront the politicians who have repeatedly stood in the way of real solutions to this crisis. In that moment, Dita stood tall in the face of a brick wall of opposition, and she spoke the truth.

Talking to grieving parents like Dita, like Christie, like Sue, Aimee, Jeff, and Tamara has helped me understand how deep the division and anger in America runs. But it also taught me about forgiveness, and helped me understand and better cope with my own grief. There's no cost that will rebalance the losses of all the friends and loved ones who aren't here anymore. That stays with me too. I did not lose a child, but that anger and pain also runs through me. It runs through all of us. And if we don't do something about it, I'm afraid it's going to tear us apart.

I'm afraid that it already is.

A year after Nathan Windham's trial, spring was starting to bloom in the sparse suburb of Hillsborough, North Carolina. The air was slightly cool and breezy. The rolling hills and dense forests along the Eno River looked lush and alive, creating dark green tunnels of low-hanging branches and leaves. It was a typical Friday afternoon for Christie, who had just dropped her two dogs off at the groomer. She looked fondly at the bright yellow portrait of Kevin hanging above her fireplace mantel, and she smiled.

"In some ways," Christie said, "I feel like Kevin's purpose was to come in and kind of blow the lid off things." Nathan's trial received wall-to-wall coverage. The image everybody remembers is Christie hugging the man accused of murdering her own son, telling him, "I forgive you." Christie believes Kevin's death has already changed many lives. "Now we're really actively involved," she said. "I think a lot more lives will be saved as a result of that one death. I wish I could have my son back, but he's doing good work."

8

GOODBYE, YELLOW BRICK ROAD

Before we look at how we can improve things, we need to understand the effects of our current—and frequently shifting—approach to the drug war. How does it play out for real people? How does it affect the folks on the front lines? The Tenderloin District in San Francisco is one of the most heavily affected areas, but in many ways, it's the rule rather than the exception. You'll find smaller-scale versions of this in most cities and towns across America. It's a red-light district, where red doesn't mean "stop." It means "go, go, go."

This neighborhood is not what I'd call the happiest place on earth. It's too messy for that. Too gritty. Maybe that's one of the reasons some people love it. It's a small slice of everything San Francisco has to offer, densely concentrated in a neighborhood that's only a few blocks wide and about six blocks long. The first morning of my visit, I left my hotel and walked along sidewalks lined with low-income services, SROs (single-room occupancy housing), methadone clinics, and social welfare offices with signs in Spanish, Vietnamese, and English. I was one of the only white people up at this hour—the only white person in the donut shop where I bought a couple raised-glazed and a cup of coffee so strong that it made my hair curl.

Outside the shop, a homeless man begged me for some change.

His hands were covered in half-healed lesions that looked like dozens of cigarette burns. They discolored his skin like the spots on a dalmatian puppy and seemed to bubble under his nails, pushing them out of their beds. One hand was so swollen that he could barely close his fingers over the money I gave him. His hat was pulled low over his eyes. A scrap of tin foil was tucked into the folded brim.

"Mind if I stand here?" I asked him. He simply shrugged and edged away from me, dragging a tattered Army-issue blanket behind him.

At first, I thought it was me he was avoiding. Then, I turned and saw a short, stocky white man with a beard wearing a camouflage windbreaker jacket printed with the logo of a group called Urban Alchemy. His neck was mottled with tattoos, and his jaw was set in the firm, fuck-you angle of an ex-convict. He told me his name was Thomas. (I've changed his name, since talking to me might jeopardize his job.) He'd been a bouncer before this, done time for a few felonies, and was no longer allowed to own a firearm in the state of California. Honestly, he didn't look like he needed a gun.

He was one of several hundred Urban Alchemy contractors, many of them ex-convicts and felons. UA collects millions of dollars in city contracts to post guys like Thomas all over the Tenderloin to look tough and keep the peace. As I talked with him, my nose caught a familiar smell—sickly sweet, and nothing at all like the donut I was chewing.

Ten feet from us, a crew of people sat cross-legged on the sidewalk smoking meth. They passed the pipe around, barely bothering to glance over their shoulders. As the pipe changed hands, a father with a first grader in tow was crossing the street. Thomas perked up and gestured to catch the attention of the people sitting on the sidewalk.

"Hey, hey!" he barked. "A kid is coming! Put the pipe away. Put it away!"

To my surprise, they did. One woman hid the pipe in her lap,

remnants of milky smoke billowing out of the glass stem. The father and son walked by without a glance at the group. They may as
well have been separated by a plateglass window. On one side, the
"open-air drug use" that I'd heard so much about in the news. On
the other, a family walking to school, cartoon lunchbox and all.

"That's what you do around here?" I asked Thomas.

"Mostly, yeah," he said. "We don't want kids exposed to that
kinda stuff."

I watched the father and his child walk down Golden Gate
Avenue—the heart of the Tenderloin, which was supposedly ground
zero for the "druggy zombie apocalypse." It was not at all what I had
expected. I'd come to see the real version of San Francisco, viewed
from the ground where people actually live. The news shock stories
didn't have much to say about this small slice of Northern California
coastline, dotted with tall glass skyscrapers. There was no mention
in the headlines of the loud trolley horns whirring every which way
and grassy hillsides in sprawling green parks; the ease of so many diverse cultures melting and blending together; tourists from around
the world shopping at high-end stores, dining at one of the city's
39 Michelin-starred restaurants,[1] marveling at downtown's art deco
buildings, and strolling down the steep, sloping neighborhoods; or
the seemingly endless rows of multicolored neo-Victorian mansions.

Over the next few days, I saw all of that—and so much more.
Mostly, I noticed how closely the extremes of wealth and poverty,
beauty and horror, health and sickness, and power and powerlessness
coexist. After I said goodbye to Thomas, I headed toward the Civic
Center, right in front of the towering City Hall building. I asked a
public works employee named Clarence where people were using
and selling drugs in broad daylight, and he told me that Hyde Street
and Eddy Street were where the action was.

"It's sad," Clarence said. "Those people need a lot of help. It's like
everyone has given up on them."

I walked up a steep hill toward Hyde and Eddy, passing the law school where Vice President Kamala Harris had graduated. I leaned against a bike rack in front of San Francisco's version of a bodega, which sells sandwiches, ice cream, and cheap snacks, along with butane lighters and tiny plastic roses inside little glass stems.

Just as Clarence promised, I saw *those* people—my people—at the corner, lining the sidewalk. They looked thin and frail; chronic substance use and illness made them seem older than they actually were. I tried to keep my eye on them, but I kept getting distracted by the cars zooming down the hill, speeding through the intersection. A stream of white Teslas, Audis, Mercedes, Jaguars, and Priuses. I even saw something called a "Waymo," and it startled me almost more than the open fentanyl use. ("Waymo," as in "I make Waymo money than you.") Somebody was sitting shotgun in the fully autonomous, white Jaguar SUV, but nobody was in the driver's seat. All the bells and whistles on the Jaguar's roof reminded me of the movie *Twister*, as though this wired-up car was speeding right into a tornado. Standing at the corner of Hyde and Eddy, seeing the open drug use and poverty as cars sped by, I felt like I'd been punched square in the gut by the city's stark, in-your-face inequality.

If trickle-down economics existed, money would run uphill in San Francisco—along with everything else. More people in the city have died from drug overdoses than from COVID-19. In 2022, the city saw a 41 percent jump in fatal overdoses.[2] During the first three months of 2023, a record 200 people died from overdoses, mostly due to illicit fentanyl used in combination with other drugs, like meth and alcohol. The mortality rate for San Francisco's homeless population is also staggeringly high. During the first year of the pandemic, the number of unhoused people dying in the street doubled.[3]

The solution? Make things worse. For almost 40 years, San Francisco has been cracking down—and driving people into those cracks, never addressing their root causes. The mayor, governor, police, and district attorney have all promised to, once again, target "large-scale" fentanyl dealing. It's the playbook they've tried so many times before—on crack, on AIDS victims, on drug users, on poor people—that it's hard to keep track of how many times it's failed. For such an innovative and daring city, San Francisco can't seem to hack the basic issues of human life. Need a car that drives itself? They've got you covered. You have nowhere to live? Can't stop using heroin? Too bad, buddy.

The blaming and shaming reeks of xenophobia, lacking the basic analysis of addiction, political conditions, and the drug market. Even San Francisco's "liberal" media is quick to point outward when analyzing the origins of the city's problems. "A housing boom in one area of Honduras . . . is being fueled by drug sales in San Francisco," crowed the *San Francisco Chronicle*. The article blamed Hondurans for the fentanyl crisis, claiming that the real estate boom in Honduras is linked to drug dealing in the Bay Area. Nestor Castillo fired back in an op-ed published in *El Tecolote*, "The piece just reeks of 19th century racist writing . . . pigeonholing Hondurans all as drug dealers who are responsible for the fentanyl crisis, while providing a subpar analysis of the complex structures that shuttle poor immigrants into urban areas, which offer little to no resources and limited economic mobility. There is no mention throughout the article, at least in any substantive way, of the broken immigration system that often drives immigrants to do work that is precarious, dangerous, or low paying."

The split between the two worlds—high and low, white and nonwhite, rich and poor, housed and unhoused—struck me again and again during my trip to the city. As a gay man, so many of my freedoms came from San Francisco. From equal rights, including the right to marry the love of my life, Sean; to in-the-streets ACT UP protesters who inspired many of the movements I'm a part of today; to the pride I feel walking down the street as myself, with nothing to hide from anyone; my life and my destiny are unquestionably tied up with the Tenderloin. As a person in recovery, I can't ignore that the city will likely be the next battleground for human rights.

And as of 2023, those rights were falling far behind. The Rainbow City is becoming an unfriendly, narrow-minded, cruel place. The streets that birthed so many progressive social movements instead seemed to be spawning something dangerous and toxic: a reinvigorated drug war. In the face of an economic, human rights, and public health catastrophe, out-and-proud city officials were deploying police, prosecution, and incarceration. Leaders like Mayor London Breed, District Attorney Brooke Jenkins, and city councilors like Matt Dorsey advocate for ineffective punitive tactics that exclude people and punish them for being sick, instead of finding a seat for everyone.

The city of queer love is pushing tough love instead. And, as usual, the people feeling the squeeze are the ones who are already in the grips of an illness that has no cure. These are people severely stigmatized by our culture, which portrays addiction as disgusting and disfiguring, morally repugnant, and deviant—much as AIDS was portrayed by the religious right in the 1980s.

To understand why this deadly story—this lie—is so effective, you have to understand the unique political, historical, and social landscape of San Francisco.

San Francisco is an American city unlike any other (except maybe New York). It's the kind of place where a fantasy of the city reaches the level of a Greek myth. Stories of the Golden City in the West so deeply penetrate our imaginations that it's hard to separate fact from fiction, history from myth, real from imagined. There isn't just one story here, and depending on the cultural or political mood at any given moment, these myths are always changing.

Not long ago, San Francisco was often depicted as the wealthiest, most prosperous, most progressive, and socially tolerant city in America. Some said it was the cradle of invention and innovation, home to more billionaires per capita than anywhere else, and an elite coastal enclave near Stanford University, where the right idea at the right time could make a young person fabulously wealthy. It was an intellectual gold rush, the land of opportunity, where the American dream lived on. Perhaps not all of that was a myth. But if it was ever real, the bright colors and big dreams of this story are fading. The bloom, as they say, is off the rose.

For almost two centuries, journalists, writers, and historians have described San Francisco as a "boom-and-bust" town. The highs are high and the lows are low—from the 1800s mining bonanza to the 1990s dot-com boom and the explosion of tech in the 21st century. But as high as those highs were, the city I visited seemed to be going bust right before my eyes.

When I was there in June 2023, the streets felt eerily quiet. Downtown has accumulated some 18.4 million square feet of vacant office space.[4] During the pandemic, young tech workers no longer had to show up in offices, and they fled the high cost of living on the coast for cheaper pastures. All these tall buildings made of tinted glass as monuments to money, innovation, and progress sat empty and unused. Ironic, right? The city bet on tech by offering companies like X, formerly known as Twitter, millions in tax breaks to build corporate headquarters. Just blocks away from skyscrapers and billion-dollar tech companies, thousands of people live outside on the sidewalk. What good is a "boom" if it only helped a small, elite group? The more I thought about San Francisco, the less sense everything made.

I wasn't the only one to notice. "How Tech Fueled the Boom and Bust of San Francisco," reads a 2022 headline from the *San Francisco Standard*.[5] In 2021 alone, San Francisco lost 25,000 college graduates to migration. At the same time, people were literally dying in the streets as fentanyl ripped through the city. As I waited for the light to change at the corner of Market and 7th, I realized I was witnessing a cultural, social, and political battle that could have massive implications for the future of American drug policy. What San Francisco decides to do with its "drug problem" would matter for all of us.

Controlling the story of San Francisco would be key to winning that fight. Over the past few years, a network of Very Online, well-funded activists has embarked on creating a new myth. Thanks to their financial backers—venture capitalists and tech tycoons—along with a web of nonprofit donors and techno-libertarians, they've been extraordinarily effective. By now, I'm sure you've heard their new story. To hear them tell it, San Francisco's latest bust, the closing of businesses, and mass migration of young workers—none of this is the result of housing prices or economics. (No, really. Promise!) Instead, these stories claim that the economic slump is all due to rampant crime, lawlessness, and chaos stemming from the city's "open-air drug scene." These mythmakers pin the blame on staggering levels of homelessness and untreated mental illness. Addiction, homelessness, and mental illness have been dubbed the "dark triad." This narrative appears on podcasts, on social media, and in the press, often without criticism or pushback. Right-wing tabloids blast negative headlines: "San Francisco Deploys National Guard in Fight Against Drug Zombies." Glossy respectable outlets like the *Atlantic* explain to their readers "How San Francisco Became a Failed City." In a *Good Morning America* segment about a mall closing, the correspondent claimed that reporting from the scene at night "was simply too dangerous." People instinctively accept all this fearmongering—and why shouldn't they? It's aligned with the other lies we're told about those same three issues.

Drugs are bad, and bad people use them. Bad people do bad things. Therefore, bad people are to blame when bad things happen. It shouldn't be so simple, but to many folks, it is. These myths and lies misrepresenting the city have backfired. Real problems were blown way out of proportion. San Francisco's real estate and business leaders (who are typically conservative) are fed up with all the overwrought and sensationalistic stories.

"They're making stuff up," Rodney Fong, CEO of the San Francisco Chamber of Commerce, said to the *San Francisco Chronicle*.

"It is absolutely unfair." People in San Francisco are sick and tired of seeing this skewed portrait.

There's a grave irony that these paid trolls and online activists don't seem to understand. Their dramatic stories, exploitative videos, and constant complaining about drug use and homelessness have actually hurt the city they claim to love so much. The story of San Francisco's demise has caused real-world social, economic, and political pain. If you love something, you don't try to tear it down.

There are several main characters behind these activists peddling drug war propaganda, mostly venture capitalists and Silicon Valley types, almost all of them middle-aged white men, and wealthy. They see themselves as having libertarian ideals, as least toward themselves and especially their own business ventures, as if to say, "Don't get in our way; government regulation hinders innovation." Perhaps because of this weird, bootstrapping ideology, this group can't seem to accept that our society has a responsibility to help the people who are worse off than ourselves. These titans of tech aren't interested in social consciousness. When it comes to people who are unhoused and mentally ill, who are suffering so visibly, so nakedly out in the open, these same venture capitalists are quick to strip them of their humanity and rights—rights that they see as inalienable for themselves.

For example, investors like Michael Mortiz spent over $300,000 for a PR campaign created by TogetherSF Action.[6] In May 2023, TogetherSF blanketed the Tenderloin with snarky billboards and mocking posters as part of their "fentalife" campaign. The posters poked fun at naloxone, mocked those who struggle with addiction, and scolded those who work in harm reduction. The propaganda belittled people who are trying their best to provide services that prevent overdoses and stop the spread of blood-borne illnesses.

The justification for this outright antagonism was bringing "awareness" to a problem that everybody is already well aware of. Sure—just like Jerry Falwell's cover story in July 1983 in the *Moral*

Majority Report.[7] He used an image of a white, heterosexual family in surgical masks with the headline "Homosexual Diseases Threaten American Families." The excuse was awareness then too—but it was a false awareness, acting as a thin veneer for bigotry.

I wasn't the only person who felt that way about it. Nuala Bishari, a columnist at the *San Francisco Chronicle*, wrote that the "fentalife" campaign font looked as though it "came off a Barbie box." Bishari also did some helpful math for us: The $300,000 spent on crude and cruel advertisements could have purchased 100,000 vials of generic naloxone, or 12,631 doses of name-brand Narcan. Or, that $300,000 could have funded 927 days of residential addiction treatment. It could also have paid for the salaries of three social workers, "who could help take the burden off our city's overworked employees and help some of the most vulnerable people with addiction issues get into housing," Bishari wrote. Instead, all this money went into a PR campaign that threw homeless people under the bus.

I've tried to understand the TogetherSF group, and the online activists and trolls that supported their campaign. It's hard to come away thinking that they are anything other than reactionary and cynical. They come off as angry and mean-spirited, constantly criticizing harm reduction, housing-first policies, and public health workers. They seem determined to rewrite history to blame all of the city's problems on harm reduction programs, ignoring the social, economic, and political calamities that, for decades, have contributed to poverty, homelessness, and substance use. As the author Maia Szalavitz wrote in the *New York Times*, "Rather than seeking an unattainable 'drug-free world,' harm reductionists focus on reducing drug-related damage. People always have and always will take drugs . . . A better approach is to target harm, not highs." I see this as similar to earlier harm reduction efforts, like the ACT UP and medical staff who handed out safer sex kits, free condoms, clean syringes, and educational pamphlets at pop-up clinics in the '80s.

People will always have sex, they reasoned. Why not make it safer, and not a death sentence?

The same reasoning doesn't seem to apply to drug users today. Instead, this venture capital-funded propaganda has turned toward the people themselves, reinforcing the idea that the War on Drugs is actually a war on (certain) people who use drugs.

The Bay Area activists involved in TogetherSF toe the same line as Michael Shellenberger, who runs a nonprofit called Environmental Progress. This group has also poured hundreds of thousands of dollars into the same network that advocates for a punitive drug war.[8] Shellenberger's funded messengers call on the city to replace public health and harm reduction with a vigorous police response. They want the police to arrest unhoused and addicted people, and force them into some unspecified form of "treatment." It's a cruel and dubious strategy, especially since the research on forced and compulsory treatment is decidedly mixed. Some studies show that forced treatment more often fails and causes other collateral harms, like trauma, death, and serious medical issues. What gets lost in this debate are the specifics. What *kind* of treatment would people be forced into? Shellenberger's team never really says. They just deploy slogans and vague platitudes about supporting "treatment" and "recovery."

This group has effectively sold the idea that San Francisco is a dystopian hellscape, and that liberals and "radical" harm reductionists are to blame. The activist groups Shellenberger funds also pop up in other cities too, from Austin, Texas, to Seattle and Portland. Together, they've formed a national alliance called North America Recovers. The collective first launched with a bizarre ad in January 2023 featuring Jacqui Berlinn of Mothers Against Drug Addiction and Deaths, a group molded after Mothers Against Drunk Driving (MADD). The ad was slapped onto a fleet of trucks that circled the streets of Washington, DC.

In the ad, which seemed to be directed at President Joe Biden, Berlinn held a poster of her addicted son. It said, "Please help my son escape addiction the way you helped Hunter." Beneath that message, the call to action: "Stop government drug sites." I assume that meant overdose prevention centers, and that describing them in such an inaccurate and creepy way would deter people from supporting safer use facilities.

A quick side note: this ad didn't last very long. North America Recovers briefly featured heavy hitters in drug policy. But after the launch featuring the cynical ad attacking the Biden family, some of the organization's listed supporters quickly disappeared from the North America Recovers website. (It's unclear what, precisely, North America Recovers has accomplished, aside from burning a lot of money on strange advertising and PR campaigns.)

As the investor behind this campaign and many others, Shellenberger has been criticized ad infinitum by economists, public health officials, and housing experts for spreading this twisted fantasy. He authored a diatribe against Democrats in his book titled *San Fransicko: Why Progressives Ruin Cities*, in which he argues that homelessness is fundamentally a problem of untreated mental illness and drug addiction. Right after my trip to San Francisco, the University of California published the largest-ever study of California's homelessness crisis. The study's findings contradict Shellenberger's bogus story of "drug tourism" and homeless people "choosing" to live in tents on the street. He says they'd rather use drugs all day than work; whereas, the study found that nine out of ten participants lost their last housing as a result of economic hardship, not drugs.

Time and again, the research contradicts Shellenberger's assertions that homelessness is about drug addiction rather than poverty. For instance, a 2023 study gave $7,500 to homeless people in Vancouver, with no strings attached.[9] They could spend the money however they wanted. What happened? The results showed that over one year, the recipients of free cash spent fewer days homeless, increased their savings, and moved into stable housing more quickly. This meant that the homeless shelter system was under less strain, which resulted in saving $8,277 per person, a net saving of $777 per person. This means that giving homeless people money *literally* pays for itself. It costs nothing. It's astonishing. Results like these ought to revolutionize the way American cities respond to homelessness, which is fundamentally a problem of poverty and a lack of cash.

Here is what the lead researcher, Dr. Margot Kushel, of the California homelessness study said: "Everything in their life gets worse when they lose their housing: their health, their mental health, their substance." Dr. Margot called it "a personal doom loop." And yet, Shellenberger repeatedly says addiction is the primary *cause* of homelessness, even though that's completely false. If drug addiction leads to homelessness, then how come states with much higher rates of addiction and drug overdoses, like West Virginia and Kentucky, have such comparatively small unhoused populations? What explains that discrepancy? In states like West Virginia, housing is cheap, abundant, and affordable. In San Francisco, housing is off-the-charts expensive. Shellenberger simply ignores inconvenient facts about San Francisco, such as the median price for a single-family home being $1.3 million. "Homelessness meets cluelessness" is how one reviewer described his book.[10]

While he's eager to throw millions of dollars at defaming and targeting poor people, Shellenberger isn't finding an especially wide audience—at least beyond the one he pays to reach. In 2022, he ran for governor of California, hoping to outflank the Democratic incumbent Gavin Newsom on a platform of arresting drug dealers and drug users, rounding up all of the city's homeless people, and forcing them to choose between jail or a sprawling "treatment" system that does not currently exist. Shellenberger only won 4 percent of the vote across the entire state, and he didn't even place top three in San Francisco County, where he campaigned the hardest.[11]

That's a good sign that San Francisco voters are not buying the tough-love, punitive and ambiguous "treatment" and drug enforcement story that he's been selling. It's a sign that this loud group is a vocal minority without popular support. But that hasn't stopped the small army of activists who support Shellenberger, who are funded by him, from agitating for a harsher drug war. Just like Trump, they blame every problem on "the radical left," and in particular, they blame "radical" harm reductionists for ruining the city.

The idea is patently ridiculous. I stopped by three different harm reduction groups while I was in San Francisco, and each one told me the same thing: they are overworked, underpaid, and are constantly running low on critical supplies. Once again, the myth wasn't aligning with reality.

However, that didn't stop the anti-homeless rhetoric. Any perceived social issue, from the murder of a cheating tech executive to the closure of a Starbucks, could be chalked up to unhoused people or substance users. For example, on April 10, 2023, a Whole Foods on Market Street, about two blocks from Twitter's corporate headquarters, permanently closed its doors. Board Supervisor Matt Dorsey, who represents the Market neighborhood where the Whole Foods was located, said the closure was caused by "addiction-driven theft" and homeless people having "outbursts" in the store.[12] Certainly, it couldn't have anything to do with the mass exodus of Whole Foods' target demographic: college-educated tech workers who need a fresh panini and kombucha on their lunch break.

That day on Twitter, I remembered endless posts coming from the angry army of trolls who take to the platform to bash San Francisco all day, every day. They took the closing of Whole Foods as confirmation of their narrative. Another spiral in the city's "doom loop." They called the city a "hellscape." They posted cruel images and videos of homeless people without their consent. They blamed everything that happens in the city on wishy-washy liberals. These keyboard warriors were building and spreading a new myth of San Francisco as "a failed city."

The new myth isn't rooted in reality. The GDP of San Francisco is over $500 billion, making it the sixth-largest economy in America.

In 2022, the Bay Area ranked number one in GDP growth, with 4.8 percent, which translates to roughly $1.3 trillion in additional growth from the year prior. Housing prices are soaring off the charts. It's almost as if big business and billionaire tech companies are the only things that *can* survive. In 2022, the median household income in San Francisco was $96,265. The following year, the average rent for apartments was between $2,781 and $4,696. How can a city simultaneously not cater to business while the average home price is more than $1 million? It makes no sense. This is not a failed city where businesses cannot survive. Anyone who says otherwise is lying.

Realistically, it's not like the closing of a Whole Foods affected anyone's life in any deep, material way. Many of these out-of-touch Twitter whiners do not live in San Francisco for the same reason a lot of people don't: because it's just too damn expensive. But you wouldn't know that from what they say online. They pounce on every little thing that happens in the city.

Instead of simply being what it was, the now-shuttered Whole Foods had become the latest symbol of decay and decline. Apparently, one shopper did not get the memo that the store had closed. I saw her tug on the locked door and throw up her arms in dismay. I kept on walking down Market. A closed Whole Foods? Who cares? Everyone, even politicians, described San Francisco the way Batman described Gotham: full of criminals and thugs, vandals and fiends, a place that's no longer safe, a culture steeped in chaos. But that was not what I saw at all.

Despite the high-drama warnings thrown around by the media, I didn't feel any less safe than I do in my hometown of Las Vegas. This goes against everything I'd heard on TV, which makes it sound like you're going to get shanked at MoMa. Centrists at CNN, Republicans on Fox News, far-right psychos at Breitbart, and tech CEOs like Elon Musk seem to have found one thing they can all agree on: San Francisco is dangerous these days. Even Florida's far-right governor and the most uncharismatic presidential candidate in recent memory, Ron DeSantis, got in on the San Francisco bashing. In a campaign video, he repeated the same myths cooked up by Shellenberger's paid trolls. "We're here in the once great city of San Francisco," DeSantis said, dressed in a black suit while standing in front of a wall of graffiti. "We came in here and we saw people defecating on the street, we saw people using heroin, people smoking crack cocaine . . . the city has really collapsed." His tone is dull, his affect bone-dry; not even *he* sounds persuaded by what he's saying.

All this propaganda sings the same tune: San Francisco is said to have been taken over by homeless drug users and greedy fentanyl dealers. It's a city where people commit crimes with impunity. It's decaying and crime-ridden, or, as Musk incoherently tweeted, "a derelict zombie apocalypse," brought on by the "woke mind virus."[13] (DeSantis also constantly drones on about the "woke mind virus." If such a virus is real, it seems to have melted their brains.)

Two blocks away, I noticed another grocery store called The Market, right next door to Twitter's headquarters. *Hmm*, I thought. The trolls online didn't mention that Whole Foods was competing with a local grocery store down the street.

Inside The Market, local artisan vendors and small family-run businesses served up delicious-smelling Korean and Filipino food made from scratch. The Market looked way better than any Whole Foods I'd ever been to. It was local—and more affordable. I browsed around the aisles and grabbed a water bottle and some dried mango slices to eat on my long excursion across the "hellscape."

Checking out at the register, I asked the cheery cashier if it was hard for this place to stay open, you know, due to the "crime" and mentally ill "outbursts" that everybody on Twitter yells about.

"Nah, it's not that," she said, raising her eyebrows. "We're doing all right. It's just not as busy as it used to be, with everybody working from home now."

I paid for my mango and water bottle, which cost a combined $7. The Market used to see a busy lunch rush, the cashier explained, as I declined a plastic bag. She told me that a lot of the tech workers around here only come to the office a couple of times a week, and many are completely remote now. After seeing the reality of the dreaded Whole Foods closure, I wondered what else might be *off* about this new story that these online activists are peddling. I left the grocery store to continue on my route, in search of the zombie apocalypse.

I ventured off toward Union Square, where people shop at high-end luxury stores. I heard a trolley's horn blaring as I wandered past Supreme, the multibillion-dollar apparel brand that sells expensive, limited edition gear. A plain white T-shirt cost $90 off the rack. Nope—no browsing in here for me. I kept pace down Market and spotted more luxury brands like Burberry. (I didn't even bother going in there.) I strolled past groups of friends and families eating at a fancy Japanese ramen shop. Across the street, I whiffed the delectable scent of pizza cooking in a fiery wood oven at a bustling Italian restaurant. I saw people sipping Negronis and eating Neapolitan pies. Businesses can't survive here, really? This was hardly a scene from a failed city. What planet was Elon Musk living on?

I kept walking down Market, approaching 4th Street, weaving in and out of crowds of tourists shopping with their families. I lost track of all the different languages I heard: Chinese, Japanese, German, Portuguese. I approached a corner and saw police stationed on both sides, across from one another. I walked to the next corner and saw another group of police posted. They were all over the shopping district, armed to the teeth and terrifying. Some wore dark cloth masks over their faces, covering everything but their eyes. Something told me these masks weren't a pandemic precaution. Maybe this was the law enforcement mobilization Governor Newsom announced—a promise to clean up the streets and sweep unhoused people into the gutters to die.

In the past few years, polling of San Francisco residents shows that people do actually feel scared when they walk the streets.[14] People feel this way even though violent crime remains at its lowest level since the 1960s. Just to be clear, that's not even really a San Francisco thing—it's an American thing. (Many Americans believe that crime is on the rise every year when it actually isn't. That's probably because they watch local news, which peddles sensationalized and violent stories to its suburban audience. There's a reason true crime podcasts are so popular.) What has risen is homelessness, drug addiction, and overdose deaths. These issues of mental health, public health, and housing are conflated with "crime."

People aren't scared of "crime." They're afraid of poverty, drug use, and mental illness. And those issues are abundant in San Francisco. The idea that San Francisco is "a failed city," crime-ridden and unsafe, flows right into this idea that businesses can no longer survive here. A Nordstrom's closed. A Whole Foods closed. Some people see this as a sign of the end times.

While overdoses continue to soar, crime rates in the city have plummeted from the high peaks set in the 1990s. This trend mirrors big cities across America. Most recently, San Francisco saw a spike in violent crime in 2013 and a spike in property crime in 2017. But both of these upticks rose nowhere close to the level of the 1990s. In 2023, the *Los Angeles Times* analyzed San Francisco crime data for homicide, rape, robbery, and aggravated assault, finding that these crimes peaked in 2013 with 7,064 cases.[15] Over nearly a decade, these types of violent crimes have declined to 4,796 cases.

When the city hunkered down for quarantine in 2020, crime plummeted further. And when lockdowns lifted, crime slowly ticked upward again. (All of this was part of a nationwide trend.)

Crime in San Francisco remained below pre-pandemic levels. However, other social issues became more apparent—and they made people really, really mad. Overdoses, petty crimes, drug dealing, and many other problems were blamed on Chesa Boudin, a progressive district attorney elected on a reform agenda. Angry activists in America's "most liberal city" formed new coalitions calling to kick Boudin out of office. For the record, crime levels barely budged from the time Chesa Boudin took office as a progressive prosecutor to the time he was recalled and replaced by a "tough on crime" prosecutor named Brooke Jenkins. She campaigned on an old-school restoration of "law and order," promising she would clean up the streets by aggressively prosecuting thieves, vandals, and fentanyl dealers.

You might have heard Jenkins's name in the news. Shortly before my trip to San Francisco, a young, Black, transgender man named Banko Brown was accused of shoplifting by a security guard at a Walgreens. The guard (also a Black man) confronted Brown in the store, and they began to fight and wrestle one another. The scuffle ended, and security camera footage showed Brown was walking away, leaving the store, when the guard shot and killed him. Brooke Jenkins decided not to prosecute the security guard who ended Banko Brown's life.

Brown's family and activists were outraged by the decision to not prosecute. Jenkins said video and testimonial evidence showed the security guard acted in "self-defense." Yet I could see with my own eyes that this wasn't true: Brown was standing outside the store, unarmed, when the security guard shot and killed him. Again, I wondered, who is San Francisco not safe for? The billboards, viral videos, and talking head TV shows imply that the city is not safe for "nice" people. They mean business owners and homeowners—the wealthy and elite—who live, work, and play there. Are *they* not safe? Well, statistically, they are going to be just fine. People who are housed and have access to health insurance are the safest in San Francisco, and they are likely to stay that way. The protections in place for them did nothing for Banko Brown. The city is safe for the tech bros. It wasn't safe for a Black transgender 24-year-old who, while dying, begged the first responders to call his dad.

The more I walked, the more it seemed like the point of San Francisco's tough-on-crime policy was to frighten poor people into leaving. Crime rates weren't higher—but I sure saw plenty of armored police. Ellen Chaitin, a retired San Francisco Superior Court judge, said placing the blame on Boudin was based on a lie.[16] The city decided to blame a left-wing prosecutor—usually, the mayor and chief of police catch some flak too. In reality, prosecutors have little control over crime rates. Brooke Jenkins's tenure as district attorney only confirms what Judge Chaitin said. Despite a tougher approach on drugs, overdose deaths have increased under her watch. In the few cases against drug dealers that Jenkins's office took to trial, her attorneys failed to win convictions. Jenkins's approach has not fixed the city's issues. And it won't—because it can't.

At the same time, an hour south, a San Jose police union leader was arrested for smuggling fentanyl.[17] If the cops are the ones dealing fentanyl, then how are cops going to solve the problem? Jenkins launched a drug war. I think it's fair to say it's failed.

If you don't believe me, check the data. It tells a very different story. Research shows there has been a tremendous increase in deaths among unhoused people in San Francisco. The first 12 months of the pandemic, from March 2020 to March 2021, 331 homeless San Franciscans died. That year was twice as deadly for the city's unhoused population than any other year on record. The mortality rate for this group is far higher than any other demographic, and the majority of those deaths occur in the Tenderloin neighborhood.[18] Again, the inequality, the sharp division between the haves and the have-nots, and the lethal punishments the privileged doled out to the poor made me feel queasy.

If you really want to break it down, San Francisco's murder rate is also much lower than that of other American cities— especially cities in deep-red states. For example, Florida governor

Ron DeSantis would never admit that Florida has a higher homicide rate than California. Over a 20-year span, from 2000 to 2020, the per capita murder rate in red states was 23 percent higher than the murder rate in blue states.[19]

The idea that liberal policies are killing San Francisco is false and manufactured. But facts and statistics are no match for the deluge of myths and propaganda. Yes, San Francisco does have its problems, just like every other big city. Car thefts, for example, increased by 42 percent from January 2019 to December 2022,[20] even though overall crime in the city dropped. But instead of looking at the facts, people cling to viral videos of drug use and homelessness that circulate on social media. These clips, tinged with exploitation and cruelty, take the place of actual evidence.

Many of the videos show people using fentanyl in public, or nodding off in parks or on benches. When I look at them—or when I see the folks on the streets of the Tenderloin passing a pipe or sleeping against the side of a building—I don't see people who deserve to die. They shouldn't be discarded. I don't see morally bankrupt folks who brought this on themselves. I see an epidemic. And, like the AIDS epidemic, which claimed millions of lives, the overdose crisis is a public health issue first.

I've often said that there's no money in harm reduction. If there was, everyone would do it. An often-cited statistic shows that every $1 spent on addressing addiction saves $7 of public funds on criminal justice costs—a return on investment that would thrill the average venture capitalist to bits. For comparison, the AIDS Global Fund has disbursed over $43 billion since its creation to support programs in over 100 countries and claims to have saved millions of lives. This includes innovations in medicine, treatment, prevention, and education. Medications like PReP, which are offered for free by many counties, help reduce infection rates. Ending AIDS finally seems possible, thanks to the dedicated efforts of many, many activists and philanthropists who have helped us literally change the culture around this widely stigmatized disease. We can never replace what was taken from us by HIV, AIDS, homophobia, ignorance, and hatred. But we can build a future that is safe for new dreamers.

Many of the same actions that work to fight AIDS apply to the overdose crisis as well. Like AIDS, it's a complex illness with a surprisingly simple—and attainable—solution. In fact, there's a lot of crossover between new HIV infections and people who use drugs. While AIDS is still often characterized as a "gay disease," that isn't necessarily true. According to the CDC, people who inject substances accounted for 10 percent (3,864) of the 37,968 new HIV diagnoses in the US and dependent areas in 2018.[21] (The same study reported that 2,492 of these cases were attributed to injection drug use. The remaining 1,372 cases were attributed to male-to-male sexual contact plus injection drug use.) People who inject and share syringes and other supplies at high rates are at the most risk, with young people having the highest rate of sharing. More than 48 percent of people aged 18 to 24 shared syringes. It's no accident that this group also has the highest rate of infection, with people aged 13 to 34 making up the largest group of new diagnoses. And before you make assumptions about who's getting sick, it's white men who receive the most new HIV diagnoses—almost half of new diagnoses, which includes infections attributed to male-to-male sexual contact and injection drug use.

If that's not what you expected, maybe it's time to revise what you think you know about HIV, addiction, and recovery from both.

It should not be a surprise that the biggest stumbling blocks are the deeply ingrained fears, prejudices, and social stigma of substance use. To get to that 700 percent return—one dollar in, seven out—we have to focus on outcomes. Saving lives. Stopping overdoses. Lowering barriers. Supporting harm reduction. Ending shame. In San Francisco, which is a microcosm of a polarized, unequal, and increasingly angry America, this is proving to be a bridge too far.

The most recent example was in December 2022, when Mayor

Breed increased policing and shut down a harm reduction facility called the Tenderloin Center. One peer recovery mentor called the Center a "sanctuary" for the Tenderloin's poorest and most marginalized residents. It was a place where, every day, over 350 people were able to get free meals, a cup of coffee, a hot shower, and use the laundry facilities. People counted on these services for their dignity and for their lives, lining up from 8 a.m. until 8 p.m., and even sleeping outside to be close to the help they needed.

The Tenderloin Center also offered a safer site for substance use. This included fentanyl testing strips, clean syringes, and medical supervision of injections. Rather than pretend people don't use drugs, or require that someone be sober in order to receive help, the Center was open to anyone and everyone. All told, the Center reversed more than 300 overdoses. If you have any experience in overdose prevention, you know that these numbers are astronomically high for such a hard-to-reach population. Again, looking at this as a return on investment, that's a payoff on par with Bill Gates's best idea. So, why shut it down?

Mayor Breed opened the Tenderloin Center in January 2022 in response to the number of overdose deaths in the neighborhood. She shut it down less than 12 months later in response to public pressure. I walked past the now-abandoned storefront at 1172 Market Street. It was less than a mile and a half from where the old Fillmore West used to be—where one of my heroes, Elton John, played sold-out shows on his white piano. Now, the Center's windows are covered in painted black plywood, as though the building was in mourning. The brick plaza out front, where people had been able to socialize, rest, and eat, was empty except for a few pigeons. I had the sense of standing on a battlefield after the shooting had stopped. Sure enough, the Center was dead—but not because it wasn't needed anymore. Instead, rates of drug use and homelessness have only increased, along with bitter political battles.

It was like watching the AIDS crisis unfold again—except this time, Anita Bryant was winning. As she famously said, "I don't hate homosexuals. I love them enough to tell them the truth: that God puts them in the category with other sinners." Replace "homosexuals" with "fentanyl addicts," and it seems like plenty of so-called progressive and even gay voters in the Rainbow City are locked in step with her attitude.

It's been hard to make sense of everything that I saw in San Francisco. The "tech boom," the power of business and real estate, has made the city unlivable for so many people, while enriching a few lucky ones. Unhoused, addicted, and mentally ill people didn't benefit during the explosion of tech money and real estate flooding the city. That doesn't sound like a "boom" to me at all. Instead, it created a deeply unequal society in which billionaires live next door to homeless families on the sidewalk. During the "boom" times, why didn't the city build up public infrastructure to head off these catastrophes? When all that wealth was being created, minting young new billionaires, why didn't that coincide with an investment in housing and health care for those who couldn't afford it? What's the point of a "boom" when so few actually benefit?

As the city became a rich playground for wealthy tech CEOs, drug use and homelessness worsened. That is not a myth. That's very real. I saw it. Towering glass skyscrapers of empty offices pierced through the low-hanging, cool pacific fog as the homeless folks living on the gray cracked concrete got pushed off one corner, and then the next, and then the next.

For all its mythmaking, San Francisco could be Anytown, America. People are in pain, using powerful opioids like fentanyl to nurse their wounds and find a temporary rush of warmth and calm, a reprieve from the agony of life on the street. It isn't pretty. It's painful to see. And after so many days spent wandering around the Tenderloin and witnessing the same pain day-in-day-out, I began to understand why people are angry. I began to understand why they just want all this to go away. But the drug war isn't a magic wand.

Arresting people for being poor and addicted has never worked. The drug war has been waged for decades here in the Tenderloin.[22] I saw the misery that all the prosecution and incarceration has produced.

San Francisco may very well be in a slump. The boom has busted. But what if that, ultimately, is a good thing? Maybe housing prices will drop. Maybe regular, working-class people who want a taste of the Golden City will come back. And instead of trying to force out the people who are homeless and addicted, instead of ignoring and neglecting them, the city could band together to help their neighbors who need housing, health care, and employment.

Yes, there are people crowded on San Francisco's sidewalks. Yes, they need help. Many of them openly buy and use drugs on the street—despite the crackdown on drug dealers that has yet to produce its promised results. They rely on help from a few harm reduction sites that are hanging on by the skin of their teeth and could get shut down at any moment. Many of them are poor, unimportant in the eyes of the powerful. But that doesn't mean their lives are not meaningful either. In a city that marches for gay rights, for AIDS, for trans pride, and for Black lives, survival is a cause that could—and should—bring all of us together. It's human, and it's right in front of your eyes on every block of the Tenderloin, hoping you'll find it in your heart to share your change.

That's my fantasy for this city. That's my wish, my vision. For now, it's entirely a myth.

9

THE CONVENIENT BOOGEYMAN

Since 2019, the number of fatal overdoses among children under the age of 14 has quadrupled. According to a study from *JAMA*, overdose deaths increased from 253 (1.21 per 100,000) in 2019 to 680 (3.26 per 100,000) in 2020 and to 884 (4.23 per 100,000) in 2021. Of the deaths in 2021, 77.14 percent were identified as being related to fentanyl.[1]

These deaths represent a new category of overdoses: people who are dying earlier on the drug use continuum. Overdoses happen to people who are younger in age. This pattern isn't new: young people have always used drugs and even experienced nonfatal overdoses since the first "initiation" into drug use often occurs in early teen years. The mortality rate is what's changing. Young people in America have often experimented and self-medicated with substances. But doing so has never been so deadly. These children's bodies are found in their bedrooms, lying on beanbag chairs, curled up under sheets that have cartoon characters on them, and sprawled on the family den rug. When their parents find them, they're baffled, horrified, stunned. How could such a horrible thing happen to a 14-year-old kid with no history of serious drug use, no access to street dealers, and no interest in self-harming or suicide?

This isn't the same as a seasoned street heroin user getting a hot shot. As Morgan Godvin told me, people who are regular users accept that there's a certain amount of risk that goes with their habit. With kids—some of whom are first-time users—that basic common sense isn't in place. The inherent dangers of illicit drug markets are unknown to them. The kids who overdose aren't consenting to using fentanyl. They're given the powerful opioid without their knowledge, in a pill pressed and marked to look identical to a pharmaceutical drug, and they die from taking a small amount they think is safe.

Parents, politicians, and law enforcement officers believe they have found a culprit: social media.

In January 2023, a group of parents, policymakers, social media executives, and law enforcement agents met for a roundtable event hosted by the House Energy and Commerce Committee—a committee newly controlled by Republicans since their party took over the House in the last election. With fentanyl spreading like wildfire, and young people increasingly vulnerable, the committee's goal was to create proposals that might protect kids online—and limit the liability protections for big online platforms like Facebook, Snapchat, TikTok, and Instagram.

Led by Rep. Cathy McMorris Rodgers (R-WA), the panel heard heartbreaking testimonies from parents and people who had lost loved ones to fentanyl. Grieving parents demanded justice for their children, but unfortunately, it's not as easy as flipping a switch and shutting down social media or going for the nuclear option in cyberspace—in the form of attacking an obscure telecommunications regulation from 1996 that protects platforms from liability. Pushing that red button would, in fact, place more lives at risk because it would mean that none of us would be able to share the critical information and resources online that drug policy reform and the recovery movement need.

The new category of fatal overdoses includes kids dying of deceptively marketed pills bought from strangers or anonymous dealers on apps like TikTok or Snapchat. Children purchase these substances without knowing what they are or what's in them. They're often sold as popular pharmaceuticals like Xanax or Percocet. But these fentanyl-laced counterfeit pills—and the deaths that result from taking them—don't appear out of thin air. Authorities do know what is out there, and they know about the danger. Health-care workers in emergency rooms, police departments, campus security officers, and the DEA all have information about the substances being sold on social media. In regions hit hard by fentanyl, the DEA might have a warning listed on their website, or even an emergency update from the medical examiner. But when was the last time a middle schooler thought to check a dot-gov website before buying anything online?

This lifesaving information isn't available where any child (or most parents) would think to look. During the pandemic, everyone got the message to social distance, wash their hands, and wear masks. Fake pills have received no such public health campaign. And yet, these fake pills are all over the place—and if you use social media, they're practically at your fingertips any time you touch your phone. The many groups and agencies that have information about where fentanyl is sold online don't work together, and children continue dying as a result.

Where do these pills come from? Law enforcement claims to be focused on arresting its way up the pyramid of drug dealers and catching the Sinaloa Cartel kingpins at the top. In a press release from 2022, DEA administrator Anne Milgram said, "The most urgent threat to our communities, our kids, and our families are the Sinaloa Cartel and CJNG [Jalisco New Generation Cartel], who are mass producing and supplying the fentanyl that is poisoning and killing Americans. The Sinaloa Cartel and CJNG are ruthless criminal organizations that use deception and treachery to drive addiction with complete disregard for human life. To save American lives, the DEA is relentlessly focused on defeating the Sinaloa Cartel and CJNG by degrading their operations to make it impossible for them to do business."

While these cartels may be part of the problem, are they actually distributing these drugs using social media—just as other types of dealers stand on street corners? We know that this bureaucratic model of drug distribution is becoming obsolete. Nowadays, the street corner is virtual, and people transfer money to dealers using Venmo. We know that most users "deal" to one another, sharing and selling small amounts of substances within their friend groups. Many of those who sell these pills are using themselves, which complicates the bright line that police and politicians like to draw between sympathetic drug users and malicious drug dealers. When drugs are bought anonymously, there's a higher risk of danger.

Owned by Snap, Inc., Snapchat is a popular social media app that enables users to exchange disappearing messages, short videos, and locations with one another. The anonymous and ephemeral nature of the platform makes it hard to trace drug dealers—in part because it doesn't seem to prioritize safety features, and in part because it isn't required to reveal internal data or other information to law enforcement or concerned parents.

At the House Energy and Commerce Committee, Spokane County sheriff John Nowels said that his office invests heavily in tech to investigate fentanyl transactions. They track dealers on Snapchat, TikTok, Facebook, Instagram, and other encrypted services. He commented that it's common for dealers to have a presence on multiple platforms—thereby advertising to a wider variety of potential customers—but point buyers to their Snapchat accounts to make the actual sale. According to CNBC, Sheriff Nowels said it's "short-lived" once dealers realize other platforms are cooperating with law enforcement.

In searching for dealers, law enforcement isn't just coming up against the design of certain social media platforms. The way an app works can protect a user's privacy—for better or for worse. Burner profiles, disappearing messages, and fake information are only part of the battle. The other barrier to finding and prosecuting criminals is the law itself. As explained by NPR, "Section 230 is a law that shields social media companies from most civil lawsuits linked to content on their platforms created by users—including users engaged in criminal activity."

While most people have never heard of Section 230, it governs every online interaction. The 20-year-old law is a section of Title 47 of the United States Code enacted as part of the United States Communications Decency Act. It protects website platforms from being held responsible for the content posted on them. What is shared—from public posts to private messages—is considered a type of speech. However, it isn't protected speech like distributing published materials or sharing your opinion in a public space. It isn't First Amendment speech. It's more like "talk." And what people say can really hurt them.

Section 230 has felt increasingly relevant since the Trump era, with people conflating their right to express their opinions online with "free speech." (Pro tip: They're not the same thing.) The assumption that saying anything, anywhere, to anyone will not have consequences is naive and ignorant. That's just not how society works. Section 230 is a way for apps and websites to distance themselves from being held responsible for what is said—or sold—by their users. For example, if a QAnon group plans and enacts a traitorous insurrection in Washington, DC,[2] the website that hosted this group has immunity. They can't be prosecuted for what people post online.

In the case of the January 6, 2021, insurrection and Capitol riots, a mob forcibly entered the Capitol building as part of a seven-part plan by Trump to overturn the election results. Their goal was to keep Trump in power by preventing a joint session of Congress from counting the Electoral College votes to formalize the victory of President-elect Joe Biden. The 9,400 insurrectionists, which included at least 19 current and former Republican state legislators, neo-Nazis wearing swastikas, Blue Lives Matter members, and representatives of other hate groups, used apps like Twitter and Telegram to communicate with one another before and during the attack.

But while the social apps were implicated in the insurrection, they weren't punished for their role in the attack. If two Proud Boys conspire against the federal government in their Twitter DMs, Twitter isn't legally liable—but it does become the social media giant's problem once people pick up their tiki torches.

The law protects social media apps like Snapchat and TikTok from being prosecuted for whatever illegal activities take place on their sites. That includes being an unintentional marketplace for the sale of fake prescription pills. If someone dies because they bought fentanyl-laced drugs on Snapchat, that isn't Snapchat's fault; it's a "buyer beware" situation. The issue is driven by ignorance, and ignorance is a good problem because it can be solved by education. This may seem like a long-shot example, but when it comes to fentanyl, arguments tend to run to extremes. There is no black-and-white solution either—just a solid wall of gray. While an overdose death, a violent and traitorous mob, and sex work may not seem to have much in common, they all come together under the same umbrella of Section 230.

So, let's backtrack for a moment. Section 230 isn't the outright villain it's made out to be, and could actually become a vital tool in combating the overdose epidemic. To understand why, we have to understand how it works—and how it doesn't. On its first major appearance in the press, Section 230 wasn't even nominally about democracy. It wasn't about drugs either. It was about sex trafficking.

One of the most recent instances of a high-profile attempt to rewrite Section 230 was called Public Law 115–164, better known as FOSTA/SESTA. Claiming to want to protect children and vulnerable people from being abducted and trafficked, advocates pressured lawmakers into passing this law in 2017. The law amended Section 230 by holding websites and online platforms responsible for user content that might facilitate sexual exploitation. Although the Department of Justice went on record warning that FOSTA/SESTA would actually make it more difficult to prosecute sex trafficking cases, it was passed anyway. (Imagine that.)

Disaster ensued. Instant crackdowns were implemented by websites, but—surprise, surprise—they failed to slow sex trafficking. In fact, the law was only used *once* by federal prosecutors, who said they didn't really need it. They were able to use other, already existing, laws to prosecute sex-trafficking offenses in the past.

However, while FOSTA/SESTA did nothing to help potential victims or catch traffickers, it had an immediate, negative effect on another vulnerable group: sex workers. According to the Government Accountability Office, the Department of Justice (DOJ) brought at least 11 criminal cases against those who control platforms in the online sex market, including three cases against those who control Backpage.com, between 2014 and 2020.[3]

Backpage.com was a centralized, moderated online hub for sex-related entertainment and services. (This was before Pornhub and OnlyFans became household names, and online sex work became as commonplace as student loan payments.) When Backpage was taken down, providers were pushed to other platforms and lost the tools that ensured their safety while working. A study by Hacking// Hustling on both online and street-based groups of sex workers showed that FOSTA/SESTA has had a detrimental effect on online sex workers' financial stability, safety, access to community, and health outcomes.[4]

Backpage functioned as a form of worker protection. Without the ability to vet clients, communicate with one another, and stay healthy, sex workers risked serious injury and death every time they accepted a gig. In the weeks following the passage of FOSTA/

SESTA, sex workers died. Three women were reported murdered after turning to street work, dozens are reported to be missing, and violence against sex workers skyrocketed. Understanding a law like FOSTA/SESTA that merely changed some language of Section 230 is an important case study in unintended consequences. It's also a warning of what might happen if Section 230 gets rewritten again by those who want to curtail another illicit market: counterfeit pills. Knowing what happened to online sex workers after Section 230 was changed holds a lesson for what could happen in the realm of drugs online.

While sex work is considered taboo, it is a common way for people to support themselves. In Portland, Oregon, which has the most strip clubs per capita in the United States, there is a running joke that you need a master's degree to dance on a pole. Many of the performers and dancers are mothers, wives, entrepreneurs, and homeowners. Stripping is steady money, with some sex workers earning six figures—easily double the incomes of the executives who throw singles at them during the lunch shift. Cam workers can earn $85,000 to $200,000 annually, with highly sought-after performers earning as much as $1,000 per minute. In-person sex work pays comparably, depending on the service and type of relationship between the worker and the client. One escort in Nevada earned more than $1.2 million in 2019. (And yes, they all advertise or promote their availability on social media.)

Before Backpage, Craigslist was the go-to space to find or market sex-related services. Until 2009, Craigslist had a section of the website called "erotic services." In this section, people openly advertised sex—selling or seeking—sometimes with an à la carte menu that included prices.

In 2009, an engaged medical student in Boston named Philip Markoff was arrested and held for murdering Julissa Brisman, whom he offered to pay for a massage; physically attacking Cynthia Melton, a stripper, whose husband intervened in the attack; and committing armed robbery against a third woman named Trisha Leffler, who also advertised massage services. Evidence discovered in Markoff's hotel room suggested a pattern of violence against sex workers.

Because of Section 230, Craigslist was not charged for Julissa's death or any other crimes committed using the site. (Markoff committed suicide while he was held for trial.) Craigslist changed the section's name to "adult services" and promised stricter screening, then eventually stopped listing ads for "adult services" in 2010. It finally shuttered its personals section altogether when FOSTA/SESTA surfaced in 2017.

While some people are quick to say that sex work is the problem, I don't think that is true. A 2015 study by Law Street Media found 58 murderers and 45 murder victims connected to Craigslist postings since 2009—after the "erotic services" page was shut down. As of 2015, there were 22 murder cases still pending, according to the study. The oldest pending case was from 2012, and eight were from 2014. This suggests that violence, danger, and lack of protection are more of an issue than two consenting adults exchanging cash for companionship.

"Social media and websites are just as important to sex workers as they are to plumbers. Anyone who does direct service deserves to know who their client is," said one escort, who preferred to keep her name private. "If you're a contractor, you're either getting your clients from off the internet or you are being referred by word-of-mouth. Is this person going to pay you on time? Do they have a dangerous dog in their house, a gun, or a bad temper? Are they going to lock you in the basement? With sex work, it's the same thing. Either Backpage is going to tell you that this person is safe, or your friends are. Without those two resources, you end up being either ripped off or murdered."

In 2017, the Yelp equivalent for sex workers was Backpage. The website made it possible to openly discuss bad dates, identify pred-ators, and check in with one another. Then, these basic protections people needed were suddenly gone.

The people endangered by FOSTA/SESTA were parents, bread-winners, and community members—middle-aged moms in six-inch Pleasers. A Rhode Island sex worker rights group called Coyote RI surveyed 260 sex workers and showed that 77 percent used sex work for their sole income, and 75 percent were supporting one to three dependents. Within two weeks of Backpage going down, a quarter of these people said they were unable to support themselves or their dependents; 6 to 10 percent were facing eviction; 30 percent had stopped screening clients; and 60 percent had taken sessions with unsafe clients they would not have normally seen. Desperation and lack of resources and support put workers and their families at risk. FOSTA/SESTA was supposed to save lives. Instead, it killed people and drove others deep underground.

To me, FOSTA/SESTA felt like a "won't somebody think of the children" attempt to harm marginalized people—like sex workers, people in recovery, and other groups—under the banner of a seem-ingly virtuous cause. But these symbolic attempts have real-world material consequences. In May 2023, the United States Supreme Court unanimously upheld Section 230 in two decisions, citing that any change to the law could break the basic functions of many websites and potentially create many risks for internet users. "The very fact that the justices are proceeding cautiously is a good sign and suggests a more nuanced understanding of these issues than many feared," Evelyn Douek, an assistant professor at Stanford Law School, told CNN.

The reality is that online platforms already limit third-party user content, suspend people's accounts, and prevent resource sharing—all in the name of following the law. Proposals to amend Section 230 fail to consider the role online platforms play in supporting margin-alized communities—including recovery and harm reduction—and present a narrow, reductionist view of engagement around substance use on platforms. Section 230, as it was originally written, provides protection not just to corporations but to companies, news organizations, creators of all stripes, political activists, nonprofits, libraries, educators, governments, and regular users—including people who work on the front lines of the overdose crisis.

When Chad Sabora started working in harm reduction, he worked out of his car. The beat-up sedan with Missouri plates was a familiar sight in neighborhoods where substance users, especially people who used IV drugs, lived. Chad had been in recovery for years and experienced firsthand how to survive the hell of addiction: He knew clean syringes prevented disease transmission, using with another person prevented overdoses, and testing drugs before using them saved lives. He also knew that often, users were interested in recovery and harm reduction resources, and that a well-timed pep talk could change the course of a person's life.

As social media took off, Chad tried to replicate his harm reduction efforts online. It should have been a success. Statistically, millions of Americans use opioids—recreationally and by prescription. Addiction affects one in three homes, and overdose rates have skyrocketed, killing hundreds every day. Naloxone, an overdose-reversing medication, is essential to saving lives. Chad was confident that he could use Facebook and other social media tools to help educate people about harm reduction, share resources, and reach people in need. Instead, he found himself silenced—by the same algorithms that target sex workers, political organizers, and drug traffickers. His educational tips were being flagged and blocked.

Sharing information is what social media is for. When a bad batch comes through town, you'll see the warnings pop up all over the place. Fentanyl disguised as Xanax, MDMA pills laced with meth. Social media is how people get the word out. It can be a life-saving tool for people who use drugs. However, that door swings both ways. The free exchange of information means that people have a chance to protect themselves and their friends from fatal overdoses.

Fentanyl is involved in 79 percent of Gen Z drug deaths, and teens are one of the fastest rising segments of the overdose crisis. They are extremely comfortable with technology; many of them have spent their entire lives online. (Kids of this generation don't even have baby books anymore, but every single moment is documented on their parents' social media pages.) Children get cell phones and social media profiles at an early age and learn about issues like cyberbullying and stranger danger in a different way than I did, way back in the 1980s. It's a different world, with new and unexpected risks—not to mention much, much higher stakes.

Bonnie Sawyer, executive director of the Herren Project, a national organization committed to the prevention of and recovery from addiction, said that in order to support young people, we should look at the protective and risk factors that lead to resilience at both the individual and community level.

She said, "Knowledge, awareness, and access to resources are powerful protective tools, but they are detrimental when they bring hysteria and anxiety. Young people today already have a full plate of social pressures, expectations, and insecurities to cope with in a world challenged by social media, war, global warming, and the pandemic."

Ed and Mary Ternan know from personal experience that these deaths are unexpected and world shattering. Their youngest son, Charlie, a college student studying economics at Santa Clara University, overdosed in May 2020, during the early days of the pandemic. He was one of many seniors who decided to stay around campus for a last hurrah—a group of around 1,500 students. Charlie wasn't naive or new to substances or partying, and a back injury meant he was familiar with prescription opioids. In fact, the pill that killed him was a fake Percocet. He was struggling with pain the day of his death and hoping to be more comfortable for a job interview he was looking forward to. However, the pill wasn't what the dealer said it was. Charlie and a friend bought from a dealer on Snapchat: they asked for Xanax, and Charlie opportunistically got some Percocet at the same time.

His friend stuck with Xanax, and Charlie took the fake Perc. He died in his fraternity house. His parents, along with Charlie's friends, relatives, community, and thousands of students, reeled from the loss.

"He was the Big Man on Campus," Ed said. "We all grieved him together. They had lights everywhere, people on the lawns holding candles. It was a big deal. We're a legacy family at Santa Clara, and Charlie came from a Catholic high school that was a big feeder school."

He and Mary knew that their son wouldn't want them to seek revenge. But they couldn't ignore the impact of his legacy on their family or the young people who were still out there taking risks. Ed and Mary founded Song for Charlie, a nonprofit that works with social media apps, families, colleges, and youth to educate people about the risks of "fentapills."

Ed said, "We're trying to get young people to learn about the new chemical drug landscape and motivate them to protect their friends. You don't want this to happen to anyone you love. It becomes an empowering message. Coming off the heels of COVID, we tried to make it clear to young people that this fentanyl crisis is not your fault. It's not their generation's fault. The grown-ups haven't figured this out in fifty to one hundred years, and they are directly impacted by our failure. We believe that you can have an impact if you own the solution."

By working closely with Snapchat—Ed sits on Snap's global safety advisory board, and several executives from different social media companies are members of the Song for Charlie board—the Ternans hope to change the way young people make decisions about drugs.

"Social media is where young people, pandemic or no, conduct all their social transactions," Ed said. "That's where they set meetups, gossip, and whisper about parents and teachers. As long as the kids are there, these drug marketers will go where the kids are. There's this narrative that persists about drug deaths, which is the 'fellow user' story. If someone dies of an OD, it's now assumed that the person who furnished the substance was partying with the person using with them, known to them, maybe a friend, addicted themselves. The narrative suggests that the overdose was an accident. Two people knew the risks; one died. But, in the age of social media, we know that this isn't always true anymore. Many drug transactions are between strangers."

Ed pointed out that the cultural landscape continues to shift, and the only way to help people is to stay ahead of those changes as much as possible. When he and Mary pursued a resolution to Charlie's overdose, they were surprised by how much information was out there about fentanyl—and how much of it was in all the wrong places. They reached out to Snap's executives, finally meeting with them in February 2021.

"We said, 'People are selling fake pills on your platform, and kids are dying. This is not good for you,'" Ed said.

Snapchat's response? "We don't allow drug sales on our platform."

The Ternans explained that the gap between what is allowed and what really happens online is potentially lethal. They explained that the drugs being sold aren't real; instead, people were unknowingly buying potent opioids. Snapchat created a research initiative that confirmed these risks. Instead of burying the data, they worked with Song for Charlie to put together an awareness program called Heads Up. If someone searches for the word "percocet," the first thing that comes up is a portal that says "No drugs, no judgment." The portal includes educational content about drugs, substance use support, and information about the risks.

The social media giant switched from making drug dealing on Snap a reported content moderation harm—something most platforms implement to passively track problematic users or inter-actions—to proactive patrolling of the site. Compared with many of the harms social media apps are trying to address, such as child sex trafficking, bullying, pornography, teen mental health, and other issues, tracking down a couple of kids buying or selling weed was a fairly low priority. However, Snap soon understood that relying on user reports wasn't enough. To actively detect drug content, Snap started using machine learning to remove it before it is seen.

"The outcome is that the number of drug ads you'd see from dealers is reduced dramatically," Ed said. "They can take it down, save it, or report it to law enforcement. They flip from a passive ap-proach to an active approach."

If what Snap is saying is true about their efforts to reduce drug dealing, this could save many lives. But social media companies and their algorithms remain a black box to the public. The only way we'll know for sure that it's working is in the years to come, if we see re-ductions in counterfeit pill deaths among young people, and if we hear fewer parents share the horror of losing a child because they bought a fake pill online. Under Section 230, social media platforms don't have to do anything to limit users' behaviors. They simply hang a sign over the bar that says "no drugs" and wash their hands of the consequences. In this context, Snapchat's initiative is the equivalent of banning drug dealers from hanging out in your bar and making sure that anyone looking for a fix knows what they're getting into.

Mary Ternan said, "We really believe that we have to reimagine the drug conversation in America in order to save lives. We've con-nected with all kinds of people from all over this issue. We come in with fresh eyes, no institutional bias, and a background in prod-uct and programming development. We don't want to be judgmen-tal or say 'don't do drugs.' Instead, we're teaching young people to avoid the harm of fake pills. Young people appreciate being given the credit to figure stuff out. They don't want to be told what to do; they just need the info. So, we point them to a place to learn more on their own and connect them with resources."

Being able to share those resources freely and without shaming users is key to saving lives. When people can't speak openly about their needs, it is impossible to get help or share information. Young people may feel that they are individually invincible, but they care immensely about their friends' safety.

"The guy online sees you as a dollar sign," Mary Ternan said. "You can't trust him to tell you the truth. When we meet with groups for Q&As and speaking events, we will say that drug selling has become more institutionalized. In Charlie's case, when someone ventures out there into the world of buying drugs online, they are one step removed from a really dark underworld. This is not like buying from your high school buddy with a big brother who can get weed from the dispensary. Charlie dipped his toe into that world one day for an hour, and it cost him his life."

Using proactive monitoring may be a solution that both protects free speech and users. Historically, efforts to clamp down on the communication of online drug sales through Section 230 carve-outs have overlooked or straight-up omitted recovery advocates' voices. (For minorities, members of the LGBTQ+ community, and others sitting at the intersection of multiple marginalized groups, the consequences of limited speech are often compounded.) Banning certain words doesn't work. Taking a black-and-white approach to stopping drug sales online is shown to be misguided for many reasons—not least of which is that people determined to buy or sell substances will always find a way around the barriers. Erasing substance-related information endangers the recovery community, and threatens to stifle productive speech that is critical for progress to combat the overdose crisis.

More speech, not less, is the answer.

Back in St. Louis, Chad Sabora noticed the impact of FOSTA/

SESTA almost immediately. He used social media to have real and meaningful conversations about substance use. However, his posts were flagged for violating the platform's rules. If he talked about the basics of harm reduction, such as fentanyl testing or naloxone, his account was disabled. Mentioning drugs—instant suspension. Even though he had a standing order from the state of Missouri and a doctor on staff at Missouri Network for Opiate Reform and Recovery, he was blocked from sharing any information about recovery online.

He wasn't saying anything untrue or spreading dangerous information, but the platforms he was using to help others couldn't tell the difference. There is no gray area on these platforms; they find and block particular words, phrases, or speech patterns. Harm reduction efforts and conversations need to be nuanced, empathetic, and specific to the individual, aiming to minimize the harms of substance use. Blanket content bans, prescribed without consideration of context and nuance, could punish those in recovery, hamstringing legitimate, proven approaches to combating overdoses.

Chad said, "I've been put in time-out just for posting about naloxone."

Proposed Section 230 carve-outs, similar to what many members of Congress consider a misguided solution to the fentanyl crisis, have undermined access to these resources, mandating takedowns of broad categories of content, and forcing vulnerable populations, including those navigating recovery, off-platform. For criminalized communities, from sex workers to substance users, the risk of exploitation and harm offline is significant. Support and resources are already limited. Censorship only creates more barriers and costs human lives.

The ongoing aftermath of FOSTA/SESTA underscores the potential consequences of blunt, broad Section 230 carve-outs. These amendments are intended to prevent harm. However, they do not live up to their stated purpose, nor are they needed to protect people—as the surge in fentanyl deaths underscores.

Most leading platforms where these conversations take place

have clear rules prohibiting the online sale and promotion of drugs and controlled substances. Those guidelines work, especially when there are real live people moderating groups, rather than word-targeted algorithms. Snapchat recently rolled out a chatbot program called My AI that can answer simple questions or respond in a conversational way to users. I entered the sentence "my friend sold me drugs," and it responded:

> *I'm sorry to hear that your friend sold you drugs. It's important to remember that drug use is illegal and can have serious consequences. If you feel comfortable doing so, you may want to talk to your friend about how their actions made you feel and encourage them to seek help if they're struggling with addiction. If you're feeling overwhelmed or need additional support, there are many resources available to help you, including counseling services and support groups. Remember, you deserve to be safe and healthy, and there are people who care about you and want to help you through this difficult time.*

This is a long way from the ban-and-burn strategies of FOSTA/SESTA. But this type of compassionate, accessible, and universal support should just be the beginning.

Companies continue to improve the scale of this shift. They should implement more measures to prevent government intervention and avoid mandating regulatory changes that could actually cause more harm. When best-practice suggestions become law and are applied without nuance, people suffer. For example, in 2016, the CDC applied new guidelines to opioid prescribing. These former guidelines were put in place in response to the overdose crisis—which only worsened, unaffected by these arbitrary thresholds. But pain patients suffered under the new limits because they were unable to get the medications they needed to manage their medical conditions. Some patients were even forced to taper off their medications. In 2022, the CDC updated these guidelines to try and mitigate the disaster they'd caused in the previous six years. That's an example of a knee-jerk regulatory reaction causing a crisis—and needing a lot of effort and money to fix it.

The same types of "guidelines" force people like Chad Sabora back to street-level support. Rather than sharing scientifically grounded, evidence-based information for free online, Chad's recovery support actions are criminalized. Like the people he helps, he is pushed into the shadows and cut off from resources. That's why Congress should be careful when crafting content moderation regulations around substance use disorders. Any legislation in this area must ensure that policymakers are engaging members of recovery and harm reduction communities to assess potential harm. Companies are likely to shut down all related conversations to avoid liability, chilling free speech in the process.

Choosing an emotionally charged subject like fentanyl, sex trafficking, or an anti-government insurrection to push another Section 230 amendment through hurts all of us. It's clear that these amendments don't stop illegal or even dangerous activity. It hasn't stopped overdoses. It has only made life harder for people desperately trying to survive. And it prevents people from helping one another.

There's a world of difference between a clean syringe exchange and a drug deal. Until our government—and our social media companies—recognizes that, we will continue to lose friends, loved ones, neighbors, and family members to preventable overdoses. Not because they wanted to die. But because they were silenced, and separated from the people who were trying to reach them.

Instead of crushing free speech and pushing social media companies to eliminate our ability to share resources, the US government should focus its efforts on things that work. FOSTA/SESTA didn't stop sex trafficking, and cracking down on Snapchat won't end overdose deaths. To save lives, policymakers should create a national strategy to combat the overdose crisis. Don't kill the conversation. Instead, we need to coordinate with localities to identify authentic places for support. We need to help platforms coordinate on identifying and removing bad actors, and work with law enforcement to identify and prosecute large-scale drug traffickers.

Like fentanyl, social media is a convenient boogeyman. However, I believe it is like any other public utility. We don't outlaw sidewalks because drug dealers use them as drop points. We don't outlaw cell phones because human traffickers use them to entice underage children into unsafe situations. Targeting a tool that's being misused is not the same as stopping the person misusing it.

Ed said, "With social media, people don't understand how those things work. There's a perception that it's magic or witchcraft, or that the people at these platforms can decide to do whatever they want. Most folks think an 'algorithm' is an all-powerful universal law. In reality, there's more to it. At the end of the day, if we're going to talk to young people, we have to go where they are, speak their language, and get them talking to each other. Where they are is social media. That's why we don't consider ourselves political advocates. There's no pounding the table about policy."

Instead of seeking revenge against drug dealers, and pressing lawmakers to "get tough on drugs" and lock everybody up, the Ternans are singularly focused on saving lives through education. They are charting a different path for parents to take, based in compassion and understanding, rather than fear tactics and punishment that have repeatedly been shown to backfire and cause more problems than they solve.

Using social media for good—to connect law enforcement, recovery, educational, and policy efforts—might just turn the tide of the fentanyl crisis. As with every other tool of transformation, it isn't about who has the loudest voice or even who talks the most. It's about ensuring that the internet remains a place where information can be free. Going in hard on a solution that limits online speech will only cause these companies to implement broad category bans (including addiction and overdose), pushing people offline and into the line of fire.

10

TEAM AMERICA

Over a four-year period, Morris & Dickson shipped 12,000 unusually large orders of opioids to pharmacies and hospitals. The Shreveport, Louisiana–based company, which was registered with the DEA, didn't seem to find anything strange or suspicious about the size or frequency of these orders; they just kept on shipping opioids, from fentanyl to hydrocodone. They are the fourth-largest wholesale drug distributor, right behind Cardinal Health, AmerisourceBergen, and McKesson—all of whom had similar violations to Morris & Dickson and were ordered to pay a combined $21 billion over 18 years to resolve claims as part of the opioid settlement that includes other drug manufacturers. Morris & Dickson rakes in $4 billion annually in revenue; their clients include pharmacies and hospitals in 29 states.

Between 2014 and 2018, the company filed just three suspicious order reports with the DEA, according to AP News. Those huge orders didn't raise any red flags; yet, alarm bells should have been ringing. Large orders tend to fall off the truck. They end up making their way into the black market. You can't "control" a "controlled substance" if you can't account for where it is, who has it, and how safe it is.

But that didn't seem to bother Morris & Dickson. Then-president Paul Dickson Sr. said in 2019 that the company's compliance program was "dang good." He also said that he didn't think a "single person has gotten hurt by [their] drugs." Apparently, that was enough of a vote of confidence for the DEA, who didn't think to double-check the distributor's records until 2023. Usually, DEA decisions and investigations take two years or less. In this case, action is more than overdue.

Paul Senior's "dang good" compliance comments were backed by Morris & Dickson's then–compliance consultant, Louis Milione. He was hired in 2018 as part of a $3 million contract that was supposed to implement an "ideal" compliance program. If the name "Milione" sounds familiar, it's because he was previously the principal director of the DEA, second-in-command to DEA administrator Anne Milgram. Milione began work as a consultant when he retired from the DEA in 2017 after a 21-year career that included two years of managing the division that oversees the sale of highly addictive narcotics—such as the ones distributed by Morris & Dickson. In the four-year gap following his retirement in 2017, Milione worked as a consultant for some of the companies he was once in charge of regulating. Then, he returned to the DEA in 2021 to work under Milgram. In July 2023, Milione quietly stepped down amid news reports about his work for Morris & Dickson, as well as Purdue Pharma.

According to AP News, when Morris & Dickson's credibility was first called into question, Milione testified that the company "spared no expense" to overhaul its compliance systems, cancel suspicious orders, and send daily emails to the DEA spelling out its actions. Considering the massive number of undocumented infractions, unaccounted-for shipments, and other violations, it might have been more accurate to say that the drug distributor spared no expense in whom it hired. The compliance system, whatever it was, clearly didn't work—which makes me wonder what Milione really provided for his $3 million.

Conflicts of interest, like hiring former DEA leadership into the private sector and using agency relationships to avoid accountability, reveal how ineffective the DEA really is. Almost a decade after the first suspicious shipment, we finally have a report—which is essentially the DEA investigating itself through the work of one of its former or current administrators or agents. And all we know is that somebody made a mistake.

We still don't know where the missing pills are.

At the same time, the DEA is hell-bent on restricting a different type of medication: buprenorphine. This medication is considered the gold standard of treatment for OUD, right up there with methadone. While not dangerous and rarely misused—in fact, the FDA approved a delayed-release injection option as well as a pill—this substance is as highly stigmatized as the condition it treats. As a result, people who need these medications must navigate a different set of rules to get a lifesaving prescription. Accessing care could mean complying with stringent regulations, including in-person doctor visits, picking up medication from certified pharmacists, or agreeing to be included in a drug user database, among other draconian measures.

Every single dose is accounted for—unlike the opioids that Morris & Dickson released into the market without the appropriate or required oversight. Yet, in spite of the scrupulous regulation of buprenorphine, the DEA is trying to make it even harder to get. On February 24, 2023, the DEA announced a set of new federal telemedicine guidelines that would roll back access to this medication. The rules would limit telemedicine prescriptions for buprenorphine to a single 30-day supply. Under the DEA's proposed guidelines, any new patient who starts their treatment via telemedicine must find and see an in-person provider in order to renew their prescription beyond the initial 30 days.

Over ten thousand people spoke out against these proposed rules in April 2023, hoping to extend telemedicine access to addiction treatment medications such as buprenorphine. At a time when more than 111,000 people die annually from opioid overdoses, creating excessive limits on prescription medications for opioid addiction seems backward. But then, that seems to be the DEA's style.

While they seem to have no problem allowing a massive corporation to ship and sell opioids without oversight, the DEA rules for telemedicine patients show that the agency is determined to make sure every single person in need of treatment for OUD has to jump through every single hoop they can think of. That is a high-stakes process for those of us who need access to care. A large multisite study in 2009 showed that 87 percent of OUD patients who tapered off buprenorphine over a 28-day period returned to opioid use within three months. A 2011 study showed that 93 percent of OUD patients who completed a shortened four-week course of buprenorphine treatment returned to active opioid misuse. A Swedish study on heroin addiction from 2003 found that one year after a six-day taper off buprenorphine, 100 percent of these patients dropped out of treatment for OUD—and 20 percent of them had died. It's clear that the potential consequences of being unable to continue buprenorphine treatment beyond 30 days are recurrence of use, overdose, and death.

The DEA exists "to enforce the controlled substances laws and regulations of the United States and bring to the criminal and civil justice system of the United States, or any other competent jurisdiction, those organizations and principal members of organizations, involved in the growing, manufacture, or distribution of controlled substances appearing in or destined for illicit traffic in the United States; and to recommend and support non-enforcement programs aimed at reducing the availability of illicit controlled substances on the domestic and international markets." In plain English, this means that their purpose is to stop drug dealers from making, growing, and selling harmful substances.

Yet, the agency shows time and time again that they can't fulfill this mission. They crack down on people trying to recover, and look the other way when opioid distributors break regulations to rake in billions in revenue. In this scenario, the person trying to get a tele-medicine prescription for buprenorphine is treated like a criminal. The corporation might pay a fine—or hire another former DEA admin as a helpful and willing consultant. The consequences are inequitable, as are the methods. The DEA claims to be "protecting people." But whom are they really protecting when they cut off access to life-saving care in the middle of a devastating epidemic?

"If we have a public health or medical concern, why is it enforced by an institution that has the power to incarcerate?" says Saeeda Dunston. She is the executive director at Elmcor Youth and Services Activities, Inc., in the East Elmhurst/Corona area of Queens, New York. As a Black woman with a background in harm reduction who runs a community service nonprofit, her work places her on the bleeding edge of the drug epidemic. It also makes her highly attuned to the racialized and carceral barriers that prevent people from getting help.

She says that the barriers created and enforced by groups like the DEA are aimed at preventing certain types of people (that is, Black and brown people, people with criminalized illnesses, and lower-income or unhoused people) from getting help. The DEA specifically targets these groups—all of which show incredible resilience and improvement when given access to the resources they need. The DEA does that by honing in on medications like buprenorphine and methadone, which are associated with addiction. Yet, these medications are much less harmful to the body than many other lifesaving drugs.

Saeeda explained that when her mother had a brain tumor, Saeeda was responsible for picking up the chemotherapy medication her mother needed to fight the cancer.

She said, "There is nothing more poisonous than chemotherapy. This medication is more powerful and more potent than any street drug. Every time I got the prescription, I would be picking up some-thing that would literally attack my mother's insides. What stops me from misusing it to harm myself or end my own life?"

The difference, she said, was the DEA.

Cancer isn't a criminal illness. You can't get arrested for having it, and your medication won't get your name added to a mandated list of known drug users. Unlike methadone, physician-directed cancer care can cause you to become very sick and weak, and even die. Cancer treatments remove body parts, decimate your immune system, and can have long-term impacts on your fertility, physical abilities, and other basic functions. Yet, nobody would think of preventing a cancer patient from undergoing every option for treat-ment, including genetic testing, cancer screenings, chemotherapy, radiation, and surgery. These are widely accepted as lifesaving inter-ventions; if you're newly diagnosed, you're rushed into the ecosystem of care and offered every treatment option that may prolong or save your life, regardless of how toxic or debilitating those options may be, because the benefits far outweigh the risks.

We can't say the same for addiction treatment. While the DEA claims to be protecting Americans from unregulated substances and shutting down cartels, it looks like what they're really doing is punishing terminally ill people for being sick. The mission is a failure. And it looks to me like the DEA needs a few doses of its own medicine.

Since its founding in 1973, the DEA has intercepted a fraction of one percent of illicit drug trades. (I'd love to know what happened with the other 99.) Using their federally granted powers, DEA agents have arrested, tortured, and murdered countless innocent people. In the *American Institute for Economic Research*, Laura Williams wrote, "The DEA's punitive prohibition of cocaine precipitated the spread of crack. The DEA's misguided attempts to reduce opiate misuse fueled an overdose epidemic."

The agency not only fueled the epidemic, but arguably, they

helped create it. As you'll read in this chapter, they've smuggled drugs, diverted public health funds, and taken bribes from drug cartels. They may be a federal agency, but they act like a cartel themselves. Corruption, big-ticket "consultants," and special deals for corporations are just scratching the surface. The DEA is fighting with itself: setting up a straw man and knocking it down, again and again, all while claiming victory and cutting itself yet another check.

Over the decades, the agency has been caught again and again taking from the community purse to bankroll a toxic, endless drug war, while preaching the gospel of the "War on Drugs." This form of deliberate incompetence is not only irresponsible. It's life-threatening.

If the DEA was really doing its job, it would be working overtime to put itself out of business. But anyone who knows about abuse of power knows that that's the last thing corrupt officials want to do. It's my opinion that the DEA's failure to end the drug war is no accident. It's the natural outcome of irresponsible programming, mass fraud and corruption, and misuse of American tax dollars— all while refusing to cop to these shortcomings so they could keep doing whatever they wanted. Whistleblower José Irizarry, a former award-winning DEA agent convicted of 19 counts of corruption and fraud in 2020, confirmed that this behavior was "business as usual" for the institution.

Irizarry told reporters that his elite "Team America" group of DEA agents abused government funding and resources, falsified reports, made up stats to make the agency look good, and used so-called work trips for personal travel and entertainment. He estimated that 90 percent of the team's travel was "bogus" but could be justified by saying it was "case-related."

"DEA is a game. Drug war is a game," Irizarry told the AP. "It was a very fun game that we were playing . . . We know we're not making a difference."

Well, the DEA *is* making a difference. But it isn't the one their mission promises. Annually, the agency blows through a budget of $3 billion. This is a fraction of the total cost of enforcement, which is estimated to be $100 billion—a number that includes $25.7 billion in state and local funds. (At the same time, Irizarry's arrest triggered an audit, which revealed that the DEA hadn't submitted annual reports to Congress about their undercover operations since 2006 or earlier.)

With so much cash, you'd think the DEA would put an agent on every street corner and in every school. Nope. Among other shady practices, the agency uses its budget to launder tens of millions of dollars a year on behalf of the world's most violent drug cartels, according to former federal prosecutor Bonnie Klapper. José Irizarry's arrest showed that agents used laundered money to track cartel connections through banks. However, in this process, they became complicit in the cartels' business operations.

Bonnie said, "For every dollar we laundered, we had to seize two. If not, we shut the operation down. Meaning if we had to launder $1 million, we better have seized $2 million . . . Launder more money, seize more money, launder more money, take more trips to Europe. Take nice trips all over the world, and seize more money."

Enabling drug traffickers and paying agents to "play both sides" while lining their own pockets is antithetical to the DEA's mission. (Of course, that hasn't stopped them.) At this point, the agency is starting to seem like a Russian doll of investigations. They investigate the investigators of the last investigation to learn if their investigation points to a need for more investigation. It's ridiculous—a circus. And while they're clowning around, juggling the facts, and making money disappear, people are dying. If the person who's supposed to stop your child from overdosing on fentanyl is helping a drug cartel move the same pills into your town—then whom can you count on to do the right thing?

"It's always the moms," Sue Ousterman said. "Society is toxic? Don't worry. The moms will fix it."

Loving her son Tyler Cordeiro through the last months of his life tested Sue's limits—and what she believed she, as a mother, was capable of. Tyler tried getting help numerous times, and he was stymied by bureaucracy and red tape, again and again. Sue stands staunchly against the renewed push for more intense criminalization. She believes more arrests and prosecution feeds into the stigma that her son Tyler felt, and in turn, that stigma creates shame and secrets that prevent people from asking for help when they need it. Stigma also permeates the health-care system, and because Tyler used drugs, she believes he was discriminated against.

He was so much more than his illness. Sue's son was her "mini-me," she said. From birth, he and Sue shared a special bond. At times, they'd look at each other and just laugh—they were so close that their thoughts were often the same, jokes and all. Tyler was a beautiful soul, authentic and kind. Like his mom, he was an advocate who stood up for people who were being bullied or excluded. His big heart had room for many friends and family members. Sue remembers how excited he was to start a family of his own someday—to be a dad.

"When he was with you, he was *with* you," Sue said.

Yet, the same compassionate nature meant he could sometimes take on the world's pain. The inner hurts that led him to substance use never quite seemed to heal. Over time, they only worsened.

Tyler was on the streets in the Kensington neighborhood of Philadelphia during the first part of the COVID-19 pandemic. He was using opiates, unhoused, and extremely vulnerable to the coronavirus. When he contracted endocarditis, which inflamed the membrane and area around his heart, his mother thought it was COVID. He couldn't breathe and had chest pains, which ended in him being rushed to the ER.

Her son's life-threatening condition forced Sue to encounter the inhumane and unethical treatment that drug users routinely face when seeking help. Tyler was so sick that she needed to advocate for him—yet, due to COVID, she was unable to be with him in the hospital. He was left in the care of people who looked down on him and neglected him, even while he was in a hospital bed.

"The doctors were not transparent with me and denied him the surgery he needed," Sue said. She frantically searched for a surgeon who would be able to give Tyler the operation he needed and had him transferred to another facility. While he was recovering, she sent him cupcakes—he was turning 24. Two weeks later, Sue was finally allowed to visit her son. In a face mask, she sat by him, talked to him, and held his hand.

"The cupcakes I sent were still on the windowsill," she said. "He spent his last birthday on earth surrounded by hospital staff who didn't have enough humanity to acknowledge his special day."

The surgery wasn't enough to save Tyler's life. He returned home with a prescription for an antibiotic that cost $1,600 for a month's supply and no painkillers. He was supposed to recover from open-heart surgery with nothing stronger than Tylenol.

"God, he was suffering. I didn't realize it at the time because he tried so hard. *So hard*," Sue said. She described Tyler's weakness when he came home to recover from surgery.

The pain was unbearable. During open-heart surgery, doctors cut through the sternum and ribs with a short electric saw. The ribs are cracked open, leaving the body exposed like a standing roast. The body's tissues flood with adrenaline—even under anesthesia, the body's systems know when they're being bypassed—which can create unbelievable pain and cramping in the muscles.

After he was discharged from the hospital in July, Tyler didn't want to be on buprenorphine. He decided to try medical marijuana to manage his pain instead. At the end of August, he was incarcerated after being picked up on a bench warrant when he was a passenger in a car that was pulled over. (The bench warrant was issued after he missed a probation appointment while in the hospital. Ironically, this probation was for a possession of paraphernalia charge when he was caught with an unused syringe in 2018. Sue believes her son contracted endocarditis from reusing syringes, and this probation was a deterrent to Tyler using safer injection practices.) As a condition of Tyler's release, he had to live in a county-approved recovery home that did not allow the use of medical marijuana. This is when he relapsed. He attempted to go to detox, but learned his Medicaid had been unlawfully terminated while he was incarcerated. The county denied him funding for detox because he had a medical marijuana card, even though he offered to relinquish it.

It takes eight weeks to be 80 percent healed from open-heart surgery. Tyler passed exactly four months from the day he had surgery. In that time, he used every resource he could access. Every one of them failed him. The medical marijuana card prevented Tyler from accessing county funding for medical detox and treatment. While medical marijuana helped him manage his cravings for opioids, the federal/state policy conflict created more barriers. The lack of funding forced Tyler's family to pay out of pocket to a facility who claimed to be an inpatient rehab. (Sue ended up reporting them to the New Jersey Attorney General's office and they are now under investigation.) The message was clear: Can't get medical help? Tough luck. You're on your own.

Sue said, "For the first time, it was clear as day that there was nothing I could do, so I said, 'I'm just going to love him.'"

"He relapsed and came home so we could make a new plan," Sue said. "He went to get cigarettes and used in the gas station bathroom."

Tyler had been gone for 30 minutes when Sue went down the block to look for him. The EMTs were already there. They only gave him one dose of naloxone—not enough to stop this fatal overdose.

"They accused me of giving him drugs. I could see my son's dead body lying on that bathroom floor, and they wouldn't let me near him," Sue said.

After Tyler's funeral, she sat down and made a list of the reasons her son had died. She wrote down every factor that contributed to his death. It included the ignorance of their family doctor, profit-hungry pharmaceutical companies, and the noninvolvement of regulators, including the county, state, and federal governments. It was a problem that was too big for one person to solve—even a mom like Sue. But she still tried to get the wheels in motion. After an intense phone call with the president of a drug-induced homicide organization, Sue was invited to attend the DEA's Inaugural Family Summit.

At first, it seemed like a step in the right direction. Two DEA agents sat at each table, while parents and loved ones listened to speakers and enjoyed a catered lunch. A young woman who worked for the agency provided outreach for families and invited Sue to come see the memorial wall of young people who'd lost their lives to fentanyl overdoses. She later reached out and asked Sue if Anne Milgram, DEA administrator since 2021, could use Tyler's story as an example of the barriers a person faces when trying to get treatment. The transparency and willingness to connect seemed promising.

Then came the regional summit. Here, the divisions between the parents and families were much more obvious. Some families stuck to the DEA's narrative that their children were "poisoned," which Sue didn't agree with. She saw the problem squarely as systemic. Her son, like many others, fell through the cracks of a system designed to traumatize and kill people, not help them heal. Sue said that the families all had the same culprit to blame for their children's deaths: the DEA, an agency that Sue says "killed all of these children." Yet, the agents she saw at the regional summit looked anything but ready to take responsibility for their part in the crisis.

"The agents looked so proud of themselves," Sue said. "They rolled out this big sign that said 'Drug Poisonings Not Overdoses.' There was no compassion. They were obviously being told to just use different words when they'd really prefer to lock people up."

Shortly after, Sue went to DC hoping to meet with Anne Milgram. As a decision-maker, Milgram's support and understanding would be key to stopping overdose deaths. Sue knew from her own experience and intensive study of drug policy relating to health care that the DEA's involvement was essential. While she was waiting to hear back from Milgram's office, Sue visited the memorial wall. It was not what she imagined.

"It was all white kids who overdosed. It felt ugly, like a wall of pride. Where are the other people who died as a result of problematic drug policy?"

Milgram never returned Sue's request for a meeting. The next time Sue saw her, it was on TV. Milgram spoke during a White House press conference on the DEA's commitment to expanding access to Medication-Assisted Treatment. Sue settled in at home to watch the update and was shocked to hear the story Milgram improvised while speaking Tyler's name.

"Tyler was poisoned by fentanyl," Milgram said. She went on to say that "the DEA's top priority is doing everything in our power to save lives . . . At DEA, our goal is simple: we want medication for OUD to be readily and safely available to anyone in the country who needs it."

Sue snapped. After learning of Sue's story on the phone, Milgram created a new, inaccurate version of Tyler's death. She was behaving as if he was a poisoning victim, not someone who died because he was denied the help he asked for. And Milgram was saying that the DEA was somehow the good guy?

Detail after detail was misused and misrepresented. Tyler—who Sue believed was killed by bad drug policy, lack of access to resources, stigma, and uninformed decision-makers—was now being painted as a victim of poisoning, all to fit into the DEA's narrative about overdose deaths.

It couldn't be further from the truth. Sue was beyond furious. After taking a couple of months to cool off, she sent Anne Milgram a message. (The complete, unedited letter follows, printed with Sue's permission.)

Dear Administrator Milgram,

I am the mother of Tyler Cordeiro. You may or may not recall speaking his name during the MAT Act press conference at the White House on January 24th of this year. In the past nine months, I have met with individuals from DEA on five separate occasions but have been denied each request to meet directly with you regarding the problematic Faces of Fentanyl display. I understand you are an incredibly busy person. Nonetheless, after publicly, yet wholly inaccurately, telling my son's story, I am again requesting an in-person meeting with you. It has taken me this long to process and properly articulate my feelings after viewing that press conference. I was excited to hear my son honored but left feeling betrayed, once again, by my government. I realize some of the words you spoke were simple mistakes, and I give grace for that. However, you made statements that were only to support your agenda, and this is, by any standard, unacceptable.

Don't worry; I am not writing to shame you, to ask you to prosecute my son's friends, or to implore you to stop using the word "overdose," or to close the border. My request today is for you to stop perpetuating discord among grieving families. The fentanyl poisoning story that DEA has latched onto is causing tremendous harm, and you have the power to end it. There is a special place for whoever thought it acceptable to patronize parents and weaponize their grief. We are individuals who are suffering from the most unfathomable pain as a direct result of corrupt politicians, harmful drug policies, and regulatory failures. The DEA has no place in our community. Our community is one of authenticity, compassion, critical thinking, and mutual respect. I urge you to stop using the faces of our children to further your agenda. If your genuine intention is to honor them, then there should be no hesitation in honoring ALL of them, regardless of the substance, with

an appropriate national memorial garden for us to gather
and honor them.

I'm sure you've heard this before, but in general, we
don't get much support from other communities. Our homes
weren't flooded with casseroles and flowers after we lost our
children. Our friends and family have mostly abandoned
us, and there is very little professional help for our unique
grief, so we take care of each other. The pain we live with
and will continue to endure until our last breath can only
be described as unnatural and inhumane. I was fortunate
to learn early on that it does not get better with time. I've
spoken with mothers in their eighties who still cry every day
over a child they lost 50–60 years ago. Accepting this reality
is the closest thing I've found to healing. The mothers who
attempt to live the life they had before or wake up expecting
to feel better only to be disappointed are suffering even more.
We redefine words like joy, success, and happiness. We are
women who have had to not only bury a child we birthed
and with whom we would gladly trade places, but we must
also confront all the secondary losses. Just last night, I was
comforting a mother who didn't understand why the members of her church had shunned her. The ripples of this grief
are never-ending. My point in telling you all of this is to
convey the complexity of what we are dealing with and how
disrespectful it is for our government to do anything other
than shield us from more unnecessary pain.

I spend countless hours with bereaved mothers, working
through and releasing any guilt, regret, and shame to allow
them to grieve authentically. I do this by helping them un-
tangle unnecessary conflicts between what they know in their
hearts (their child was suffering) and what the failed war on
drugs taught them (their child was morally deficient). One of
the most significant barriers to this work is the new trend in

using the term poisoning. Yes, our drug supply is poisoned due to the iron law of prohibition, but that is not the context in which this term is being used. This is a way for families to separate themselves from the moral failing narrative, prolonging the realization that it's a false narrative, creating more harm, and further complicating the healing process. I wrote about this recently in USA Today.

So, you can imagine my disbelief when you ended your speech by saying my son was poisoned by fentanyl. I understand that saying this supports your agenda, but your agenda needs to be put aside when you speak the names of the dead children that your agency has failed to protect. My child is no longer here, not because of some cartel in Mexico or China, but because of harmful drug policy, greed, a corrupt criminal justice system, incompetent government officials, and a capitalist health-care system that is not worthy of the word care . . . all run by individuals who are profiting from our pain or whose salaries are paid with our taxes.

When I received the request for you to use Tyler's story, I was told it was regarding barriers to treatment. I provided details to your staff member by the name of Dane regarding the barriers in a document for your reference. I was not aware this was a press conference on the MAT Act, which I support the passing of, but none of his barriers were to buprenorphine. In fact, he said buprenorphine blocked him spiritually; he wanted to receive ibogaine treatments. Every barrier we faced can be traced back to problematic drug policy. I notified multiple politicians and prosecutorial agencies regarding the criminals who claimed to be "treating" my son's addiction. Two and a half years later, the treatment facility is finally being turned over to the FBI for an investigation, yet it is still open for business. We are tired of prosecutors only taking the winnable cases. I wonder how many more white-collar criminals the Department of Justice is going to allow to harm innocent families before prosecutorial discretion is seen for what it really is: negligent, racist, classist, and allows the wealthy to commit crimes against humanity.

The vengeance-filled angry parents who are being preyed on by politicians are not an accurate representation of the majority. They are the ones struggling the most. I urge you to stop the gaslighting, tokenizing, politicizing, and otherwise interfering with their grief journey. Please respect and appreciate that you can't comprehend the pain we are feeling and allow us to heal. Someday, these families will realize that we were all failed by the same bad actors, and they will clearly see how our government continued to victimize them.

In a recent interview, you spoke of the DEA's authority to investigate and charge a Chinese national for trafficking fentanyl precursors and are willing to waste five million taxpayer dollars to bring him to "justice," yet [you] have done nothing to hold accountable the diabolical Sacklers or countless other pharma criminals living right in our backyard. Somehow, it's acceptable to allow them to continue supplying medications to uninformed citizens. Until enforcement actions are taken against the bad actors within our government and the wealthy businessmen sitting in American boardrooms plotting the genocide of a generation, we are forced to assume our entire government is being led by individuals who prioritize greed over human life.

Ms. Milgram, the distrust of the government will not improve until there is an acknowledgment of the failures. Just as our individual physical, spiritual, and emotional wounds need to be acknowledged and accepted to heal, so do our nation's failures. It is simply not possible to solve a problem until the problem is transparently addressed. Your agency may have responded to inquiries by Congress, but there has never been an explanation to the victims, let alone an apology for

*our pain or a valiant effort to fix the problematic drug pol-
icy, prosecutorial neglect, and regulatory failures. In fact, it's
nauseating how the state attorneys general are campaigning
for office based on stealing victim restitution and framing it as
solving a crisis they caused.*

*Your strategy will never work. In Luzerne County, PA,
there have been over 15 suicides in the women's correctional
facility because they aren't doing anything to treat the withdrawal from fentanyl and xylazine. Us parents try to raise a
hundred dollars here and there to help pay for their funerals,
while the county is using opioid settlement funds to build a
new jail and purchase new weapons. No matter how hard you
manipulate the data, this is not a criminal justice issue. I spent
my Sunday getting wound care supplies to a 25-year-old girl,
who recently had her arm amputated, and who needed her
legs wrapped because she has maggots feeding off the necrotic
skin. She will likely never receive the care she needs because of
the stigma generated by drug criminalization. This is a hu-
manitarian crisis being inflicted on suffering individuals by
our own government. Good Samaritan laws are being overpowered by drug-induced homicide laws, which will result in
fewer people calling for help. Such laws are directly fueled by
the "poisoned by fentanyl" narrative your agency continues to
prop up. Cops are wasting hundreds of thousands of taxpayer
dollars on unnecessary drug testing equipment, yet it's illegal
in many states for a person with a substance use disorder to try
to stay alive by checking their substances.*

*There is an army of us who are incapable of engaging in
petty politics. We consider the increase in early loss of life a call
to action, the universe's last straw, if you will. Our country has
lost its way. It is divided, dysfunctional, and toxic; it is not
a safe environment for vulnerable populations. We were told
our children were losers, weaklings, junkies, unworthy of love,*

causing us to betray the most primal human instinct, and
making us complicit in their deaths. There is nothing clearer
than the hindsight that comes after losing a child to a prevent-
able, premature death. The great majority of bereaved parents
are open-minded and undeterred in using our fierce, uncon-
ditional love to find real solutions. If you are serious about
ending this crisis, value our pain, and respect our experience,
then speak to the parents who are out here doing the work,
but come with the urgency of 300 individuals dying every day
because we don't have time to tangle with your red tape.

The US War on Drugs killed our children. Most of the
soldiers who died during combat volunteered to fight for our
country, and their families knew the risks. Our children did
not volunteer, and they were not equipped for the battle. They
were struggling and then abandoned by their families, pun-
ished only for their suffering, and left to die alone in their
homes, public restrooms, jail cells, or behind dumpsters. Non-
sensical drug policy, greed, and the government regulatory
agencies are to blame for Every. Single. One.

Regards,
Susan Ousterman

Two weeks later, the DEA hosted a press conference on Zoom—
Sue believes her letter lit a fire under Anne Milgram. The families
were invited to watch the press conference. But the announcement
wasn't about making lifesaving policy changes. It was a declaration
of war on drug cartels. Milgram described how the DEA "proac-
tively infiltrated the Sinaloa Cartel and the Chapitos network, obtained unprecedented access to the organization's highest levels, and
followed them across the world." She went on to say that cartels were
"feeding people to tigers."

"I would rather watch Tyler be eaten alive than die slowly for six years," Sue said. "Feeding people to tigers? Really? This is about watching people suffer."

Anne Milgram, who runs a DEA plagued by scandal, has yet to respond.

The missteps the agency has made over the years are astounding. From replacing McGruff the Crime Dog with an anti-fentanyl mascot in an orange hazmat suit, to publicizing an "emoji drug decoder"—so frightened parents will see a tree or star in their kid's texts and choose to support federal intervention—to sweeping corruption committed by DEA agents never held accountable for their actions under the rug; the list goes on and on. It's fearmongering at its worst because it focuses on the lowest-hanging fruit possible, sensationalizes the impact of drugs, and categorically fails to solve the problem. It's happened again and again, and it will keep happening as long as the budget for bad decisions is still there.

Some of these actions are laughable, while others have truly frightening implications for our personal freedoms. For example, under legislation considered by Congress, social media platforms and other user-to-user services could be legally required to turn private, protected messages over to the DEA if they're connected to an "unlawful sale or distribution of fentanyl, methamphetamine" and "the unlawful sale, distribution or manufacture of a counterfeit controlled substance." (Presumably, this includes any messages that include the emojis on the DEA's little decoder chart.)

According to the Electronic Frontier Foundation, the law would make it so that "providers are required to report to the DEA when they gain actual knowledge of facts about those drug sales or when a user makes a reasonably believable report about those sales. Providers are also allowed to make reports when they have a reasonable belief about those facts or have actual knowledge that a sale is planned or imminent. Importantly, providers can be fined hundreds of thousands of dollars for a failure to report."

This type of illegal interference in our right to privacy is a smoke screen from the DEA's serious behind-the-scenes screwups. Whistleblowers alerted the US Office of Special Counsel, the president, and Congress that the DEA failed to secure the Haitian harbor of Port-au-Prince and was not limiting the flow of substances through the port. DEA agents seized a small amount of the illicit cargo—and let the rest go. Special Counsel Henry J. Kerner said, "Since the U.S. government expends resources for DEA to operate in Haiti, it is incumbent on the agency to be as effective as possible in its mission to disrupt the flow of illegal drugs into the United States."

Attempts to investigate the agency's dysfunction tend to come up conveniently shorthanded. An external audit that cost over $1.4 million glossed over internal corruption and focused instead on the agency's success stats for undercover money laundering and special vetted units overseas—the same "Team America" unit that whistleblower José Irizarry confirmed was misusing funds, manufacturing statistics, and enabling drug cartels through laundering money themselves.

Senator Chuck Grassley, an Iowa Republican on the Senate Judiciary Committee, said, "This report is stunningly vague in its actual evaluation of known problems at the DEA and remedies to fix them. This speaks to the agency's broader effort to evade oversight. The agency has attempted to dodge my oversight inquiries, but I intend to push forward."

This doesn't diminish the losses that pile up day after day. The DEA is complicit in every single fentanyl death, either because it aided and abetted cartels, or because it failed to warn Americans of what the agency already knew about fentanyl. For example, many unsuspecting people died after taking counterfeit pain pills purchased at drugstores in Mexico. An *LA Times* investigation published on March 11, 2023, showed that "both the U.S. State Department and the DEA have known since at least 2019 that some pharmacies in Mexico are selling pills made of powerful drugs such as fentanyl and methamphetamine and passing them off as legitimate pharmaceuticals." The State Department finally learned of the threat after congressional lawmakers called for action and warned the public—but it was three years too late for many people.

The DEA has yet to take public action to combat this problem, and the number of people who actually died from the counterfeits is unknown. Yet, isn't that the DEA's purpose? Their one job is to find and stop illicit drugs—to save lives by preventing potentially harmful substances from entering the mainstream and killing people. For $3 billion a year, you would think that we would at least have some data. But no. Story after story exposes the fact that the absolute value of American lives, at least according to the DEA, is zero.

For an agency that wields such immense power, the DEA has surprisingly little oversight or accountability. Their narrow focus on fentanyl seems to miss the point. There are so many threats to American life and health and bigger, more obvious villains in the crisis. So, why choose fentanyl? By honing in on fentanyl, the DEA can spend billions of dollars of its already-bloated budget either terrorizing normal, everyday people and their families or laundering money on behalf of foreign cartels. I suggest that it is *because* of the DEA's incompetence—which they weaponize by persisting in an unwinnable war against an untraceable, inexhaustible substance. In 2022, firearms became the number one cause of death for children and teens in the United States. But nobody seems to be taking on a problem like gun violence—a problem that could actually be solved.

"I don't want anybody to die from anything. There are more mass shootings every day in the United States," Saeeda Dunston said. "Guns kill more young people than fentanyl. So, why can't we have a conversation about that if we're so universally concerned about youth and safety? Why can't we rewrite these regulations and policies to benefit the community?"

Doing so would limit the DEA's reach and power—and force

them to be accountable for the deadly outcomes of their harmful drug enforcement policies.

Saeeda pointed out that the DEA has specifically targeted Black communities for decades, if not longer. "During the crack era," she said, "even Black activists and preachers called for drug users to be locked up. They criminalized their own community, buying into the messaging pushed by the state and federal governments that addiction was a criminal choice, not a mental illness.

"Twenty years later, most of those people have recanted," she said. "They're saying 'we wish we didn't do that.' That's the definition of insanity, isn't it? To do the same thing over and over, expecting a different result. That era is here again now. If we continue to try the same policies and principles the DEA applied in the '80s and '90s, we will get the same result. And we'll wonder why, years later, people are still sick and suffering.

"Rather than moralizing," she said, "it is important to speak the truth and choose language that is clear in its meaning and intention." Raised by parents who were an editor and a reporter, Saeeda is sensitive to the power of words and how they can influence processes and the people affected by them. As an anti-racist, she prefers to focus on systems rather than individuals—and she knows that transforming or dismantling those systems takes time.

She said, "You can know things are racialized by the way we talk about them. The narrative of the 'accidental' overdose did not exist until these systems realized they needed a compassionate approach to addiction for white 'victims.' But for Black and brown folks, the same disease, the same behavior, the same tragedy becomes criminal. It's a repeat of the story we've heard again and again. One person is a 'victim' and 'those people' are the problem."

The word "victim," she says, is problematic in itself when talking about fentanyl. Many families, as Sue Ousterman noticed, claimed that their child was "poisoned." Yet, Saeeda says, the terminology of poisoning is very specific. Used in a clinical setting, fentanyl is a godsend for people recovering from surgery. On the street, it's "poison." The lack of nuance in the language we use to talk about drugs and overdoses avoids the fact that the child who tragically overdosed and died was affected by a systemic issue.

She points out that carceral responses don't make sense in these situations. Prisons are not treatment centers, hospitals, or detoxes— yet, white families who are new to advocacy and hurting from the loss of their child often cosign the narrative that locking up sick people is the best way to save their lives. They lean on the state to intervene and use police power—including violence, prisons, and in- carceration—to navigate what is, in reality, a public health problem.

Sue explained that the solution would be to detangle federal agen- cies and carceral systems from the way addiction is treated. "We get relief when we advocate for actual justice," she said. "Your heart grows like the Grinch's when you lose a child. You see the racism. You see the bias. You can really feel your child guiding you, and that is the immortal work of advocacy. I want to bring all the families into that space and tell them that this is their opportunity to make real change."

She said that most people who lose their loved ones to overdoses don't bury them. Instead, they keep their child's ashes in a box so they can see them, carry them, and talk to them every day. "To lose someone like this is to grieve continuously. We walk the earth griev- ing every day," she said. "I feel Tyler in nature, and I know I'm doing what he would want me to do. Truly, he was amazing."

One day, she says, she hopes to establish memorial gardens across the country to honor the victims of the drug war. She calls these me- morial spaces the "Vilomah Gardens," which take their name from a Sanskrit word that means "against the natural order." No person should have to bury their own child, she says. The unfathomable and unnatural loss is compounded by the lack of serene places to inter the dead. She couldn't imagine leaving her son's body in a gloomy cemetery or crypt.

"They deserve beautiful places," Sue wrote. "We can feel their lights continue to shine through the natural world around us, and embrace not only our grief, but the joy they brought to our lives."

Tyler Cordeiro is on the wall of faces in the DEA's museum exhibit—even though his mother knows he doesn't belong there, amid the names and smiles of people who are "forever 17" and "forever in our hearts." Tyler would want his face shown everywhere, but Sue decided to celebrate his life privately as well.

She took Tyler's ashes to southwestern Virginia, where their family has a small piece of land. Among the sloping foothills of the Blue Ridge Mountains, there is a large stone with Tyler's tag name "TCORD" inscribed on it. The last traces of his earthly body are beneath it, laid to rest by his mother's hands in the most peaceful place they'd ever laughed, and hugged, and soaked up life together.

The Story of a Chinese Drug Company

In today's fentanyl market, deep-pocketed drug traffickers have collided with even deeper-pocketed chemical suppliers. These two elements bonded, creating an entirely new and monstrous compound.

In March 2023, executives at a chemical company called Amarvel Biotech flew to Thailand from their headquarters in Wuhan, China, to meet with a new buyer who was promising big business. Prior to this meeting, the buyer transferred $5,000 worth of untraceable cryptocurrency as a down payment for an order of precursor chemicals—chemicals the buyer said were for the sole intention of producing fentanyl. "You know I making fentanyl," the buyer, in broken English, said to the seller over an encrypted messaging app. "I know," the Wuhan-based seller replied. In a later message, the seller promised "you'll be happy with our product."

The executives and sales force at Amarvel Biotech promised that they could handle just about any amount of precursor the buyer wanted. If the buyer wished to order metric tons of lab-made chemicals, Amarvel was eager to not only manufacture and ship it, but also offer advice on how to process the chemicals into fentanyl. The company's chemists even provided processing tips for maximizing the amount of fentanyl that precursors could create.

"We have a lot of customers in America and Mexico," a saleswoman from Amarvel told the buyer. "They know how to produce."

This interaction is a window into the rapid transformation of America's drug supply, with synthetic, lab-made drugs taking over the agricultural, plant-based drug market. This switch created entirely new supply chains and distribution routes for drugs such as fentanyl. We're way beyond grow operations and small-time production. Now, fentanyl production can span more than 45 countries and involve thousands and thousands of new players across multiple industries. This has magnified and punctuated the job of drug enforcement as an impossible profession chasing unattainable goals. Every parcel of fentanyl that DEA and border agents seize can be immediately manufactured again and replaced in a lab without a hiccup.

In text messages, the Chinese sellers said they needed to be careful not to mention the word "fentanyl" in writing. In 2019, facing international pressure, China banned all exports of the substance. However, many of the chemicals used to make fentanyl are not technically illegal, since they are widely used for other purposes throughout the chemical industry and can be made in massive quantities all over the world. For example, if a company in China happens to get busted, other countries like India that also have a sprawling chemical industry could just as easily fill the void and produce and ship precursor chemicals. As American law enforcement focuses on China, drug policy analysts already see a move to India taking place.

This fact alone complicates any drug enforcement efforts that target the global fentanyl supply chain. Fentanyl is a boundless product. Hundreds of farmers, thousands of acres of land, and millions of gallons of water can be replaced by a single chemist in a makeshift tent-turned-drug-lab—a chemist who is replaceable themselves, and can vanish at a moment's notice.

The latest trend in fentanyl production speaks to this endless game of whack-a-mole. For years, federal authorities operated under the assumption that Chinese chemical companies shipped fentanyl precursors to traffickers in Mexico, which resulted in more heat on Mexican drug trafficking organizations. Many Republicans, for instance, are rallying behind the outrageous idea to bomb Mexican labs while "shutting down the border," whatever that means. In a twist, underground fentanyl labs have begun to pop up in Canada. An hour outside Vancouver, police seized 2.5 million doses of fentanyl and 528 gallons of chemicals stored in a shipping container. In another Vancouver-area home, police found glass beakers and barrels of chemicals used to make massive amounts of illicit fentanyl. Near Toronto, just thirty miles north of Niagara Falls, New York, Canadian authorities discovered the largest secret fentanyl lab to date, enough equipment and chemicals to make millions of doses that could be shipped around the world or even driven across the Canadian border into the US. As American law enforcement is focused on China and Mexico, the spread of labs to Canada illustrates how, with the right tools, fentanyl can be made almost anywhere.

That's what border agents, DEA agents, and local law enforcement are all up against. Essentially, it's a network of ghosts. Disrupting the drug supply is like chasing your own shadow.

In April 2023, after the first meeting in Thailand, the buyer transferred $40,000 more in cryptocurrency to Amarvel, enough to purchase about 200 kilograms of chemicals. The buyer wanted the product to be shipped to New York, but an executive at Amarvel said it was easier to ship to California.

"New York has been strict in checking the precursors," explained the Amarvel executive in an encrypted text message. "For the sake of safety, this time it is sent to California."

Amarvel claimed to have a sophisticated system for sending restricted chemicals and avoiding detection. To get around customs inspections, the Wuhan lab could add a benign molecule to the chemicals to avert any suspicions. They would then give instructions on how to later remove that chemical during the manufacturing process. The Chinese company also used clever packaging and labeling, disguising chemical shipments as "Nature's Nuts," dog food, or motor oil. The likelihood of authorities searching a giant cargo ship carrying thousands of containers and finding a small package of chemicals labeled "dog food" is far beyond the old needle-in-a-haystack situation.

The first $40,000 purchase of chemicals was just a trial run. After all, two hundred kilos is nothing for an industrial chemical company, which is capable of producing many, many times that, over and over again. If the chemicals from China arrived in America undetected, then the buyer would put in another order—only this time, they wouldn't want kilos, they would want *tons*. There's roughly 900 kilograms per ton. If handled properly by a trained chemist, just one full order of chemicals from China could create millions upon millions of doses of fentanyl, all destined for the street and worth far more than the initial $40,000 investment.

Experts believe the government only confiscates a small fraction of illicit drugs that flow into the country. So if the authorities seize 10 million counterfeit fentanyl pills, that means there's hundreds of millions more pills that they didn't find. Now, back in the day, the drug supply had limits. Cocaine, heroin, marijuana, and other plant-based drugs were finite. There could be long stretches where the supply ran dry. But in this brave new world of synthetic drugs, the days of drug droughts are over.

The supply is bottomless. The supply is cheap. The supply is everywhere.

The lab in China manufactured 210 kilograms for the buyer with ease. The 462 pounds of off-white and tan powder were packaged in boxes in Wuhan and shipped to a warehouse near

Los Angeles. The trial run worked. The drugs landed. Now, it was time to go bigger.

Before placing the next order, the buyers and sellers planned to meet on the small South Pacific island of Fiji on June 8, 2023. They planned to discuss the details of the next shipment. But during the Fiji meeting, the saleswoman from Amarvel expressed worry about their deal. Chinese companies felt like enforcement was heating up.

"Recently American government seized some Mexican group, and they followed the routes to China," she said. She sketched out the dizzying structure of the global fentanyl supply chain. Shipments of illicitly made fentanyl originate in China's gigantic chemical industry, after passing through the hands of criminal organizations in Mexico that turn those chemicals into fentanyl. Once in America, the fentanyl is delivered and distributed across major cities that act as hubs, and from those hubs, fentanyl flows in every direction. Larger shipments can be hidden in any of the thousands of trucks carrying cargo across the border in California, Arizona, and Texas. This network is rapid, efficient, and adaptable.

Still, the saleswoman at the Chinese chemical company was right to worry about their operations. The unprecedented death rate from fentanyl pushed American law enforcement to focus their efforts on disrupting that first layer in the supply chain: chemical companies in China. If these companies feared that they could be arrested, prosecuted, and imprisoned in the States for doing business with fentanyl traffickers, then maybe they'd get out of the drug business. But so far, there has been no Chinese "El Chapo." The threat of extradition was just a threat—for the moment.

Back in Fiji, the saleswoman had no idea how spot-on her fears were. It turned out the buyers she'd been meeting and dealing with this whole time were undercover DEA agents working a global sting operation. That meeting would be her last one as an Amarvel employee. She and the other executives would become the first Chinese nationals prosecuted for fentanyl trafficking. Fijian police arrested and detained the Amarvel team, who were promptly taken into US custody. From Fiji, they were flown to Honolulu, Hawaii, where they would face an American judge in court the very next day.

In June 2023, the Department of Justice announced that they'd successfully dismantled the Amarvel company, along with two other companies based in China accused of manufacturing fentanyl precursors and sending them to Mexico and America. This bust marked a new shift in the American government's war on drugs—which, as I've discussed at length throughout this book, has struggled to adapt to the new realities of the fentanyl era.

But would taking down one chemical company in China make any difference? We'd soon find out.

On the day of their big announcement, federal prosecutors and DEA agents labeled fentanyl the "single deadliest drug threat the United States has ever encountered." Stateside, federal officials issued their press releases announcing victory. US Attorney Damian Williams for the Southern District of New York said, "Today, we target the very beginning of the fentanyl supply chain: the Chinese manufacturers of the raw chemicals used to make fentanyl and its analogues. We've charged a Chinese precursor chemical company. And that's not all. We've charged and arrested some of the individuals who work at the company. That includes a corporate executive and a marketing manager. They're in American handcuffs. And they're going to face justice in an American courtroom."

Attorney General Merrick B. Garland also issued a statement about the DOJ's first ever drug prosecution against Chinese nationals for fentanyl trafficking.

"When I announced in April that the Justice Department had taken significant enforcement actions against the Sinaloa Cartel, I promised that the Justice Department would never forget the victims of the fentanyl epidemic," he said. "I also promised that we would never stop working to hold accountable those who bear responsibility for it. That includes not only going after the leaders of the cartels, their drug and gun traffickers, their money launderers, security forces, and clandestine lab operators. It also includes stopping the Chinese chemical companies that are supplying the cartels with the building blocks they need to manufacture deadly fentanyl."

The DOJ's unsealed indictments read like a gritty crime screenplay. They documented an elaborate, high-stakes sting operation with all the makings of a Gene Hackman thriller: big wire transfers, encrypted text messages, shady warehouses in New York and California, bricks of off-white and tan powder, undercover DEA agents, and secret meetings in exotic locales like Thailand, Fiji, and Beijing. The indictment sketched out a classic tale of the good guys catching the bad guys.

But there was also something about this massive operation that felt very different. There were no people in the story. There weren't any shoot-outs or dramatic raids or drug kingpins living in a sprawling palazzo surrounded by lions, tigers, and hired guns. No helicopters carried soldiers into hostile territory. No bad guys carrying AK-47s hid out in a secret lab, concealed within a dense jungle.

The offender was a registered, licensed Chinese chemical company.

The "drug traffickers" in this case weren't hiding at all. It was just the opposite. They were blatantly advertising their services on the internet—the same way every business does. Amarvel Biotech had online storefronts and even a Facebook page marketing its entire operation. Facebook posts advertised "custom packaging solutions" that disguise illegal chemicals with benign packaging ("Nature's Nuts"). The chemical company guaranteed its customers safe shipping of illegal chemicals to California.

A month before the Fiji arrests, the DOJ and DEA also announced the success of Operation Last Mile, a yearlong effort to disrupt fentanyl trafficking that resulted in more than 3,000 arrests and the seizure of some 44 million fentanyl pills and more than 6,500 pounds of fentanyl powder. And before that, Attorney General Garland announced new indictments against a global fentanyl operation run by the Sinaloa trafficking organization, which included the sons of El Chapo (known as "the Chapitos"), along with more than two dozen others. (The leader of Sinaloa, El Chapo, has been serving a life sentence in a Brooklyn prison since 2019.)

On paper, that sounds like "mission accomplished," right? But the supply is only one side of the ledger. El Chapo may be in prison, but that hasn't slowed down illicit drug sales or overdoses. Fentanyl is still flowing. People are still dying. Supply-side drug enforcement isn't producing the outcomes law enforcement claims it does.

By 2019, the Justice Department indicted multiple Chinese nationals on drug trafficking charges, accusing one father-son operation of producing and shipping synthetic opioids to 47 states. American policy toward China became increasingly hawkish under Trump, who accused the Chinese government of being complicit in the illegal fentanyl trade.

"He said he was going to stop fentanyl from coming into our country—it's all coming out of China; he didn't do that," Mr. Trump said, referring to Chinese president Xi Jinping. "We're losing thousands of people to fentanyl."

The truth was that America was losing tens of thousands of people to fentanyl.

Facing economic pressure, China eventually banned the export of fentanyl.[1] In theory, it sounds like such a policy would solve the problem. But it's the same supply-side drug policy that America relies on—the same approach that continues to fail, even by its own logic and objective measures. Drug enforcement's basic goal is to reduce the consumption of drugs by disrupting every level of the supply chain: manufacturing, distributing, and selling. But what results are we getting? Governments banning the production, importation, and sale of illegal drugs is *supposed* to apply pressure on the illicit market. The enforcement of these laws is *supposed* to increase the cost of doing business for criminal drug trafficking organizations. None of this has worked with fentanyl, which remains cheap, abundant, and highly potent—the exact opposite outcome that drug laws are supposed to achieve.

Aggressive drug enforcement, focused squarely on curtailing the supply, has not made a dent in the deadliest overdose crisis in American history.

11

BREAKFAST OF CHAMPIONS

At first, Anne Fuqua tried using traditional treatments like physical therapy, Botox, and oral and intrathecal medications to manage her chronic illness. Her dystonia—a highly painful and life-altering neurological movement disorder that causes twisting, frozen, or abnormal postures and painful muscle cramps—was getting worse. Until she was in high school, her family assumed she had mild cerebral palsy. However, by the time she started nursing school in her hometown of Birmingham, Alabama, the disorder had taken on a life of its own. It was eating up Anne's life, one hour at a time.

To manage it, Anne was on a heavy regimen of opioid pain relievers. She coped with painful kidney stones and elevated liver enzymes as the result of these prescribed painkillers; if she didn't take the medications, pain caused her blood pressure to soar to critical levels.

"My medication was breakfast of champions, lunch of champions, and dinner of champions," she said. "I was taking them as prescribed, but the last few months, I was puking my guts out. At the same time, I was terrified of these medications I was taking."

With such an unpredictable condition, Anne struggled to find medical providers who understood how to treat her. She found it hard to walk or stand. There were periods where she could do well on her own, but every couple of years her symptoms flared like lightning strikes, and she ended up back in the hospital. Frail and unable to keep on weight, Anne said she looked like someone with late-stage anorexia. Because of the way her chronic pain affected her mobility, she was recommended a pain management option called an intra-thecal pain pump. The pump is implanted into the spinal cord and delivers powerful doses of medicine directly to the pain receptors in the spine. It's supposed to interrupt pain signals and is often used for people with cancer and chronic pain to help them live normal, functional lives.

The treatment was Anne's best shot at relief.

However, Anne's spine was damaged during the surgery, leaving her with what is called a mild incomplete spinal injury. The dystonia-related damage to her spine worsened and developed into inflamma-tory arthritis within her spinal cord. With patients who experience this degree of pain, there isn't much doctors can do to help. Her qual-ity of life suffered gravely. With no possible cure, the only option was more medication.

"They wind up giving us IV opioids for however many days," she said. "Eventually, your body just calms down and the pain goes away. Dystonia is like Parkinson's in some ways, because you have limited dopamine, and self-regulating pain is very hard. After a bad flare, I took this treatment for nine days. They said I was the worst case in the hospital."

In spite of her nursing degree and her daily experience with high doses of opioids, Anne said she didn't really understand much about the science of opioids and how the drugs worked. Her pain didn't disappear; it just became more tolerable. No single pain treatment she tried helped for any significant amount of time. She rotated from muscle relaxants to opioids to Botox injections to IV treatments, all while hoping her liver and other organs wouldn't fail. Fentanyl was the magic answer for Anne—because she could take it once a day in small doses to manage her pain. It worked quickly, effectively, and without too many side effects.

Fentanyl is widely (mis)perceived as a terrible drug. It's labeled a "poison," a toxin like anthrax that can kill with a single touch. I hear many people say that there is "no safe way to use fentanyl" or that there is "no safe dose of fentanyl." These are myths driven by fear. All too often, fentanyl on the street is conflated with the safe, regulated, and highly effective medical-grade fentanyl that patients like Anne take. These false claims ignore the millions of people for whom fentanyl is not a deadly poison but a lifesaving medication.

While not everyone copes with the extreme degree of pain that Anne does, chronic pain is a widespread issue in the United States. Pain is the number one reason that people see a doctor; it carries complex health implications, especially when someone has co-occurring disorders. A study published in February 2022 by researchers from Brigham and Women's Hospital and Massachusetts Eye and Ear, both Harvard University hospitals in Boston, suggested that 50 million Americans experience chronic pain. That's 20 percent of American adults, making it the most common chronic condition in our country. The 2019 edition of the National Health Interview Survey found that 50.2 million adults (20.5 percent) reported pain on most days or every day. The majority of these folks used massage or physical therapy to deal with their pain. Five to eight million of these chronic pain patients said they regularly rely on opioids.

Anyone who's experienced chronic pain knows that treatment, just like the illness itself, is a moving target. (For example, massage on its own may help mitigate a chronic illness, but it isn't a cure.) In the 2022 study, respondents "reported limitations in daily functioning, including social activities and activities of daily living."[1] People with chronic pain reported missing significantly more work days than people who didn't have pain. For some people, like Anne, managing the pain itself becomes a full-time job—or more than full-time.

Finding a doctor who can provide adequate and appropriate pain relief is also a struggle. Physicians today have an aversion to prescribing opioids. They fear being flagged by surveillance systems like Prescription Drug Monitoring Programs (PDMPs), which track every controlled substance they prescribe. Doctors have been forced to think more like lawyers, regulators, and police than like health-care professionals. Using medicine to heal patients has taken a back seat to risk management.

By the time Anne was able to see a doctor who not only knew how to treat her pain but was also willing to use opioids to do it, she was fully reliant on a wheelchair. Pain and muscle spasms prevented her from walking; she couldn't stand alone, even while leaning against a wall and holding on to the edge of a table. Her last flare-up of dystonia had put her in the hospital for ten days, on more IV opioids. She felt like all the progress she had made was erased.

She said, "I was at that point where nobody could do anything with me. Nobody wanted to help because it was a risk to them. My medical risk put them at risk. Even when I tried to go to urgent care, they would turn me away. If I tried to go in, a nurse would get me in the parking lot and say, 'You can't come in.' Every time I went to the doctor, I was afraid that this was the time they would decide I was a fiending junkie and throw me out."

The doctor who finally helped Anne was able to prescribe compound medications tailored to her needs, including fentanyl. That medicine eased her pain and helped her regain control of her movements. He prescribed sublingual fentanyl tablets and fentanyl patches, since she was barely able to swallow pills. Double-acting medications, some of which she took off-label according to medical guidance, were also helpful. Transformative, even. Anne said that she went from "being a shaky, jerky mess who couldn't stand up straight to looking almost normal."

Although she said her movements were still unreliable, and she couldn't walk far or fast, she could now handle stairs on her own.

For once, she was off the roller coaster. She didn't need constant hospitalization. Periodically, her body would become jerky again—muscle spasms dislocated her shoulder and gave her concussions—but it was a small price to pay compared to her untreated chronic condition or ineffective pain management.

However, a reactionary, hard-line story about fentanyl was taking hold. Rhetoric about fentanyl's dangers on the street kept heating up—and once again Anne's independence was in jeopardy. The CDC implemented new rules about fentanyl, making it harder to access. In 2016, the CDC released first-of-its-kind guidelines for prescribing opioids for chronic pain. This was "intended to enhance patient and community safety by providing guidance on best clinical practices . . . outside of active cancer, palliative, and end-of-life care," according to a paper written by a panel of pain medicine experts published in *Pain Medicine* in April 2019. Since Anne was a chronic pain patient who did not have cancer, nor was she at the end of her life, her prescription was targeted by the CDC.

The new CDC guidelines were supposed to "protect" pain patients, but now they resulted in burdensome limitations and, often, the denial of pain relief. The permissive prescribing practices that were in place prior to 2011—which resulted in almost everybody receiving 30 days' worth of oxycodone for anything from a toothache to a stubbed toe—had vanished. The era of controversial, high-volume opioid prescribing ended. In its place were new restrictions, implemented without flexibility and often without enough information to make patient-centered decisions. Overnight, it seemed we shifted from one extreme to the other.

The CDC prescribing guidelines published 12 core recommendations and principles, which emphasized that opioids are *not* first-line therapy for chronic pain, to avoid the concurrent use of opioids and benzodiazepines, and to always aim for the lowest dose possible—all in the name of "reversing the opioid epidemic."[2] It sounds okay in theory, but pain management is also a highly complex medical specialty; these guidelines were meant for general practitioners and primary care physicians, not pain specialists treating patients like Anne. Caution and nuance were thrown to the wind. Those in authority wanted to see a big reduction in opioid prescribing, no matter the outcome.

In a twisted way, the rollback of prescription opioids created a whole new set of problems. In an interview with CBS, Dr. Stefan Kertesz (Department of Medicine, University of Alabama at Birmingham School of Medicine and Medicine Service) sized up the situation.[3]

"The problem is that you cannot always resolve a crisis by going precisely backward from how you got into it," Dr. Kertesz said. "Even though some patients might benefit, many others suffer from mental health crises, overdose, suicidal ideas, or actually dying by suicide."

One phrase comes to mind: *The cure is worse than the disease.* Other medical experts agreed with Dr. Kertesz.

"When access to prescription opioids is heavily restricted, people will seek out opioids that are unregulated," said Grant Victor, an assistant professor in the Rutgers School of Social Work and lead author of a study published in the *Journal of Substance Use and Addiction Treatment.* "The opposite may also be true; our findings suggest that restoring easier access to opioid pain medications may protect against fatal overdoses."[4]

The worst outcomes of the new guidelines for patients like Anne manifested in an inflexible system of pain care, with abrupt and mandated opioid tapers enforced by pain contracts and legalese. Medical ethics and patient-centered care be damned.

As you can imagine, this caused so many problems and produced such a loud public outcry that the CDC was forced to change course and update the guidelines in 2022. Both doctors and laypeople have mixed opinions about this change. On the one hand, many of the pre-2016 policies were co-written by opioid manufacturers like Purdue

Pharma and sought to increase corporate revenue by irresponsibly pushing addictive pills to the unsuspecting public through miseducated doctors. On the other hand, for people who needed daily access to painkillers, more permissive policies were a godsend. Either way, the people advocating for the CDC's new guidelines in the press weren't much for nuance—like Dr. Andrew Kolodny of Physicians for Responsible Opioid Prescribing.

Kolodny, who is not a pain specialist, is one of the many people who majorly overestimate and overemphasize the role of doctors and pain patients in the American overdose crisis. The truth is that overdose deaths in America were on the rise long before Purdue Pharma injected OxyContin into the market. From 1979 to 2016, drug overdose deaths in America *doubled* every eight years.[5] The culprits included methamphetamine, cocaine, prescription drugs, heroin— and now, illicit fentanyl. How could one evil pharmaceutical company—a company that wasn't even producing its blockbuster opioid until 1996—be responsible for all of this death?

These facts haven't stopped a cadre of paternalistic doctors from taking on lucrative gigs as expert witnesses in multibillion-dollar opioid trials. On the stand, their arguments are often simplistic and reductive, ignoring the historical patterns and trends of drug use in America. In their stories, it's as though time starts in 1999, and nobody used drugs before then. They point to charts that show an increase in opioid prescribing on one line next to another line showing an increase in overdose deaths.

Now, Statistics 101 states that correlation does not equal causation. However, in major news articles and on cable news, doctors like Kolodny still play the blame game. They argue that prescribers, pain patients, and prescription opioids are the primary suspects—even though the vast majority of deaths today occur in the illicit drug market and are the result of dangerous drug combinations. Dr. Kolodny, when pressed, will offer mixed messages.

"I can't point to data, but I believe that for the vast majority of people who become stuck on opioids, their prescriptions began because of injury or surgery," he said in a 2018 interview with the *Chicago Tribune*.[6] If he can't point to data, maybe he shouldn't be pointing in the first place.

The inconvenient truth is that deaths today resulting from *just* opioids, and *only* prescription opioids, remain quite rare. Yet, many doctors like Kolodny refuse to acknowledge the complexity of drug use in America. Yes, too many opioids were being prescribed to far too many people. But it's also true that rapid dose reductions and forced tapers were and are dangerous. Now, far too many people have been pushed into a dangerous marketplace where they've died from unregulated substances.

Strict interpretations of CDC guidelines were a death knell for people whose lives depended on access to reliable pain management. Pain is complex. One-size-fits-all treatment plans are not the solution. In the CDC's updated version of their guidelines, doctors and specialists noted that the original guidance was wildly misapplied across the country. Namely, what were meant to be *suggestions* for prescribing and dosing in primary and general care were taken up by lawmakers and politicians into strict thresholds written into black letter law. Violating these "guidelines" could now result in harsh penalties.

The logic of the drug war has invaded health care.

In some cases, the implementation of the 2016 guidelines was downright medieval. Thirty-eight state legislatures, the federal government, law enforcement, Congress, state medical boards, hospitals, and countries worldwide read these guidelines as a call for opioid prohibition. Doctors who worked with this population or had high numbers of opioid prescriptions were flagged by PDMPs and threatened with legal repercussions, including job loss and incarceration. With a single-minded focus—to reduce the overall volume of opioid prescriptions—the new, more cautious prescribing regimen cut off pain patients who were otherwise stable. Even if you already had a prescription and established care with a doctor, your care would be disrupted. One writer described this as "a lethal combination of bureaucratic arrogance and do-goodery, with the [CDC] foolishly trying to stop substance abuse by making prescribing more difficult and, thus, the drugs more challenging to acquire on the black market."

The CDC's approach not only backfired, it exploded, spreading shrapnel deep into the most vulnerable populations. From forced tapers to clinics shutting down overnight, pain patients were thrust into a chaotic clinical environment that treated them like "drug-seekers" rather than people with disabilities in need of specialized care. The already stigmatized medications that folks depended on were placed even further out of reach. As you may have guessed, it was a practical and ethical disaster that did nothing to stop a tidal wave of overdose deaths.

A white paper by Professors Kertesz and Adam J. Gordon (professor of Medicine and Psychiatry at the University of Utah School of Medicine and chief of Addiction Medicine for the Salt Lake City Health Care System) questioned the ethics of the prescribing rollback. The professors pointed out "suboptimum" results of "incentivized involuntary termination of opioids in otherwise stable patients," meaning that the patients were suffering. Emphasizing dose reduction wasn't a sign of success, they pointed out. It was actually a sign of a system-wide failure to treat people with complex medical needs. Real patients were reduced to numbers on a chart. As long as those numbers were going in the right direction on a line graph, nobody had to worry about anything else. They wrote:

> *Central to the present analysis is that policies cannot be comprehensively rational; rather, they emerge from a range of actors and agencies constrained in their ability to assimilate complex data, evaluate the data objectively and to command necessary resources in an iterative, rapid response fashion. The*

*imbalance between strong prescription control and weak pain
and addiction treatment [means that] opioid prescriptions
have fallen, but harms to pain patients and overdose deaths
have risen.*

Discouraging initial and continuous prescriptions for opioids
does reduce the total number of prescriptions. That's a no-brainer. But
what about the quality of life for people who need those medications?
For Anne, the new limits made her hard-won independence vanish.
The few doctors who could and would work with pain patients left
their practices due to law enforcement actions or the threat of losing
their licenses. Federal and local law enforcement shut down legitimate
pain clinics without warning. Basic pain services were limited or elim-
inated. Many doctors were sued, arrested, and imprisoned.

The Supreme Court even weighed in on the opioid prescribing
chaos in the case of *Ruan v. United States*, involving the criminal
convictions of two doctors who were accused of running opioid "pill
mills." The court moved in favor of doctors and pain patients, ruling
that doctors who are considered to be prescribing excessive amounts
of opioids cannot be convicted of a crime if they believe they were
doing so to genuinely help patients. It's easy to judge a doctor by
looking at their prescribing numbers with no context. But those
numbers aren't an accurate measure of the quality of care, especially
for people with chronic pain.

For pain treatment, Anne relied on compounding pharmacies,
but even pharmacies began to face many of the same barriers as doctors. Pharmacies sued over the "opioid epidemic" started refusing to
fill opioid prescriptions. Prior to the lawsuits and tightening regulations, Anne could get many of her medications from the Walgreens
near her house. After the lawsuits and the mass prescription rollback? No such luck.

"I exhausted their yearlong supply in ten weeks," she said. To get
her medication, she needed to cross state lines to find fentanyl—the

same drug that, according to the media, you can easily buy online or on any street corner in America. If that were true, Anne would have been able to get her prescription from a grocery store cart's handle or a bucket of Halloween candy. Instead, she spends hundreds of dollars every month chasing down the prescriptions she needs to live. She was told that she bought the last medical fentanyl patch available at Walgreens in the state of Alabama one time, a supply that would only last her five days. She catches the Greyhound bus to pharmacies in other states, in her wheelchair, hoping they'll fill her legal, legitimate prescription. Her whole life—and the independence she cherishes—now revolves around an absurd and unnecessary quest to obtain the medication that keeps her alive.

Even the good days are hard ones for Anne. She's not the only one treading water in a shrinking pool of resources. Some days, the struggle to feel functional is too much. Anne is not just tougher than most of the people I've ever met. She's also smart, educated about medicine and the health-care system, and supported by a community that cares about her. But even someone who is so strong and determined gets worn down over time.

We talk a lot about overdose deaths. That's where the headlines are, and it's important to raise up those losses and understand what causes them. At the same time, there's a silent cost of the opioid crisis that rarely appears in the news. These are the deaths that aren't on the front page and might appear as a footnote in an obscure white paper. They are deaths within the pain community—not overdoses, but suicides.

According to the *Journal of Pain Research*, "Data suggest that the overdose crisis is largely an unintended consequence of drug prohibition."[7] The crackdowns that are supposed to "protect" people can actually kill them. For people who need medical fentanyl, prohibition and inflexible barriers are death sentences. Following the 2016 guidelines, everyone—even oncologists caring for cancer patients—cut back on opioid prescriptions by 20 percent or more. Unsurprisingly, low-income patients and people without private insurance are most affected by these changes. A study from the *Journal of Clinical Oncology* found that the number of opioids prescribed to Medicare patients declined 38 percent while the number of emergency room visits for these same patients increased by over 50 percent.[8] The connection is obvious. Abandoning pain patients has lethal consequences.

It may come as no surprise that suicide rates for people with chronic pain are astronomical. A 2018 study analyzed the link in over 123,000 people who died by suicide between 2003 and 2014. Nine percent of the people who died had evidence of chronic pain, and many had complex or multiple health conditions. Over 54 percent of the people who died experienced one health condition, while 16 percent had two health conditions, and almost 6 percent of people had three or more health conditions. A 2021 study affirmed these results, showing that chronic pain was associated with not only a higher risk of depression but also an increased risk of suicidal behavior.

Many people take their own lives because they can no longer cope with the misery of untreated chronic pain. The barriers to treatment are too high. The medications stop working, or are unobtainable. The strain of feeling like a burden on loved ones and caregivers becomes too much. And pain, if you didn't know it in your bones, is exhausting. Waking up every morning in a body that hurts or doesn't work the way it should is terrible. Chronic pain kills, not because of the way it's treated—but because of the way it *isn't*.

Yet the CDC doesn't seem to see the connection. CDC Deputy Director Anne Schuchat, MD, says that suicide is a preventable public health problem, but the department isn't doing much to prevent it—at least when it comes to the pain community.

"Unfortunately, our data shows that the problem is getting worse," Schuchat said. "Our report found that physical health problems were present in about a fifth of individuals as circumstances considered to lead up to suicide. That doesn't differentiate whether it was intractable pain versus other conditions that might have been factors."

The CDC can learn more about these tragedies by listening to the stories of those in the community. Back in 2014, Anne started writing down the names of her friends who ended their own lives, all chronic pain patients who killed themselves after losing access to medical care. As of 2023, she has documented 932 suicide deaths. Of these, 235 deaths include the person's full name or a news article, suicide notes, family accounts, or medical records. Some are anonymous, referring only to a medical case report.

Anne has contemplated ending her own life multiple times. She said, "I am happy to be here as long as I can be on my own and have a good life. But if I lose access to my current treatment and don't find a miracle cure or someone who's willing to help me, I can't keep doing this. I'm grateful I even have medical options. Most people have not been that lucky."

12

Americans like to think we're exceptional. In many ways, we are. Yet, we aren't necessarily the greatest all the time. In the wealthiest, freest, most powerful nation on the planet, Americans also experience staggering inequality when it comes to wealth, maternal and infant mortality, racial health disparities, life expectancy, incarceration, literacy, and education.

Call it the American paradox. Our country spends more money on health care per capita than any other country in the world, and yet we're not very healthy. Americans take more antidepressants than any other nation, and we feel increasingly anxious and depressed. Our nation is home to more guns and rifles than actual people, with horrifying levels of violence, murder, and mass shootings. Nations described as "developing" have more doctors and health-care resources than states like Mississippi.

I would say that when it comes to drug use, America truly *is* exceptional. Our rates of drug use, drug overdose, and substance use disorders are extreme global outliers. On these fronts, America is number one. We consume more pills, powders, uppers, and downers than any other country. We spend more than $150 billion on weed, cocaine, heroin, and methamphetamine each year—about the same amount that we spend on alcohol. Drugs are American as apple pie. And our demand for drugs is at the heart of it all. Fentanyl is shining a spotlight on what I think of as a uniquely American problem. In the words of physician-historian David F. Musto, addiction has always been a quintessentially "American disease."

You can't fight basic human behavior (like drug use) or basic human needs (like health care and housing). The refusal to accept these things has fueled America's longest war. What would it mean for America to change its approach and stop waging this failing war? A "drug-free world" has never existed, and it never will. Enforcement can sometimes disrupt it, but as one drug market is taken down, another one pops up. Shutting down a chemical company producing fentanyl precursors in China is not a victory—there are thousands more in India to fill the gap. The same exact pattern is played out with even more dangerous drug combinations, like xylazine, also known as "tranq dope." Whack-a-mole continues unabated.

Stopping fentanyl and overdose deaths relies on a long game of treatment, prevention, education, health care, harm reduction, and recovery support. To truly combat this unprecedented fentanyl epidemic, our government must invest in reality-based education and prevention that helps people, especially young people, understand the truth about substances; we must invest in helping as many people as we can to stay alive and survive their addiction; and finally, we must dramatically expand treatment to help as many people as possible recover.

America is very much a work in progress. That's not a criticism; it's a fact. And honestly, it gives me hope. Progress means potential. It means that together, we can work to make things better.

Looking at the fentanyl crisis as a systemic problem, not an individual issue, is the beginning of this change. Substance use disorders and drug use connect to every challenge we face as a society. Addiction is a factor in employment, disease, child and family welfare, poverty, immigration, and criminal justice. Drug policy that doesn't take this into account is ignoring reality—a reality that has existed for the last century in this country. Instead, we need to focus on what fuels *demand* instead of obsessively fixating on the *supply* side of the equation. Otherwise, we'll keep spending trillions of dollars waging a futile war on the supply.

Whose problem is fentanyl anyway? It's as hard to pin down as the boogeyman. The DEA complains that Mexico and China are at fault; these countries refuse to help American authorities stop the tsunami of fentanyl crashing onto our shores. Mexico's president Andrés Manuel López Obrador (known as AMLO) dubiously contends that Mexico neither has a large demand for fentanyl, nor does it actually produce the drug. Both Mexican and Chinese governments shoot back that fentanyl is not their problem. They say it's America's problem.

These claims are clearly false. Mexican drug traffickers manufacture tons of fentanyl. The synthetic opioid also wreaks havoc on Mexico's side of the border, harming residents of Mexican border towns like Mexicali and Tijuana. Chinese authorities also reject the American accusation that China-based chemical manufacturers ship raw materials and precursor chemicals to illicit traffickers. The Chinese embassy has said that America's response to the fentanyl crisis is inadequate, calling the epidemic "rampant," while the American government does little to address it.

We're locked in a global, geopolitical stalemate over drug policy. America blames Mexico and China. Mexico and China blame America. Even though China and Mexico are bending the truth when they say their respective nations have nothing to do with the production or distribution of fentanyl, they aren't completely off base in their diagnosis of the American crisis. Fentanyl arrives in America through a massively complex global supply chain. The drug and its precursors pass between multiple countries. When someone dies, no single entity is to blame.

The truth is that fentanyl is all of our problem.

Broadly speaking, there are three targets of drug policy: 1) cutting off the source of production, 2) disrupting channels of distribution, and 3) reducing demand. America has lopsidedly invested in the first two strategies. On the third one, demand reduction, we've barely scratched the surface.

Now, reducing demand does not mean *erasing* demand. That's impossible. Carl Erik Fisher, an addiction psychiatrist who is also in long-term recovery, said it best: "By accepting that addiction has been and will continue to be a part of human life, we can abandon dreams of eradicating it. The primary goal should not be victory or cure, but alleviating harm and helping people to live with and beyond their suffering."[1]

These three policy strategies won't necessarily end drug use once and for all, but they do make a real and positive difference by materially improving people's lives. America has only briefly, in fits and starts, tried to enact a robust demand-side strategy. In the 1970s, there was a very brief window when President Nixon's administration spent more on medicine, treatment, and public health—only to reverse course and cave to "law and order" politics that disproportionately invested in prisons and jails.

Every president since has followed in his footsteps. Thus, drugs are perpetually locked between two poles, in a stalemate battle between medicalization and criminalization. Police, prisons, and punishment have been America's go-to strategy.

On top of this, people don't want to keep paying for a permanent crackdown. Polling consistently shows that a majority of Americans have soured on harsh and brutal enforcement tactics. A decade ago, 63 percent of Americans believed ending mandatory minimum drug sentences to be "a good thing," and only 26 percent believed the federal government should prioritize prosecuting people for using "hard drugs." More recent polling finds that Americans still believe the War on Drugs is a resounding failure.

But fentanyl and the synthetic drug supply complicate how

Americans feel. Due to fentanyl's shocking lethality, some doubt about the drug war's failures has begun to creep in. Some politicians have capitalized on fentanyl deaths as a wedge issue and accused other lawmakers of being soft on crime and weak on the border. (As ever, toxic partisan politics get us nowhere fast.) Now, polls show that most Americans blame individual "drug dealers" for the fentanyl crisis. In the same poll, Americans blamed China and Mexico for fentanyl; they tied for second, after drug dealers. I suspect the findings from this poll have something to do with the ubiquitous political campaign rhetoric calling for a *literal* drug war against China and Mexico.

Trump's former attorney general William Barr argued for labeling drug cartels as terrorist organizations. He wrote in the *Wall Street Journal*, "America can no longer tolerate narco-terrorist cartels."[2] Representative Dan Crenshaw of Texas introduced a bill in the House called the "Declaring War on the Cartels Act." On *Meet the Press*, Ohio senator J. D. Vance said he wants to use the military to disrupt fentanyl traffickers in Mexico. "I want to empower the president of the United States, whether that's a Democrat or Republican, to use the power of the US military to go after these drug cartels," Vance said. The Heritage Foundation, a conservative think tank, wrote that "China is poisoning America with fentanyl," while urging the White House to punish China for supplying drug cartels with fentanyl precursor chemicals.

To hear these folks tell it, today's war on drugs has multiple enemies being fought on multiple fronts. They make it sound like we have to soldier up against drug traffickers in Mexico, chemical manufacturers in China, and drug dealers in America.

Yet, they're not the only voices in the debate. While one side is agitating for war against Mexico and China, the other side asks the government to stop wasting so many precious resources on military and law enforcement. The goal of drug policy shouldn't be to dominate, destroy, and win the battle against drugs. If that's the case, we've already lost. Instead of pursuing another failed forever war, we must make a truce and find a path of coexistence.

What would happen if we laid down our weapons of over-prosecution and mass incarceration and picked up tools like health, medicine, and harm reduction? What would happen if we scaled back budgets for prisons, rolled back extreme mandatory minimum penalties, defelonized personal possession, and committed to robustly funding public health, mental health, and community services?

Thankfully, we don't have to invent this future. Other countries around the world have already given up on their wars against drugs. They've laid down their arms and picked up tools that save lives. If America can start believing that other nations' solutions could work here too, then we might be able to get ourselves through this tragedy. Looking and listening to research and strategies that are effective in other countries might help pave the way.

The Portugal Model

When forward-thinking drug policy enters political discussion, most Americans conjure up images of the small European nation of Portugal. (My analysis of the Portugal model is in Chapter 6.) Does drug decriminalization mean ending the drug war? It's a bit more complicated than that.

Drug decriminalization is exactly what it sounds like. It's neither a drug-free utopia nor a free-market drug-friendly free-for-all. Possession of personal quantities of drugs is reduced to the equivalent of a minor infraction. It becomes a *civil* violation, not a *criminal* one. This changes the way that crimes are prosecuted, the types of punishment that someone may face if they're convicted, and other factors.

Drug decriminalization is a strategy that largely focuses on protecting drug users from excessive and unnecessary punishment. People often confuse decriminalization with legalization, but they are different. The latter is what many US states have done with marijuana in recent years. (This is similar to how some states sell liquor.) With marijuana legalization, anybody above the age of 21 can walk into a store in 23 states and purchase weed that is taxed and regulated. Decriminalization is very different, especially because it is not an endorsement of the substance being sold. The government does not profit from decriminalization; it does make money on legalized substances, which are heavily taxed. While decriminalization does help keep drug users out of jail, it is also limited in its health benefits.

That's why Portugal decided to couple decriminalization with a system of treatment, health care, and harm reduction. This Portugal model is far from perfect. Experts complain that the treatment infrastructure lacks funding and has been actively undermined through budget cuts. Police complain that they've cited the same people numerous times for possession; even with publicly funded resources, nothing changes. Portugal's approach is just one model, and one example of what rolling the drug war back looks like—and it's proven to work when it gets an adequate slice of the budget and the long-term support people need to recover, including housing, treatment, and health care.

Norway—Safety Net

In 2020, after the pandemic shutdowns, both Norway and the US saw a surge in drug-related mortality. A 2022 study in the *Scandinavian Journal of Public Health* analyzed how both nations responded to this unprecedented health crisis.[3] It found a 46 percent increase in overdose deaths in America and a 57 percent increase in Norway. Both countries implemented restrictions on movement, such as shelter-in-place orders; both countries experienced a big jump in overdose deaths. But what each country did next is where things get interesting.

In the immediate window after lockdown, both countries saw overdoses spike. But the study found that Norway experienced a "more rapid return to baseline" and had fewer overdose deaths per capita compared to the US. What explains this divergence? It doesn't just fall on good drug policy (though that does help). As I said earlier, the health and well-being of a nation comes down to the entire structure of the country and its style of governance. In the case of Norway, their system has many advantages over America's, which meant that they were ready to prevent overdoses long before the surge of deaths arrived. The infrastructure to save lives was already in place, waiting to be used.

In 2014, Norway created a National Overdose Prevention Strategy funded by the Norwegian government. Here is a quick summary of this strategy published in the journal *Addiction*:

> The strategy has garnered pan-political support during the last 8 years. The strategy includes multiple elements, such as a focus on low-threshold access to opioid agonist treatment (OAT), ample access to harm reduction services, including take-home naloxone and safe drug consumption rooms. Additionally, a funded research-based monitoring strategy allows identifying new priority areas within the strategy, as overdose prevention is "chasing a moving target." Also, national prescription guidelines for opioid treatment of chronic pain are issued by public health agencies.

Sounds pretty nice, right? Norway is also home to a bountiful "Nordic-style" social welfare system, also known as a "safety net." (San Francisco is an example of a city without a safety net.) In this system, those who struggle with poverty, unemployment, homelessness, and chronic health conditions receive tremendous care and resources from the Norwegian government. Plus, Norway has a universal health-care system that can be accessed by anyone at any time, including those who need addiction care. That means lifesaving medications such as methadone and buprenorphine are made widely available. Both medications massively reduce the risk of a fatal opioid overdose. Just by having a strong safety net in place, Norway is off to a much better start for weathering an overdose crisis.

Broad political support is also crucial to Norway's success. In America, the politics around drug policy and especially harm reduction are toxic, conflicting, and extremely expensive. In contrast, the major political parties in Norway all support harm reduction strategies—often without moralizing about substance use or mental health. In the US, these strategies routinely receive accusations of "enabling" and "coddling" people who use drugs, even though they have been proven to work time and time again. Adequate support systems are described as "radical" in America, and thanks to right-wing myths of "welfare queens" and rhetoric around "entitlement," we lack a safety net that could help those struggling with addiction. For example, Medicaid expansion is one of the single most effective ways of reducing drug-related harms. But several deep-red states have refused to expand Medicaid, which offers health-care-like addiction treatment for low-income people. No safety nets allowed.

The differences between Norway and the United States are stark. The former focuses on overdose prevention and health care rather than militaristic supply reduction. Norway has invested precious resources in public health infrastructure for people who use drugs, which creates a certain flexibility and agility to respond quickly in an emergency like a pandemic.

When the Norwegian government realized that overdoses were surging during the early months of the shutdown, it quickly went to the source to try and figure out how to help. From the original study comparing the US and Norway, here is how the authors described Norway's response:

Of note, Norway had a vastly superior pandemic contain-
ment, with an overall mortality rate of about one-tenth of that
of the US. This may have facilitated a quicker re-instatement
of healthcare and other services. Furthermore, a more rapid
return to baseline, and much lower overdose death numbers
in Norway at baseline may reflect a more evidence-based approach to minimizing drug-related harms in general. Services
that are available in Norway, such as safe consumption sites,
remain largely banned in the US. Furthermore, universal
access to healthcare ensures better access to medications for
OUD, in which disparities in access remain very sharp in the
US. Also, a series of responsive actions were taken by Norwegian governmental organizations during spring and summer
2020, including weekly meetings with user organizations rep-
resenting PWUD [people who use drugs].

The last bit is particularly illuminating. To put it into perspective, Norway's "weekly meetings" would be the equivalent of the
White House reaching out to local harm reduction groups to offer
help and figure out what our community needs.

It's hard to imagine such a thing ever happening in America. The
White House is very concerned about "optics." When Biden was accused of "distributing crack pipes," his administration quickly scaled
back funding for clean smoking supplies. Norway isn't perfect, but its
government doesn't waver in its health-focused response. It was aware
that its population of drug users was at risk by disruptive pandemic
policies, so the government made efforts to reach out to organizations
led by people who use drugs to try and minimize harm during the
height of the pandemic.

The study's authors also mentioned one more crucial difference
between Norway and the United States: attitudes toward incarceration. The authors observed, "Extreme rates of incarceration in the US
have also been linked to a higher risk of overdose, especially in the

context of the entrance of fentanyl to the street drug supply. Norway's lower rates of incarceration may have been beneficial in this regard."

The Swiss Model

In Switzerland, more than 60 percent of opioid users are engaged in some form of treatment. In the US, only 13 percent of people with substance use disorders receive any treatment at all, and only 11 percent of people with OUD receive medications that protect them from overdose and support their recovery. Why do we have such a drastic gap in treatment retention and engagement? It largely stems from a crisis in Zurich during the 1980s and 1990s, which served as a catalyst for an innovative and pragmatic approach to addiction that dovetails with today's movement for a "safer supply."

Zurich is the largest city in Switzerland, home to a global system of finance and a reputation as a picturesque and ultra-wealthy metropolis. In the 1980s, that reputation took a bruising thanks to "Platzspitz," otherwise known as "Needle Park." The drug scene in Zurich 30 years ago very much resembles San Francisco's crisis today. A 2017 history of Switzerland's heroin crisis described Zurich's Needle Park like this:

> Gained notoriety as the situation spiraled out of control, with hundreds of dealers and addicts packed into the park, and many people desperately needing urgent medical care on a daily basis. A number of doctors volunteered their time, at first against the will of the authorities, to treat drug users with infected, weeping wounds or in cases of overdoses, and to hand out clean needles.

This park became a massive open-air drug scene where people injected in full view of the public. Drug users suffered from infectious disease, injection wounds, and fatal overdoses. Sound familiar? Many cities in America, from coast to coast, are struggling to respond to these very same trends today. The conditions in Needle Park horrified local residents, and politicians reacted by sending in heavy police forces to clear the park.

In 1992, Needle Park officially closed after police installed a heavy barricade. The crackdown led to a chaotic scene as drug users fled the area with nowhere to go, settling in an abandoned railway station nearby. Local residents again complained of the chaos created by the open drug use and drug dealing. In 1995, police shut down the new spot.

Realizing the troubling pattern would keep repeating itself, the Swiss did something different this time around. After shutting down the second Needle Park, the government invested in a new approach, which, surprise, surprise, focused on harm reduction, health care, and treatment. According to the history of Needle Park, "Needle exchanges were set up, clean injection rooms with medical staff on hand, a methadone prescription program and even a heroin prescription program now exists for heavily dependent addicts."

You read that correctly: prescription heroin, also known as diacetylmorphine. On the surface, it's a radical and controversial idea. But think about it this way. In the US, people have three addiction medications to choose from: methadone, buprenorphine, or naltrexone. Each of these has its own pros and cons; many people with complex opioid addiction histories have tried some or all of these options. Studies show that roughly 40 percent of people offered medications like methadone and buprenorphine continue to use illicit opioids.

When it comes to treatments, the more options available, the better. Moreover, fentanyl has made treatment much more difficult and complicated. Due to the intense tolerance that results from fentanyl addiction, many people struggle with a painful transition to these medications. Switzerland pioneered a strategy for those who'd tried multiple medications before and still struggled to find recovery. That's where diacetylmorphine comes into play.

Reserved for only the most entrenched and severe addictions, diacetylmorphine works like this: instead of receiving daily doses of methadone at a clinic, some people in Switzerland show up to a clinic two to three times per day to receive pharmaceutical-grade diacetylmorphine. Over time, the hope is for people to reduce their consumption as their lives become more stable through the treatment.

While radical, the basic principle here is simple. By prescribing a safe, regulated, and monitored dose of an opioid in a clinical setting, the person transitions from opioid addiction to opioid dependence. Think about it. People no longer have to purchase illegal drugs in parks from drug dealers. They no longer have to steal and hustle to fund their addictions. They no longer risk infectious diseases from unsanitary conditions. They no longer face the threat of incarceration and punishment. Most crucially, they are no longer vulnerable to the potency and purity of substances sold in unregulated markets. It's that volatility that puts people at risk of overdose.

People also receive much more than the prescribed drug at Swiss clinics. They are offered a whole range of health care and social services, including mental health treatment, housing, and help with employment opportunities. Instead of being trapped in the painful cycle of life on the street, people get their independence back. Results of rigorous clinical trials repeatedly find impressive outcomes from diacetylmorphine treatment programs. One study summarized the body of evidence:

> Results showed substantial improvements in physical and mental health status, social integration (including a reduction of drug-related criminal activity), as well as reductions in illicit drug use. Furthermore, a cost-benefit analysis indicated that the monetary savings due to the listed benefits from heroin-assisted treatment (diacetylmorphine) outweigh the financial costs of this form of treatment.

Now, you might be reading this and thinking, *"Is Ryan Hampton really endorsing diacetylmorphine treatment?"* Don't take this as a policy endorsement, but rather as an observation. If we're to get serious about solutions, we cannot ignore the fact that Safer Supply is working in other parts of the world. The US may not be ready for it, but it does work in other countries.

The Swiss model has proven to be tremendously effective. Between 1991 and 2010, overdose deaths in Switzerland plummeted by 50 percent, HIV infections declined by 65 percent, and new heroin users decreased by 80 percent, according to the *Stanford Social Innovation Review*. Despite these impressive results and many years of clinical research, diacetylmorphine and treatments like it are unavailable in the United States. A comprehensive report from RAND analyzed diacetylmorphine treatment and concluded that America could benefit from a pilot program to further explore this approach.

Canada—Activism and Solidarity

Vancouver, British Columbia, is the harm reduction mecca of North America. Following in Portugal's footsteps, British Columbia also decriminalized personal-use quantities of drugs in response to surging overdose mortality, stating: "From January 31, 2023, until January 31, 2026, adults in BC are not subject to criminal charges for the personal possession of small amounts of certain illegal drugs."

Vancouver has more harm reduction services than any city in America. It is recognized as a global leader in drug policy activism and reform. The services available in Vancouver—from supervised consumption sites, drug-checking programs, naloxone distribution, and even "safer supply" programs—are all the result of hard-fought battles.

The Vancouver Area Network of Drug Users is a group of people who used drugs organized into a highly effective coalition. They demanded dignity, respect, and autonomy for marginalized and stigmatized people who are at grave risk for experiencing drug-related harms. Their goal was to create a supervised consumption site—and they set it up before it was legal. Vancouver's Downtown Eastside neighborhood has had a sanctioned supervised consumption site since 2003.

Despite these victories, Vancouver is still struggling to keep up with a toxic drug supply and excessively high overdose deaths. Activists are still fighting for more resources. And it's a complex battle that goes beyond fentanyl and its many analogues. The street fentanyl supply in Vancouver is increasingly cut with a wide assortment of downers, depressants, and tranquilizers, from xylazine to benzodiazepines.

As the drug supply continues to spiral out of control, Vancouver activists have looked to Switzerland's diacetylmorphine playbook. Diacetylmorphine, hydromorphone (Dilaudid), and yes, prescription fentanyl are now on offer as treatments to help people transition out of the toxic street supply and into safer clinical settings. This "exit-ramp" approach is crucial for the era of synthetic drugs. As long as people are trapped purchasing illegal drugs of unknown potency and purity, there will be more casualties. Although "safer supply" programs are actively treating patients in BC, capacity does not yet meet demand.

Dr. Scott MacDonald is the lead physician at Vancouver's Crosstown Clinic, a Swiss-style practice that prescribes a variety of opioid addiction treatments in both oral and injectable forms. Many of the patients report that their lives have improved dramatically, thanks to the clinic's unique and innovative program. Almost all of the patients had severe substance use disorders and cycled through multiple treatment episodes during their lifetimes. It wasn't until Crosstown started offering the Swiss Model that some finally found stability.

That stability was threatened by the pandemic. Dr. MacDonald's clinic responded by pushing the boundaries of diacetylmorphine programs, allowing his patients to receive "take-home" doses so they could avoid having to show up to the clinic multiple times per day. Patients reporting their experiences in May 2023 emphasized their newly felt freedom, even folks who had been receiving medication treatment for over a decade.

Their experiences highlight the sacrifices people must make in order to stay alive and healthy. From the outside, people might see a life that's still too limited by substances. But from the individual's perspective, they're healthier and living stable lives, thanks to the treatment.

In learning about these radical approaches, I've had to reconsider my own preconceived notions—and that's as someone who is considered to be progressive on the harm reduction front. What I've learned has helped me come to the realization that the opioid drug supply is vastly different from the heroin I was injecting in the 2010s. There was a good 10 years of my addiction where I didn't want treatment. I missed fentanyl by a hair; had it been on the scene when I was active, I would be dead. Safer Supply gives people the opportunity to stay alive. Many people transition to longer-term options and treatment triages at various points in their lives, including full abstinence. The idea isn't to choose one option that works for everyone. It's to provide as many choices as possible so that everyone can find something that supports their unique recovery path.

Vancouver activists say not enough patients can access these programs, and they are still fighting to scale up. The Crosstown Clinic has a little more than one hundred people on its diacetylmorphine and Dilaudid programs, compared to the more than 85,000 people across British Columbia who are using illicit substances and are at risk of an overdose.

Back in my beloved Red, White, and Blue, our government remains laser-focused on the fentanyl supply chain. Sadly, this overlooks both robust demand-side resources and options for alternative treatments that have proven successful all over the world. A recent article in the *Economist* gave one of the most realistic assessments of today's war on drugs:

> The trouble is that trying to disrupt drug-trafficking is akin to battling a Hydra. In Greek mythology, when Hercules severed one of the serpent's heads, two more grew in its place. If China stops exporting precursor chemicals, more will come from India. If the DEA destroys the Sinaloa cartel, the CJNG may become public enemy number one. If San Diego's border crossings become impassable, Tucson in Arizona may take over as the channel—indeed, that may be happening already. "We are not making progress," says David Trone, a Democratic congressman from Maryland who co-chaired a bipartisan commission on synthetic-opioid trafficking.

We are not making *any* progress. The drug war has become a literal war. It's a war we refuse to give up, even though we're constantly losing. The death toll is well into the millions, surpassing casualties in the wars of Vietnam, Iraq, and Afghanistan combined. We have the highest drug overdose death rate in the world. Yet, we refuse to change course. Those who succumb to the all-too-human desire to use drugs are still being punished for it. A dire public health emergency is still being fought as a war between good and evil.

Chuck Ingoglia, president and CEO of the National Council for Mental Wellbeing, pointed out that policy and health outcomes are deeply intertwined. He said, "While policymakers lead from behind and struggle to catch up, people pay with their lives. Time after time, we know how the story of the overdose crisis will end before it's over—in tragedy. But until policymakers learn to address the cause of our overdose crises rather than the symptoms, our policies will remain reactionary."

American presidents have declared wars on poverty, crime, cancer—you name it. These domestic policy wars began when President Lyndon B. Johnson declared the "war on poverty" in the 1960s, but nobody back then seriously thought the president would deploy troops or invade Detroit. Declaring war on a thorny, urgent issue plaguing society was more of a signal to the public. It was a metaphor that meant that "victory" would require a massive mobilization of resources and sustained effort over time.

In the 21st century, the American government seems to have completely forgotten that the War on Drugs was always symbolic. President Johnson's war on poverty was to be fought and won by deploying empathy and help for those who were struggling. In the age of fentanyl, where fearmongering reigns supreme over calm and rational deliberation, the drug war has been stripped of its metaphorical and symbolic meaning.

Instead of implementing a strategy focused on helping people—as in Norway, Switzerland, Portugal, and Vancouver—America's response to fentanyl is hasty, rushed, and ineffective. Drug busts and global investigations into traffickers and suppliers simply don't translate into help for people who are actually suffering. As the DEA budget balloons to above $3 billion, drugs are still cheap, abundant, and deadlier than ever. Law enforcement continues to receive more and more resources, but people struggle to access even the most basic semblance of public health, such as quality, effective treatment.

Some American lawmakers, such as David Trone of Maryland, are starting to understand where we've gone wrong.

"Keep people alive," Mr. Trone repeatedly says to his colleagues. "That's the answer." And he knows the stakes: Trone lost his young nephew in 2016 to a fentanyl-related overdose. When more than 100,000 people are dying each year, implementing new and innovative strategies that save lives can make a huge difference.

Other countries have already done it. We can do it too.

13

BLAZING A NEW PATH

America is in desperate need of new ideas, values, and frameworks when it comes to preventing overdose deaths. As it stands, drug policy is dominated by the lens of crime and punishment, which labels all kinds of drug use as a criminal activity. As long as the government is obsessed with "eradication" efforts, we'll keep on chasing a fantasy of a drug-free world that never has, never will, and never can exist. The writing's on the wall. It's time to radically reimagine our national approach, or we'll keep getting the same fatal results.

The definition of insanity is doing the same thing over and over again and expecting different results. We're seeing this same pattern play out in policy. Drug use not only remains widespread and prevalent, but almost every notable outcome is trending in precisely the wrong direction. Rates of drug overdose deaths are at their highest in recorded history. The availability and potency of drugs keep rising while prices plummet. (In some markets, deadly potent counterfeit fentanyl pills cost less than $5 on the street, making them cheaper than a loaf of bread or gallon of milk.) If drug laws actually worked, substances would be expensive and difficult to find. We wouldn't have wave after wave of new "drug epidemics."

Despite throwing billions of dollars into our endless drug war, the supply continues to increase. While it's true that more fentanyl than ever is being seized at the US–Mexico border, that is simply because there is an astonishing amount of fentanyl being produced. When the street drug of choice was cocaine or heroin, which required long growing seasons and harvests, larger seizures did have some ability to make a dent in the market; they could impact availability and price. Fentanyl flips that script and makes law enforcement's strategy both inefficient and ineffective.

Former insiders agree. After leaving his job with the DEA, former high-ranking agent Chris Urben was candid about this dirty little secret. He told Reuters, "With the amount of death and destruction that fentanyl is causing, we can't look at those seizures as successes."[1]

Claiming that the tiny percentage of drugs that do get seized protects "communities against the scourge of fentanyl" is a fallacy too. Even Republican senator Lindsey Graham says the drug game "will never be won at the border."[2] In these final pages, I want to answer these questions the best I can and imagine a new drug policy modeled on compassion and human rights, based on the pragmatic principles of public health, harm reduction, and recovery that emphasizes overdose prevention.

We've got to leave the past behind and blaze a new path forward that protects human life. It's time to think about drugs through the lens of human rights—not criminal justice. Just imagine that, instead of building more jails and prisons, the ultimate goal of drug policy was to build a healthy and happy society that advances human potential. What would this look like? What institutions need to be built, and which should be reformed? What changes do we need to make? Whatever they are, we have to make them—or our loved ones will continue to die.

America was founded on the pursuit of happiness for all, and our American dream promises the opportunity to live free from tyranny and oppression. I still believe in the promise of that dream. I've put my faith in our highest ideals. That's why it's so painful to see how the drug war breaks these promises and dashes so many dreams. Drug overdose deaths are a major contributor to America's plummeting life expectancy in the 21st century, as well as rising rates of self-medication, depression, and suicide. I believe that preventing overdoses through better policy can dramatically turn these dark trends around.

Too many Americans are in pain—that much is clear. Mental health studies highlight that many of us feel alone and adrift, as if there's no way that life can get better. The worst of it is that people feel like they don't matter. That nobody cares about them. Drugs, and opioids in particular, help us cope with pain. The solution to this loneliness is not going to be found in packing the streets with police officers; it's not in prison cells, or in courtrooms. Life for too many of us already feels like a prison.

Billboards that say "think positive" aren't going to cut it either. People must feel like they matter and hope that a better life is possible. Better drug policy is part of this profound cultural shift. It may not happen overnight, but I believe that offering people meaningful, accessible support is the solution. Everyone deserves a safety net—even if they never need to use it.

To survive, people must know and feel deep in their bones that there is light at the end of this long, dark tunnel. There are brighter days ahead, and I believe we can get there. Here's how.

Changing policy is one thing. Changing how people think and feel is something else entirely. To learn more about a new framework for thinking about drugs in general, I looked to the United Nations in Vienna, where 193 countries met to find solutions to thorny global problems. The United Nations Office on Drugs and Crime provides research, guidance, and support to governments on a range of drug-related issues, from dealing with organized crime and illicit drug trafficking to balancing supply- and demand-side strategies. The UN also proposes the kinds of ideals and values that underlie effective drug policy. The most interesting distinction between the UN's approach and the American perspective is their emphasis on human rights.

Human rights are inherent to all human beings regardless of race, sex, gender, class, or creed. In essence, they are about advancing the universal conditions that promote human potential. They also encompass freedom *from* systems of oppression that would stop people from flourishing, such as slavery, tyranny, and unjust execution of authority.

Drugs and human rights are inextricable in America. Every single day in our nation, a person loses their freedom for possessing drugs, and some 300 people die from a drug overdose. More than a million people are arrested on drug charges each year. People lose jobs, scholarships, housing, and even contact with their children because of drug-related crimes, however petty or minor. Do our current drug laws violate human rights or do they promote human flourishing? If you've read this far, I think you know my answer.

On June 26, 2023, the International Day Against Drug Abuse and Illicit Trafficking, UN experts signed a scathing letter calling out the drug war as an affront to human rights. The letter identified the global war on drugs as a war on people—specifically Black people. It said: "In various countries, the 'war on drugs' has been more effective as a system of racial control than as a tool to reduce drug markets . . . Policing interventions based on racial profiling remain widespread, whilst access to evidence-based treatment and harm reduction for people of African descent remains critically low."

Just one month after the UN published their letter, something horrifying happened in Singapore, a nation that is notorious for its highly punitive approach to drug policy. Possession of just 15 grams of heroin, or about half of an ounce, can result in the death penalty. Being caught with 500 grams of marijuana, roughly one pound, is also punishable by death there. This is a blatant violation of international law and human rights.

On July 28, 2023, the Singaporean government executed 45-year-old Saridewi Binte Djamani for drug trafficking—the first woman to be executed by the state in nearly two decades. According to Singapore's Central Narcotics Bureau, she was charged, convicted, and put to death for possessing "not less than 30.72" grams of heroin, an amount that could fit into a sandwich-size Ziploc bag.

The American media was horrified and outraged at the news. *The death penalty for drugs? That would never happen here.* Well, not so fast.

As more and more states have pivoted to prosecuting overdose deaths as homicides, and even charging suspected dealers with first-degree murder, getting the death penalty for drug charges becomes a very real possibility. Former president Donald Trump, the center of gravity in the Republican Party, repeatedly called for capital punishment for drug sellers. In a 2018 speech in New Hampshire, one of the first states hit hard by fentanyl, Trump said, "If we don't get tough on drug dealers, we're wasting our time, just remember that, we're wasting our time, and that toughness includes the death penalty."

He doubled down only a few years later. Announcing his 2024 run for president, Trump made executing drug dealers the centerpiece of his terrifying campaign. "We're going to be asking everyone who sells drugs, gets caught selling drugs, to receive the death penalty for their heinous acts," Trump said. "Because it's the only way."

While the United Nations is calling on the world to adopt drug policies grounded in human rights, our wannabe politicians are flirting with the ultimate punishment for drug crimes. This is what I mean when I say we need to overhaul our views of drugs. What does it say about our nation that so many people support cruel and unusual punishment for drug crimes, and our civic representatives feel empowered to spew this hatred in public speeches?

The 2020s are a national test and critical inflection point for not just American drug policy but for the future and direction of the nation as a whole. Our costly, ineffective drug war is leading us down a road to barbarism. We're not listening to the United Nations' call to implement treatment and support over punishment. More than ever, it's vital to lay out a bold vision for a new kind of drug policy that centers on compassion and human rights.

A New Way Forward

Drugs cut across nearly every facet of human society. They touch almost every element of our lives, at every level; they affect individuals, families, and communities, as well as local, state, and federal governments and infrastructure. From education to employment, health care to housing, and police to courts, drug policy touches it all. This means that the stakes of failure are vast. The way forward seems enormously complicated. And no single person—including me—has all the answers.

I've interviewed dozens of experts over the course of writing this book, including grieving parents like Ed Ternan and Susan Ousterman and addiction doctors and toxicologists like Tamara Olt and Ryan Marino. I've heard stories from street drug users in cities across America. I've also heard inspiring stories of resilience and recovery from people like Morgan Godvin. After hearing so many different perspectives, a broad picture has come into focus. Our differences may vary, but what we all agree on is that the disaster we're living through was created by humans—and it can be fixed by humans. We all agree that if we apply the principles of public health, harm reduction, and recovery, and steer policy toward preventing overdoses, protecting human life, and advancing health and well-being, we can save many lives. We agree that stigma and discrimination against people who use drugs is one of the most critical obstacles to progress, and criminalization of substance use is a major driver of that stigma. It is clear that we must end the criminalization of drug use and change our perceptions of people who use drugs in order to break this stigma and bring America into a healthy future.

That's a tall order. It could take decades to accomplish our goals. Changing hearts and minds while simultaneously building a new infrastructure grounded in human rights requires monumental effort and focus. We need a massive mobilization of resources.

When I talk to policy experts, they say that policy and lawmaking in America is particularly difficult right now. We're a diverse, geographically massive nation with a complex system of government. However, we already have a blueprint for the same kind of united response that will stop overdoses: the COVID-19 pandemic. During this period, every level of government responded with urgency. The Treasury printed a historic $5 trillion in rescue funds. Government-funded research developed effective vaccines, paid for hundreds of millions of vaccine doses, and sent families a monthly allotment of free testing kits. Coronavirus was swiftly declared a public health emergency, and rather than risk millions of lives by ignoring the threat, Americans did something about it.

To be clear, it wasn't all sunshine and puppy dogs. Public health interventions, such as masks and vaccines, became unnecessarily polarized by cynical partisanship. COVID-19 deniers spread conspiracy theories. Some people dosed themselves with horse dewormers rather than take an FDA-approved vaccine. Our national strategy wasn't perfect—but at least the majority of us tried.

I can't say the same about the public health emergency of overdose deaths. That scale of response has yet to materialize, much less approach the effectiveness of our pandemic response. Imagine a response to overdoses at that level of health care and public health infrastructure. If the government can pay for millions of COVID-19 vaccine doses and send tests to every family for free, then there is no reason why the government cannot do the same to address overdose prevention.

We all know overdose deaths are endemic, but the exact nature of the crisis and what to do about it gets swallowed up by heated rhetoric and toxic politics. The so-called debates around overdoses are just so much hot air and wasted breath. What if, rather than arguing about morality, our leaders went all in on overdose prevention and protecting human life? What if we all started to look out for the most vulnerable in our country?

Building a Better Drug Policy: Going All In On Overdose Prevention

1. FREE UNIVERSAL NALOXONE

   The single most important thing we can do right now to save as many lives as possible is make naloxone free and universally available to everyone. Just as every public space—including schools, restaurants, bars, and airports—is equipped with EpiPens and defibrillators, every first-aid kit should have naloxone. This is a no-brainer. A survey from the Kaiser Family Foundation found that more than 80 percent of respondents support broadening access to naloxone.

   I can already hear the pundits yelling *But who's gonna pay for it?* The truth is that naloxone is a very old generic drug; invented in 1961, its patent has long expired. It costs a nickel per dose to manufacture. Yet, pharmaceutical companies have price-gouged naloxone as surging overdoses led to increased demand. (One company, Kaléo Inc., priced its naloxone product at $4,000; the company was sued by the Department of Justice and had to pay a slap-on-the-wrist fine of $12.7 million.) Drastically expanding access and availability to naloxone, including controlling the medication's price, ought to be one of the very first moves our government makes in this emergency. This will not only

improve health outcomes but also send a message to the
public that saving lives and reversing overdoses is all of
our responsibility. It would mean that the government
is taking this crisis seriously and that we all should too.

Thus far, the government has not led by example.
A 2022 study in *The Lancet* found that almost every
single state has a naloxone shortage.[3] Bystanders rarely
have naloxone on them and can't respond to overdoses
that occur in front of them. We must fill the naloxone
gap and stock this safe, affordable, and highly effective
drug everywhere possible—for free.

2. **REAL-TIME DATA**
    Collecting accurate data in real time is crucial for any
    response to a public health crisis. During the pandemic,
    many news outlet websites shared infection stats from
    Johns Hopkins's data dashboard. You could check for
    updates as easily as checking the weather. Real-time
    data collection made it possible to track the number
    of reported cases, hospitalizations, and deaths in my
    county. Several years later, I can still log onto the CDC's
    website and see how many COVID-19 cases are in
    Clark County, Nevada.

    Yet, I cannot find real-time data on drug overdoses,
    drug-related hospitalizations, or emergency room vis-
    its. It's appalling that after all these years into a public
    health emergency, overdoses aren't treated as seriously
    as other life-threatening health issues. We don't even
    know the true number of people seeking treatment for
    substance use disorder, or how many people are using
    fentanyl or meth or other drugs in America. Good data
    is essential to staying ahead of this crisis and under-

standing what's happening on the ground, instead of re-
acting to waves of deaths with months-old information.

3.   **ADDICTION TREATMENT ON DEMAND**
The pandemic brought America's for-profit and pri-
vatized health-care system to its knees. Hospitals and
emergency departments were overflowing. Exhausted
health-care workers risked their lives to treat those
suffering from a deadly virus. Addiction magnifies the
same structural and policy weaknesses—but we can
close those gaps by offering addiction treatment on
demand.

It's not that America doesn't spend enough money
on health care; the problem is *how* we spend it. In 2021,
America spent 18.3 percent of its GDP, or $4.3 trillion,
on health care. We can afford to treat addiction, but
with so many costs and access barriers, it's nearly impossible for the average person to get—especially when
they're in crisis. Only 13 percent of people who meet
the criteria for a substance use disorder receive any kind
of treatment at all; just 11 percent of people with an
OUD receive effective medications.

On top of that, even though mental health parity
laws state that addiction treatment must be incorpo-
rated with other types of medical support, treatment is
still almost entirely segregated from mainstream care.
To save lives, this segregation must end. Insurance must
cover care for both acute and chronic addiction in the
same way physical conditions are covered. Rather than
only offering intense, short-term support, health care
must adapt to provide the long-term follow-up and progressive care that chronic illnesses require.

High-cost, low-quality treatment can no longer dominate the market. Nobody struggling with problematic drug use or a substance use disorder should have to Google "rehab near me" only to end up in a predatory treatment center. Too many people take disastrous trips to the Rehab Riviera in Malibu, where their "treatment" is to spend $1,000 per day petting horses on a ranch. (The horses are sober.) Others try the Florida Shuffle and leave sick and drained, with their insurance billed for thousands of dollars.

The goals for treatment must change as well. Treatment options should be decided by a knowledgeable medical provider in consultation with their patient, and centered around the individual patient's health and well-being. To protect vulnerable people and build a better treatment system, America must scale up a robust and highly trained addiction treatment and recovery workforce. Peer mentors with lived experience, expert medical providers, and qualified caregivers are key to ensuring that someone gets help and stays engaged in their own treatment.

4.   **INNOVATE TREATMENT**

Treatment for addiction is complex, and much different from taking an antibiotic for a bacterial infection or getting a vaccine to lessen the symptoms of an airborne virus. It takes time to get better, and while certain medications can support recovery, they are only one part of an effective treatment plan. To increase people's chance of survival, we need meaningful innovation in addiction care.

There are many different pathways toward recovery—and it still isn't enough. We need more options and new tools, methods, and medications. For example, it's common for people who use opioids to also use stimulants such as methamphetamine. They might receive medication to treat their OUD, but what kind of treatment do they get for their stimulant use? Unfortunately, there are very few options aside from counseling. Why isn't there a methadone or buprenorphine equivalent for methamphetamine addiction?

The government transferred billions of dollars for coronavirus research during the pandemic and ought to do the same for substance use disorder. The National Institute of Health's budget is over $40 billion; the National Institute on Drug Abuse, which funds the bulk of the world's addiction treatment research, is just shy of $1.5 billion. With more investment in funding and research, we can unlock new pathways to help people recover.

5. **GOING BEYOND TREATMENT**

Community and a sense of belonging are equally, if not more, important than medical treatment. The standard timeline to transition from chaotic drug use and addiction to stability and recovery should be a year or more. In the current acute care model, treatment is brief and might only last a few hours per day for a few weeks, a month, or even less. Research overwhelmingly shows that our standard 28-day model is ineffective, and short-term spin-dry rehabs often set people up to overdose and die. Extending the recovery timeline to 18 months and incorporating housing, long-term support, and recovery services are shown to increase the likelihood of recovery more than tenfold.

To provide a lifesaving network that can support people during recovery, we need to think beyond treatment. We must invest in communities that create a sense of belonging and purpose. (One example of this is 12-step meetings, which represent a cohesive social support group.) Just as treatment requires multiple pathways, so does what happens *after* treatment. We need a robust, inclusive peer infrastructure with a wide diversity of recovery community organizations that are warm, inclusive, and welcoming. This is even more important because not everyone who recovers from a substance use disorder utilizes formal treatment, faith-based programs, medication-assisted treatment, abstinence-only recovery, group therapy, or self-help programs. Anyone can benefit from social groups that support a recovery lifestyle.

6.   **END HOMELESSNESS, HOUSTON STYLE**
As an advocate, I've crisscrossed this country many, many times. Whether I'm in Portland, San Francisco, Phoenix, Denver, Austin, or Burlington, Vermont, it's impossible to ignore that more people are living in tents than ever—and many of them are using substances. I don't think it's an accident that rates of homelessness happen to coincide with fentanyl taking over the heroin markets. Now, many activists, journalists, and politicians mistakenly suggest that fentanyl *caused* higher levels of homelessness. They're wrong. Conflating addiction and overdose with homelessness is a perspective that misses the forest for the trees. The basic fact is that homelessness has risen in every place where the housing supply is low, and rent costs have increased. The primary causal factor is rising prices. Period.

The only American city that has come close to figuring out how to fix this is Houston. While other cities condemn people to shelters, subject them to frequent arrests and harassment, and demolish encampments only to see them pop up again blocks away, the nation's fourth-largest city went all in on housing first. In one decade, Houston moved more than 25,000 homeless people into their own apartments and houses. As a result, Houston's overdose death rate is also much lower than many other major cities. Once people are housed, they can access the health care and services they need the same way the rest of us do: from the privacy of their homes.

7. **POLICE AND LAW ENFORCEMENT**

The paradox of the drug war is that the cost of drugs on the street remains low, while drugs themselves remain widely available. And yet, one out of every five people in jail or prison is there on drug offenses.[4] Drug war–style policing has clearly failed to accomplish its stated goals. Rather than persist in a mission that isn't working, I think it's important to talk about the role police can play. We must refashion drug policy through a pragmatic, public health lens—and that includes policing.

This change wouldn't be a first for our nation. Legalizing alcohol was a milestone in how police ended the criminalization of a substance. Brandon del Pozo, a former chief of police-turned-epidemiologist, wrote, "Legalization [of alcohol] ended policing of an illicit market, but the dangers of impaired driving, the disruptive and sometimes violent results of intoxication, and the consequences of alcohol use disorder continue to require emergency interventions."

Rather than dedicate too many resources to fighting drugs, police can focus on more serious crimes that disrupt everyday life, like property crime and violence.

When I talk to police officers, they say they want to protect the public and promote safety. If police start viewing drugs through a public health framework, they will see that they still have a crucial role in helping people access social support and health care. Just as when we ended the alcohol prohibition, police would still have a role in promoting health and safety if we defelonized drug use and simple possesion.

8. **URBAN AND RURAL HARM REDUCTION**
    A one-size-fits-all drug policy is shown to be a death sentence for anyone outside the predetermined "norm." To save lives, we must have policy that is tailored to the unique needs of people in specific regions. Urban and rural harm reduction solutions will look different, but both can benefit from the principles of a compassionate and human rights–centered approach. For example, New York City's two overdose prevention centers have rescued more than 1,000 people from fatal overdoses. These sites do so much more than monitor drug use and reverse overdoses. For many New Yorkers, these sites are places that welcome them with open arms and kindness—a sign of the change our nation so badly needs.

    Harm reduction is about meeting people where they're at. In the case of rural harm reduction, that often means literally. I've witnessed innovative grassroots overdose prevention solutions in rural towns that operate mobile harm reduction programs. In West Virginia, Kentucky, and North Carolina, I've seen the best of what harm reduction in our country can look like. Despite shoestring budgets and hostile political climates, these frontline workers have found a way to offer compassion and kindness to the most vulnerable among us. They park their vans in a friendly parking lot (such as a community center or church) and distribute naloxone, clean syringes, HIV and Hep C testing, and even perform drug checks to alert people to what they're actually using. The most important thing they do is show up for people without judgment. Doctors, nurses, social workers, volunteers, and peer workers in rural towns form deep bonds with people who've been arrested, harassed, and judged by every other institution in their life. Again, that's something our country could do with a lot more of.

Whether rural or urban, local, state, and federal governments must defend and stick up for these life-saving harm reduction programs. These programs must be funded and supported to scale up to meet the needs of the local communities.

9. **LEAVE NO ONE BEHIND**

"Justice for all" means *all* of us. Everyone. In building a new culture of drug policy and recovery, we must lead with equity in order to create the most welcoming and diverse community possible. We need to build communities of recovery and support that are tailored to the multiracial mosaic that makes up America. Our policy choices must be rooted in equity toward groups that America has historically not made room for. Substance use can and does happen in every community, from BIPOC to LGBTQIA+.

As a gay man in recovery, I feel most at home in LGBTQIA+ friendly groups. I feel profoundly grateful to have found a group that accepts me for who I am and welcomes me. I can't imagine my recovery without finding a group that represents me. Everyone deserves that. We can't build new systems and structures while leaving folks behind, which means we need to think beyond "traditional" or "fundamental" resources and center the experiences of people who are underserved and underrepresented.

Even as I propose this list of changes, the challenges we're up against can't escape my mind. The present conditions are atrocious. We have all these tough laws on the books, tons of awareness efforts, soaring campaign speeches, daily press releases, and marches and rallies around the country—but does any of it even make a dent?

Sometimes, it feels like the pain of trying is simply too great. If the drug war is really a war, we're not just losing. We're being crushed. Polling shows roughly three in ten Americans have either been addicted to opioids, or have a family member who has been in the past. One-third of Americans report feeling afraid that someone in their family will die of an overdose, while more than a third express concern that a family member might ingest fentanyl accidentally. Most Americans today share the perspective that addiction ought to be treated as a health and medical issue. Public awareness isn't our primary barrier anymore.

Without question, the biggest barrier I see ahead of us is politics.

In such a polarized moment, addiction is a rare subject on which most of us agree. And yet, progress remains elusive. In every election cycle, Democrats and Republicans continue to fight and bicker about the southern border. The issue of drugs continues to be politically weaponized. Based on survey data and nationally representative polling, this partisanship is not only unnecessary, it's leaving people angered, embittered, and resentful. Inflammatory rhetoric has boiled over, creating panic and fear that fogs our judgment. If we want to implement new and innovative policies that will save lives, we have to lower the volume of toxic partisanship and political infighting. Whether rural or urban, liberal or conservative, Democrat or Republican, there is enough common ground to work together, make progress, and save lives. I fully believe this, and I stand by my words. Maybe it's possible to stop this powerful force if we can work together and see our shared purpose and similarities.

And unless we come together, we won't just lose the War on Drugs. We'll lose the people we love most, and we'll lose ground against the rising tide of overdoses. I can talk about advocacy, policy, and infrastructure plans until I'm blue in the face. I can't ignore that we're conditioned as a society to tolerate 300 overdose deaths every day as yet another grim fact of 21st-century American life. There's a dull ache in the pit of my stomach that nags at me, telling me that we're stuck in an endless drug endemic. If fentanyl seems bad, we'll soon be coping with newer and deadlier synthetic substances.

Faith on its own is not enough to create the changes we need to save our nation and ourselves. It takes action, grit, and courage. It takes people you can count on, folks who pick you up on the days when you wonder if it's worth going forward. Even if my policy proposals don't materialize for decades to come, I trust that my community will persist in our goal of stopping overdoses.

Even as we suffer losses and grieve for our loved ones, our ideas and our spirit will never die.

What I know is this: America is in pain.

And while there's no immediate cure for what we've got, we deserve to heal together.

ACKNOWLEDGMENTS

First and foremost, I want to acknowledge the peer workers, harm reductionists, family members, and service providers who work to end overdoses and save lives. I hope this book is a testament to your dedication and persistence under some of the most difficult circumstances. Without you, we are truly lost. Thank you for all you give, every day, to the people who need help most.

Each of my books has been a labor of love, and this one is no exception. Thank you, from the bottom of my heart, to my family: my husband, Sean, my mother, Barbara, and my sisters Lorraine, Katy, Michelle, and Kimberly—and my in-laws, Laura and Bruce Johnson. Knowing that I can always count on you gives me the courage I need.

Thank you to this book's "other mothers," including my editor Kevin Reilly at St. Martin's Press, as well as Laura Clark, Ken Silver, Lizz Blaise, Niko Eickelbeck, and the entire team at the imprint. From the time I brought them *American Fix* in 2017, this imprint has put our cause front and center. Their belief in this book and its urgency is something I'll forever be grateful for. My incredible co-writers and friends Claire Rudy Foster and Zach Siegel gave their love, time, and talent to bring this book to life, while publicists

Elizabeth Shreve and Tim Sullivan shared it with the world. I am so appreciative of your commitment to this project.

For their unwavering support and faith in me, I want to thank my friends, coconspirators, and colleagues. From perfectly timed pep talks to the best hugs in the galaxy, these folks got me through more times than I can count. Thank you to Garrett and Melissa Hade, Kristen Williams, Jessica Geschke, Jaclyn and Jordan Brown, Chris Thrasher, Nick Boatman, Tom Coderre, Courtney Allen, Jimmy Hill, and Mikey Bacon.

And thank you to the entire team at Mobilize Recovery and the Recovery Advocacy Project for centering the voices of those most impacted through your meaningful advocacy and action. You inspire me every day to bring my best self to the fight.

NOTES

3. America's Longest War

1. "New ACLU Report: Despite Marijuana Legalization Black People Still Almost Four Times More Likely to Get Arrested," *ACLU Magazine,* April 20, 2020, https://www.aclu.org/press-releases/new-aclu-report -despite-marijuana-legalization-black-people-still-almost-four-times.

2. James M. Markham, "The American Disease," *New York Times,* April 29, 1973, https://www.nytimes.com/1973/04/29/archives/the-american -disease-origins-of-narcotic-control-by-david-f-musto.html.

3. "Alcohol 'more harmful than heroin' says Prof David Nutt," BBC, November 1, 2010, https://www.bbc.com/news/uk-11660210.

4. Wayne Hall and Megan Weier, "Lee Robins' Studies of Heroin Use Among US Vietnam Veterans," *Addiction*, September 20, 2016, https: //pubmed.ncbi.nlm.nih.gov/27650054/.

5. Nora D. Volkow and Eric M. Wargo, "Overdose Prevention Through Medical Treatment of Opioid Use Disorders," *Annals of Internal Medicine,* June 19, 2018, https://www.acpjournals.org/doi/abs/10.7326/M18– 1397.

4. Newton's Third Law

1. "Drug Enforcement Administration Announces the Seizure of Over 379 Million Deadly Doses of Fentanyl in 2022," DEA, December 20, 2022, https://www.dea.gov/press-releases/2022/12/20/drug-enforcement -administration-announces-seizure-over-379-million-deadly.

2. Glenn Kessler, "J.D. Vance's Claim That Biden Is Targeting 'MAGA Voters' with Fentanyl," *Washington Post*, May 11, 2022, https://www.washingtonpost.com/politics/2022/05/11/jd-vances-claim-that-biden-is-targeting-maga-voters-with-fentanyl/.

3. "Drug Overdose Deaths in the U.S. Top 100,000 Annually," CDC, November 17, 2021, https://www.cdc.gov/nchs/pressroom/nchs_press_releases/2021/20211117.htm.

4. Emma Court, "Hidden Fentanyl Is Driving a Fatal New Phase in US Opioid Epidemic," *Bloomberg News,* December 13, 2022, https://www.bloomberg.com/graphics/2022-us-fentanyl-opioid-deaths/?leadSource=uverify%20wall.

5. Aaron M. White, PhD, "Alcohol-Related Deaths During the COVID-19 Pandemic," *JAMA*, May 3, 2022, https://jamanetwork.com/journals/jama/fullarticle/2790491.

6. Roni Caryn Rabin, "Alcohol-Related Deaths Spiked During the Pandemic, a Study Shows," *New York Times*, March 22, 2022, https://www.nytimes.com/2022/03/22/health/alcohol-deaths-covid.html.

7. "Substance Use and Overdose Prevention Timeline," FDA, accessed November 7, 2023, https://www.fda.gov/drugs/information-drug-class/timeline-selected-fda-activities-and-significant-events-addressing-substance-use-and-overdose.

8. "Timeline of Selected FDA Activities and Significant Events Addressing Substance Use and Overdose Prevention," FDA, September 27, 2023, https://www.fda.gov/media/126835/download.

9. Maia Szalavitz, "We're Waging the Wrong Battle Against Opioids," *Undark Magazine,* September 22, 2023, https://undark.org/2022/02/04/opinion-the-wrong-battle-against-opioids/.

10. Alexander Y. Walley, Dana Bernson, Mark Larochelle, Traci Green, Leonard Young, and Thomas Land, "The Contribution of Prescribed and Illicit Opioids to Fatal Overdoses in Massachusetts, 2013–2015," *Public Health Reports*, October 2, 2019, https://journals.sagepub.com/doi/full/10.1177/0033354919878429?.

11. "Drug Overdose Deaths in the United States, 2001–2021," CDC, accessed November 7, 2023, https://www.cdc.gov/nchs/data/databriefs/db457.pdf.

12. Barry Meier, "F.D.A. Bars Generic OxyContin," *New York Times*, April 16, 2013, https://www.nytimes.com/2013/04/17/business/fda-bars-generic-oxycontin.html?_r=0.

13. "Drug Overdose Deaths in the United States, 2001–2021," CDC, accessed November 7, 2023, https://www.cdc.gov/nchs/data/databriefs/db457.pdf.

14. Theodore J. Cicero, Matthew S. Ellis, Hilary L. Surratt, and Steven P. Kurtz, "The Changing Face of Heroin Use in the United States: A Retrospective Analysis of the Past 50 Years," *JAMA Psychiatry*, July 1, 2014, https://pubmed.ncbi.nlm.nih.gov/24871348/.

15. Erin McCormick, "Killed by a Pill Bought on Social Media: The Counterfeit Drugs Poisoning US Teens," *The Guardian*, December 23, 2021, https://www.theguardian.com/us-news/2021/dec/22/teen-fentanyl-deaths-pills-social-media.

16. Second Peek Investigations, accessed November 7, 2023, https://www.secondpeekinvestigations.com/.

6. In Search of a New Model

1. Ashley B. Craig, "W.Va. Police Academy Gets New Training Center," *Police1*, April 28, 2012, https://www.police1.com/police-products/fitness-mental-health-wellness/articles/wva-police-academy-gets-new-training-center-UleRZAUd6ukD4EeL/#:~:text=The%20structure%20cost%20about%20%241.85,Michael%20Baylous%20said.

2. Mark McMullen and Josh Lehner, "May 2023 Economic and Revenue Forecast," Oregon Office of Economic Analysis, May 17, 2023, https://olis.oregonlegislature.gov/liz/2023R1/Downloads/CommitteeMeetingDocument/274107.

7. "I Forgive You"

1. Samantha Kummerer, "NC Law That Punishes Drug Dealers Not Widely Used Despite Increase in Overdose Deaths," ABC11 Raleigh-Durham, May 25, 2023, https://abc11.com/overdose-deaths-nc-death-by-distribution-law-drug-dealers-investigation/13299752/.

2. Rosa Goldensohn, "They Shared Drugs. Someone Died. Does That Make Them Killers?," *New York Times*, May 25, 2018, https://www.nytimes.com/2018/05/25/us/drug-overdose-prosecution-crime.html.

3. Brandon Morrissey, Taleed El-Sabawi, and Jennifer J. Carroll, "Prosecuting Overdose: An Exploratory Study of Prosecutorial Motivations for Drug-Induced Homicide Prosecutions in North Carolina," Social Science Research Network (SSRN), March 20, 2023, https://papers.ssrn.com/sol3/papers.cfm?abstract_id=4389026.

8. **Goodbye, Yellow Brick Road**

1. Dan Rosenbaum, "The Guide to San Francisco's Michelin-Starred Restaurants," *San Francisco Travel*, July 7, 2023, https://www.sftravel .com/article/guide-to-san-francisco%E2%80%99s-michelin-starred -restaurants.

2. Amanda Hari, "San Francisco Hits New Record for Accidental Overdose Deaths," KRON4, May 14, 2023, https://www.kron4.com/news /bay-area/san-francisco-hits-new-record-for-accidental-overdose-deaths/.

3. Caroline Cawley, MPH, "Mortality Among People Experiencing Homelessness in San Francisco During the COVID-19 Pandemic," *JAMA Network Open*, March 10, 2022, https://jamanetwork.com/journals /jamanetworkopen/fullarticle/2789907.

4. Roland Li and Sriharsha Devulapalli, "Map of Downtown San Francisco Shows Every Empty Office Space," *San Francisco Chronicle*, May 12, 2023, https://www.sfchronicle.com/sf/article/downtown-empty-offices -business-tech-17911258.php.

5. Anna Tong, "Easy Come, Easy Go: How Tech Fueled the Boom and Bust of San Francisco Office Work," *San Francisco Standard*, July 8, 2022, https://sfstandard.com/2022/07/08/how-techies-fueled-boom-and-bust -of-sf-office-work/.

6. Nuala Bishari, "What's the Point of Those New 'Fentalife' Ads in SF's Tenderloin?," *San Francisco Chronicle*, May 18, 2023, https://www .sfchronicle.com/opinion/article/sf-tenderloin-fentanyl-ads-18106984.php.

7. Heather Murray, "Fearing a Fear of Germs," *Perspectives on History*, October 2, 2020, https://www.historians.org/research-and-publications /perspectives-on-history/october-2020/fearing-a-fear-of-germs-how-did -the-surgical-mask-transform-from-a-sign-of-bigotry-to-a-sign-of-care.

8. "2022 Grantees," *Environmental Progress*, accessed on July 7, 2023, https://environmentalprogress.org/grantees.

9. Ryan Dwyer, Anita Palepu, Claire Williams, Daniel Daly-Grafstein, and Jiaying Zhao, "Unconditional Cash Transfers Reduce Homelessness," *Proceedings of the National Academy of Sciences of the United States of America*, September 5, 2023, https://pubmed.ncbi.nlm.nih.gov /37643214/#:~:text=Exploratory%20analyses%20showed%20that%20 over,via%20reduced%20time%20in%20shelters.

10. Peter Dreier, "Homelessness Meets Cluelessness," *The American Prospect*, March 18, 2022, https://prospect.org/culture/books/homelessness -meets-cluelessness-shellenberger-review/.

11. "California Governor Primary Election Results," *New York Times*, June 15, 2022, https://www.nytimes.com/interactive/2022/06/07/us /elections/results-california-governor.html.

12. Eric Ting, "A Whole Foods in San Francisco Closed. Now a Political Fight Looms," *SF Gate*, April 11, 2023, https://www.sfgate.com/food /article/san-francisco-whole-foods-close-politics-17891559.php.

13. Elon Musk, "Rightly so. The disaster that is downtown SF, once beautiful [sic] and thriving, now a derelict zombie apocalypse, is due to the woke mind virus," May 15, 2023, Twitter: https://twitter.com/elonmusk /status/1658334514462982144?s=51&t=FsGnfsBxtDayg3TbKIPhoA.

14. Rachel Swan, "How Safe Do You Feel in S.F.? Here's What 21 People Told Us," *San Francisco Chronicle,* April 29, 2023, https://www .sfchronicle.com/bayarea/article/sf-public-safety-survey-17904901.php.

15. Summer Lin, "Elon Musk, Others Claim San Francisco Crime Out of Control. But the Numbers Tell a Different Story," *Los Angeles Times*, April 7, 2023, https://www.latimes.com/california/story/2023–04–07 /is-crime-really-that-bad-in-san-francisco-experts-rebuff-crime-narrative -after-cash-app-founders-death.

16. Ellen Chaitin, "I'm a Former SF Judge. Breed and Jenkins Are Failing on Drugs," *SF Gate,* May 18, 2023, https://www.sfgate.com/politics-op-eds /article/former-judge-blasts-breed-jenkins-18104403.php.

17. "Police Union Director Fired After Opioid Smuggling Arrest," Associated Press, April 7, 2023, https://apnews.com/article/california-police -union-executive-fentanyl-smuggling-22d48dadae46d2629eaf4a9d9c6 7048e.

18. Barry Zevin, MD, Caroline Cawley, MPH, Jenna Birkmeyer, MPH, and Kenny Perez, MPH, "Homeless Mortality in San Francisco," San Francisco Department of Public Health, August 8, 2022, https://nhchc.org /wp-content/uploads/2022/08/Homeless-Deaths-in-San-Francisco-for -NHCHC-2022-cleaned.pdf.

19. Kylie Murdock and Jim Kessler, *The Two-Decade Red State Murder Problem,* Third Way, January 27, 2023, https://www.thirdway.org/report/the -two-decade-red-state-murder-problem.

20. Megan Rose Dickey, "San Francisco Car Thefts Rise As Overall Crime Declines," *Axios,* March 21, 2023, https://www.axios.com/local/san -francisco/2023/03/21/san-francisco-car-thefts-overall-crime-trends.

21. "HIV Among People Who Use Drugs," CDC, accessed August 9, 2023, https://www.cdc.gov/hiv/group/hiv-idu.html.

22. Nate Gartrell, "'Basically What's Happening Here Is the Creation of a Deportation Pipeline': DA, Critics Say Tenderloin Initiative Is Being Used to Dodge Sanctuary Laws," *Mercury News*, December 27, 2020, https://www.mercurynews.com/2020/12/24/da-critics-say-anti-drug-tenderloin-initiative-is-being-used-to-dodge-sanctuary-city-laws-deport-undocumented-immigrants/.

9. The Convenient Boogeyman

1. Joseph Friedman, MPH, Morgan Godvin, BA, Chelsea Shover PhD, Joseph P. Gone, PhD, Helena Hansen, MD, PhD, and David L. Schriger, MD, MPH, "Trends in Drug Overdose Deaths Among US Adolescents, January 2010 to June 2021," *JAMA*, April 12, 2022, https://jamanetwork.com/journals/jama/fullarticle/2790949.
2. Russ Choma, "The FBI Received Highly Specific Tips About Violence Set for Jan. 6—But Declined to Act," *Mother Jones*, October 31, 2021, https://www.motherjones.com/politics/2021/10/washington-post-january-6-red-flag-warnings-fbi/.
3. *Sex Trafficking: Online Platforms and Federal Prosecutions,* Government Accountability Office, June 21, 2021, https://www.gao.gov/products/gao-21-385.
4. Danielle Blunt and Ariel Wolf, *Erased: The Impact of FOSTA/SESTA,* Hacking//Hustling, January 1, 2020, https://hackinghustling.org/wp-content/uploads/2020/01/HackingHustling-Erased.pdf.

10. Team America

1. Emily Feng, "'We Are Shipping to the U.S.': Inside China's Online Synthetic Drug Networks," NPR, November 17, 2020, https://www.npr.org/2020/11/17/916890880/we-are-shipping-to-the-u-s-china-s-fentanyl-sellers-find-new-routes-to-drug-user.

11. Breakfast of Champions

1. Jason Yong, Peter Mullins, and Neil Bhattacharyya, "Prevalence of Chronic Pain Among Adults in the United States," *Pain*, February 1, 2022, https://pubmed.ncbi.nlm.nih.gov/33990113/.
2. Deborah Dowell, MD, Kathleen R. Ragan, MSPH, Christopher M. Jones, PharmD, DrPH, Grant T. Baldwin, PhD, and Roger Chou, MD, "CDC Clinical Practice Guidelines for Prescribing Opioids for Pain—United States," CDC, November 4, 2022, https://www.cdc.gov/mmwr/volumes/71/rr/rr7103a1.htm.

3. Kurtis Ming, "Call Kurtis Investigates: Patients Say Pain Pill Crackdown Left Them with 'Excruciating Withdrawals.' How Are They Months Later?," CBS News, May 18, 2023, https://www.cbsnews.com/sacramento/news/pain-pill-crackdown-withdrawals-opioids-call-kurtis/.

4. Grant Victor, Bradley Ray, Brandon Del Pozo, Kaitlyn Jaffe, Andy King, and Philip Huynh, "Buprenorphine and Opioid Analgesics: Dispensation and Discontinuity Among Accidental Overdose Fatalities in the Indianapolis Metropolitan Area, 2016–2021," *Journal of Substance Use and Addiction Treatment*, April 25, 2023, https://www.sciencedirect.com/science/article/abs/pii/S2949875923001030?via%3Dihub.

5. Hawre Jalal, Jeanine M. Buchanich, Mark S. Roberts, Lauren C. Balmert, Kun Zhang, and Donald S. Burke, "Changing Dynamics of the Drug Overdose Epidemic in the United States from 1979 Through 2016," *Science*, September 21, 2018, https://www.ncbi.nlm.nih.gov/pmc/articles/PMC8025225/.

6. John Keilman, "Hospitals Cut Back on Opioids to Battle Addiction Epidemic," *Chicago Tribune*, January 23, 2018, https://www.chicagotribune.com/news/ct-met-hospital-opioids-20180116-story.html.

7. Jeffrey A. Singer, Jacob Z. Sullum, and Michael E. Schatman, "Today's Nonmedical Opioid Users Are Not Yesterday's Patients; Implications of Data Indicating Stable Rates of Nonmedical Use and Pain Reliever Use Disorder," *Journal of Pain Research*, February 7, 2019, https://www.ncbi.nlm.nih.gov/pmc/articles/PMC6369835.

8. Andrea C. Enzinger, MD, Kaushik Ghosh, PhD, Nancy L. Keating, MD, MPH, David M. Cutler, PhD, Mary Beth Landrum, PhD, and Alexi A. Wright, MD, MPH, "US Trends in Opioid Access Among Patients with Poor Prognosis Cancer Near the End-of-Life," *Journal of Clinical Oncology*, July 22, 2021, https://pubmed.ncbi.nlm.nih.gov/34292766/.

12. America, Number One

1. Carl Erik Fisher, *The Urge: Our History of Addiction*, New York: Penguin Random House, 2022.

2. William Barr, "The U.S. Must Defeat Mexico's Drug Cartels," *Wall Street Journal*, March 2, 2023, https://www.wsj.com/articles/the-us-must-defeat-mexicos-drug-cartels-narco-terrorism-amlo-el-chapo-crenshaw-military-law-enforcement-b8fac731.

3. Joseph Friedman and Linn Gjersing, "Increases in Drug Overdose Deaths in Norway and the United States During the Covid-19 Pandemic," *Scandinavian Journal of Public Health*, February 4, 2022, https://journals.sagepub.com/doi/10.1177/14034948221075025.

13. Blazing a New Path

1. Jackie Botts, "Fast, Cheap, and Deadly," Reuters, August 9, 2023, https://www.reuters.com/graphics/MEXICO-DRUGS/FENTANYL/dwvkadblovm/.
2. Anderson Cooper, *CNN Town Hall*: "America Addicted: The Fentanyl Crisis," CNN, March 3, 2023, https://cnnpressroom.blogs.cnn.com/2023/03/03/cnn-townhall-america-addicted-the-fentanyl-crisis/.
3. Michael A. Irvine, Declan Oller, Jesse Boggis, Brian Bishop, Daniel Coombs, Eliza Wheeler, Maya Doe-Simkins, Alexander Y. Walley, Brandon D. L. Marshall, Jeffrey Bratberg, and Traci C. Green, "Estimating Naloxone Need in the USA Across Fentanyl, Heroin, and Prescription Opioid Epidemics: A Modelling Study," *The Lancet Public Health*, February 10, 2022, https://www.thelancet.com/journals/lanpub/article/PIIS2468-2667(21)00304-2/fulltext.
4. Wendy Sawyer and Peter Wagner, *Mass Incarceration: The Whole Pie 2020*, Prison Policy Initiative, https://www.prisonpolicy.org/reports/pie2020.html.

INDEX

ABOUT THE AUTHOR

Sean O'Donnell

RYAN HAMPTON is a national addiction recovery advocate, author, media commentator, and person in long-term recovery. He has worked with multiple nonprofits nationwide to end overdoses and served in leadership capacities for various community organizing initiatives. Hampton is in recovery from a decade of active opioid use and is a leading voice in America's rising recovery movement. He is the author of *Unsettled* and *American Fix,* and he lives in Nevada with his husband, Sean, and their boxer dog, Quincy.

In many countries, laws and systems increase the harm caused by drugs. The fear of abuse by authorities pushes people away from lifesaving care.

Evidence shows that treating people like criminals because they use drugs just makes their health worse. Yet people who use drugs are overrepresented in prisons, where proven services are often scarce. This approach just puts more barriers between people and the care they need.

Growing levels of stigmatization, marginalization, and poverty have led to high rates of HIV and low access to health care. We have the chance to tackle these issues and create a brighter and more equitable future—for everyone, everywhere.

To learn more about how you can support a more compassionate and health-centered response, please visit the Elton John AIDS Foundation at

www.eltonjohnaidsfoundation.org.